The Boys' Life

OF

ROBERT E. LEE

THE
BOYS' LIFE
OF
ROBERT E. LEE

BY

STANLEY F. HORN

ILLUSTRATED FROM PHOTOGRAPHS

GROSSET & DUNLAP · PUBLISHERS

New York

THE BOYS' LIFE OF
ROBERT E. LEE

Copyright, 1935, by Harper & Brothers
Printed in the United States of America

Table of Contents

Foreword

WHEN I was a boy I hated a book with footnotes. It always seemed to me that their only usefulness was to get my attention off the thread of the narrative and make me look over in the back of the book or down at the bottom of the page so that the author could prove his authority for some statement he made. I made up my mind then that if ever I wrote a book it would have no footnotes; and in this book I am sticking to that determination. Despite this absence of footnotes, however, I can give my readers the blanket assurance that every statement made herein is based on reliable authority and may be fully authenticated.

THE AUTHOR

The Boys' Life

OF

ROBERT E. LEE

CHAPTER I

The Lees of Virginia

O N A drizzling, gray day in April, 1865, General Fitzhugh Lee and a member of his staff on horseback were sloshing down the muddy road that led from Appomattox to Richmond. The Confederacy had collapsed. Even the ever-cheerful Fitz Lee was, at least temporarily, subdued and downcast. Coming around a turn in the road they met a Confederate soldier on foot, a private in the Army of Northern Virginia. He saluted the officers and, when asked where he was going, explained that he had been home on a furlough and was on his way back to join his command. Sadly they told him the bitter news: "You might as well turn around and go back home. It's all over. Lee has surrendered!" "Lee surrendered?" the ragged soldier repeated, unable to believe such an astounding piece of news. And when the officer reaffirmed that tragic fact the still incredulous soldier retorted: "You must be wrong about that. Maybe that damned Fitz Lee might have surrendered, but Marse Robert sho' ain't surrendered."

That was the typical attitude of the man in the

ranks of the Army of Northern Virginia, that daunt-
less body of lean, weather-beaten infantrymen who
for three years, regardless of long marches, short
rations and hard fighting never lost faith in their
leader, Robert E. Lee. "Marse Robert" they called
him affectionately, and without question they followed wherever he led them.

Nor was it in the private soldier alone that he inspired such blind confidence. His officers soon learned
to respect him for his military genius and to love
him for his courage, his fairness and his self-effacing
modesty. Stonewall Jackson, himself one of history's
greatest leaders of men, said: "Lee is a phenomenon.
He is the only man I would follow blindfold." After
the war tributes were lavished on him, as a soldier
and as a man, not only by his former companions in
arms but also by those who had opposed him on the
battlefield. Historians and military experts have vied
with each other in heaping praise upon him.

Theodore Roosevelt said: "The world has never
seen better soldiers than those who followed Lee;
and their leader will undoubtedly rank as, without
any exception, the very greatest of all the great captains that the English-speaking peoples have brought
forth."

Lord Wolseley said: "He was the ablest general,
and to me seemed the greatest man, I ever conversed
with; and yet I have had the privilege of meeting
von Moltke and Prince Bismarck."

Sir Frederick Maurice ranked Lee above Wellington—a great tribute from a British authority—and said, further: "Napoleon, Alexander, Hannibal, Caesar, Gustavus, Turenne, Eugene and Frederick—to that select band of great commanders the name of Robert E. Lee must be added."

Col. Henderson, the great British military biographer of Stonewall Jackson, said simply: "Lee stands out as one of the greatest soldiers of all time."

Extraordinary tributes these; but Robert E. Lee was, truly, an extraordinary man.

Lee was a soldier, not only by choice but by birth and training. The Lees had been prominent in the annals of chivalry in the old country long before the first of the family emigrated to America. Launcelot Lee fought at Hastings under William the Conqueror; Lionel Lee followed Richard the Lion-Hearted in the Third Crusade to the Holy Land, and his armor hangs to-day untarnished in the Tower of London; Sir Henry Lee was made a Knight of the Garter by Queen Elizabeth; and in St. George's Chapel, Windsor Castle, still hang the Lee family banners surmounted by the Lee arms, with their motto: "*Non incautus futuri.*"

The first of the family in the New World was Richard Lee, who came to Virginia in the early part of the seventeenth century. Members of the family took an active and leading part in the affairs of the colonies and in the deliberations leading up to the

Revolution; two Lees signed the Declaration of Independence; and when the war began, one of the first to draw his sword for America was Henry Lee, soon known to immortality as Light-Horse Harry.

Henry Lee's record in the Revolution was spectacular. Early in the war he engineered the surprise and capture of the British forces at Paulus Hook, New Jersey, an affair carried off with such dash and skill that the Continental Congress voted him a special gold medal for his services. George Washington looked on him as one of his ablest lieutenants. When it was necessary to send reinforcements to the Revolutionary forces in the South under General Nathaniel Greene, Washington unhesitatingly sent Lee's Legion; and its exploits against Cornwallis amply repaid the commander's confidence.

Light-Horse Harry Lee, after the war was over, entered into politics and showed qualities of statesmanship equal to those he displayed on the battlefield. He was elected governor of Virginia and later served as a representative in Congress. It was while he was in Congress that George Washington died, and Henry Lee prepared the resolutions on his death in which appeared the deathless phrase: "First in war, first in peace, and first in the hearts of his fellow-citizens." And it was a fair sample of Henry Lee's habitual bad luck in his later years that he was sick and unable to read the resolutions he had written, so that history for many years gave credit for the

[4]

famous words to the colleague who read them for him.

That was in 1799, when Henry Lee's star was at its zenith. With the turn of the century came a turn in his fortunes, and his latter days were filled with trouble and sorrow. A heavy blow was dealt him when Robert Morris, the financier of the Revolution, went into bankruptcy owing Lee some $40,000. This unexpected misfortune made it impossible for him to meet the demands of his own creditors, and his troubles rapidly mounted. Desperately he turned to land speculations in the hope of recouping, but these ventures resulted disastrously. His creditors became more insistent. Unable to pay, he went to a debtor's cell in the county jail. His health slowly failed him. His wife was deeply distressed by his multiplying misfortunes, and her sadness of heart and her illness were accentuated at this time by a series of deaths in her own family.

It was at this inauspicious time that Robert Edward Lee was born. The date was January 19th, 1807. The place of his birth was Stratford, that stately old mansion in Westmoreland County, Virginia, which had been for nearly two centuries the seat of the Lees of Virginia.

Stratford was built somewhere between 1725 and 1730 by Thomas Lee, grandson of Richard, the first immigrant. Thomas's first home was a plantation known as Mount Pleasant, but this house was destroyed by an incendiary fire set by rebellious convict-servants. In rebuilding his home, Thomas selected what he thought was a better site, on the high banks of the Potomac; and there Stratford was built. The building enterprise was aided by Queen Anne, then on the throne of England, who "sent over a bountiful present out of her own Privy Purse." None stood higher in the royal regard than the Lees.

Stratford, still standing after the lapse of more than two hundred years and now maintained as a public historical shrine, has the distinction of having been the home of more men of historic and political fame than any other of the famous mansions of Virginia. Here have lived members of the old House of Burgesses and of the King's Council, delegates to the Convention of Seventy-six, signers of the Declaration of Independence, members of the Continental Congress, governors of Virginia, and generals in both the Revolution and the War Between the States.

It is an imposing and sturdy old brick mansion house, built in the shape of the letter H, and containing eighteen spacious rooms, with high ceilings and elaborately carved woodwork. The ground floor is really a very high basement floor, and entrance to the principal part of the house is gained by a long flight of stone steps on the outside leading to the second story. The entrance doorway gives access to a big central hall, about thirty feet square, and the other rooms are in the two big wings, which measure about thirty by sixty feet. From the center of each of the wings arise four stout brick chimneys, united at the tops by brick arches; and between these chimneys on the roof there were built summer houses where the beaux and belles of Colonial days could enjoy the fresh breezes from the Potomac, and where on festive occasions a band of musicians would play for the entertainment of the guests. The architectural arrangement of the four chimneys afforded opportunity for a secret room on the second floor, said to have been used in the early days as a refuge from Indians.

The Stratford estate was arranged in the form of a quadrangle, with the big house in the center and four single brick out-buildings at each of the four corners—kitchen, office, stable and milk-house, each about thirty by forty-five feet. The kitchen had an enormous open fireplace, measuring twelve feet wide, six feet high and five feet deep—big enough to roast a whole ox. Adjacent to the kitchen was the vegetable garden, surrounded by a high brick wall; and at the foot of the garden was the large brick family vault. Through the trees there was a vista of the Potomac flowing lazily to the sea.

Here it was that Robert Edward Lee first saw the light of day on that cold morning in January 1807, in the same room in which had been born before him two other distinguished members of the Lee family, both of whom had signed the Declaration of Independence—Richard Henry Lee and Francis Light-foot Lee.

Henry Lee was married twice. His first wife was his third cousin, Matilda Lee, and Stratford was Matilda's inheritance from her father, Philip Ludwell Lee. When she died in 1790 she left two children: Lucy, born in 1786; and Henry, born in 1787. His second wife was Anne Hill Carter, daughter of Charles Carter of Shirley on the James; and this marriage brought together two of the most famous and prominent families of the Old Dominion. The young heiress of Shirley traced her lineage directly back to old "King" Carter, one of the outstanding figures of the early Colonial life of Virginia, who lived in baronial splendor on his great estates. She was truly to the manor born. Of this second marriage five children survived: Charles Carter, born in 1798; Anne, born in 1800; Sydney Smith, born in 1802; Mildred, born in 1811; and Robert Edward, born in 1807.

Following the birth of his youngest son, the affairs of Henry Lee went from bad to worse. His struggles against unmerciful disaster kept him constantly in hot water; and he must have hailed with delight the coming of the War of 1812 as a means of permitting him once more to exercise his talents in the field where he had made an unsullied name for himself some thirty years before. True, the war was not an entirely popular one among all the people;

and its chief opposition came from the Federalists, of which party Henry Lee had always been a member; but with him patriotism came before party, and there was never any question in his mind about drawing his sabre again in defense of his country's rights. The governor of Virginia, promptly upon the declaration of war, offered him a commission as Major-General, and he just as promptly accepted it. But, sad to relate, it was destined that Henry Lee should never achieve his ambition to serve his country again on the battlefield. Hardly had his commission been issued him than he went to Baltimore on a visit, and there he became embroiled in an affray that well-nigh cost him his life.

Baltimore was one of the places where there was a strong division of sentiment as to the advisability of the war that had just been declared by President Madison; but the supporters of the President were in the majority, including the city officials. Among the opponents of the war was a young man named Alexander Hanson, publisher of *The Federal Republican*, and he boldly denounced the war as "unnecessary, inexpedient, and entered into from partial, personal motives." The appearance of his paper in which this defiant editorial appeared was the signal for a great burst of indignation on the part of Madison's supporters in Baltimore, which indignation culminated in the organization of a mob which went to Mr. Hanson's newspaper office and literally tore the building down, wrecked his printing equipment and forced him to flee the city and take refuge in a nearby town. Hanson, however, despite his lack of patriotic fervor, was made of courageous stuff; and he straightway laid his plans to return to Baltimore and re-establish his paper. It happened that the day of his return was the day of Henry Lee's arrival in the city. It also happened that Hanson's father, who had been chancellor of Maryland for many years, had been a friend of Lee's; and when the visiting general heard of the troubles of the son of his old friend, Judge Hanson, it was characteristic of him to seek him out and offer his help.

Young Hanson, though foolhardy, was no fool. He realized the danger of the step he was taking in returning to Baltimore and renewing his defiance; and he had gathered about him a group of his friends, including young John Howard Payne, later famous as the author of "Home Sweet Home," and made preparations to defend himself and his house against the threatened attack of those who opposed his anti-war views and meant to silence him. This little group of defiant Federalists hailed with the greatest joy the timely visit of General Henry Lee. He was still remembered for his Revolutionary exploits; and it was felt that with him in the house the danger from mob violence was materially lessened. On his part, General Lee never hesitated about the course he would take, once he learned of the impending danger to his old friend's son. He did not stop to lecture him on his folly; he did not consider his own safety; he rolled up his sleeves and joined in the defense of Hanson's house against the mob that was already muttering in the street.

The Baltimore Riot stands out as one of the most disgraceful and tragic affairs in the history of that city. The municipal authorities made only the feeblest effort to disperse the mob or to rescue the objects of its fury once the Hanson house was actually besieged. They made a half-hearted and futile attempt to rescue the beleaguered occupants of the house; but their sympathies were really with the mob—and the mob knew it. Knowledge of the authorities' weakness increased their fury and boldness. Cries of "Kill the damned Tories!" resounded in the street—strange denunciation in the ears of one like Light-Horse Harry Lee who had given his best years to winning his country's independence!

The rioting continued all night, without bloodshed but without any abatement of its violence. With the coming of morning the mayor of Baltimore came and offered to give the besieged group a haven of safety in the city jail, protected by militia, until the mob could be dispersed. This offer was accepted, with more or less misgiving, and the Federalists spent the day in jail quietly. But when night came the mob gathered again, drove off a craven militia, and battered down the jail's gates. The little group of terrified men attempted to escape through the front door, but as they emerged they were set upon by the infuriated mobsters and there ensued such a bloody butchery as has seldom disgraced any American city. The victims were slugged and slashed and kicked into insensibility until there was a pile of bleeding, unconscious men just outside the jail door. Members of the mob vied with each other in visiting indignities on the helpless victims. Their faces were hacked with knives, hot candle grease was dropped into their eyes, they were kicked and clubbed. One of the mob, seeking to slash General Lee's nose from his face, let his knife slip; and although the General escaped the ignominious mutilation intended, he received a great gash in his face close to his eye which threatened to end his life then and there.

But at last the horrid night was over. The mob exhausted itself in its orgy of brutality and at length dispersed. Doctors were called and treatment accorded those still alive, among them General Lee. He was taken to a hospital, where his wounds were dressed, and later he was removed to the home of friends in the country. It was two weeks before he was able to speak; but finally he recovered sufficiently to be able to be taken back home—a broken and dejected old man.

"Home" to Henry Lee and his family was now no longer Stratford Hall on the Potomac. Stratford descended from Matilda Lee to her son Henry; and in 1810 the property was formally transferred to him, and General Lee and his second wife and their little family moved to Alexandria, the sleepy little village just across the Potomac from Washington. No doubt it was a sentimental wrench to their feelings to leave behind them Stratford, the traditional home of the Lees of Virginia, even though it had grown somewhat shabby and seedy during the years of their declining fortunes. But, in a way, Anne Carter Lee probably found life somewhat happier when they took up their residence in a modest brick house on a quiet street in Alexandria. Her health was wretched; but she had a little life income from the estate of her father, and the outlook must have been brighter for her comfort and happiness in Alexandria than it had been on the run-down estate in Westmoreland County.

It made little difference to Henry Lee, now a shattered shell of an old man, who was never again to know health or happiness anywhere. After his return to Alexandria and his partial recovery from his wounds, he attempted to carry out some of the duties of his military office in the prosecution of the war, but the best he could do was in an advisory capacity. It soon became obvious to him and to everybody else that his days of actual usefulness were over; and his chief concern became the regaining of his health. He was advised that a long stay in a tropical climate was the only hope for him in his physically shattered condition; but, of course, in the midst of a war it was difficult to arrange such a trip. Finally, however, through the direct intervention of President Madison arrangements were made for him to sail for the Barbadoes, special dispensation being made for a vessel to land him in what was then the enemy's territory. By the summer of 1814 his health had recovered sufficiently to encourage him to think of returning home; but by then the American coast was blockaded and return was impossible. By the time the war was over his condition had again declined; shipping difficulties continued; and, for one reason and another, he continued to wander among the tropic islands of the West Indies, a sick, suffering and heart-sore old man, far away from those he loved. He kept up a regular correspondence with his family, and in 1816 he wrote to his son, Charles Carter: "I begin to hope that I may live to see you, your dear mother and our other sweet offspring." But it was not to be so.

It was the spring of 1818 before he finally was able to find a means of returning. The schooner *Betsy* was leaving Nassau for the port of Savannah, and the weary and homesick old warrior eagerly took passage in her. There was a new note of gladness in his letter home announcing his preparations to return; he sent a present of two books to Charles Carter, who was then in school at Harvard; and with a lift in his heart he boarded the *Betsy* and she pointed her bowsprit for the Georgia coast.

But as the *Betsy* coasted up the seaboard, Henry Lee's illness grew worse. "Where are we?" he miserably asked the schooner's skipper; and when told that they were off Cumberland Island on the coast of Georgia, he asked that he be put ashore there. On Cumberland Island was located Dungeness, the sea-island plantation home of Lee's old commander, General Nathaniel Greene; and although General Greene was dead, Lee knew that in the home of his old general's family it would be possible for him to find a haven in his extremity.

Accordingly a boat was put over the schooner's side; stout sailors' hands carried him and his little trunk through the booming surf and set them ashore at Dungeness; and there the Greene family, though astonished at his unexpected advent, made haste to put him to bed and give him the best medical attention. As he grew weaker he grew more irritable, and one day when one of the old family servants came into his bed-chamber without knocking he angrily threw a boot at her head. She, a privileged character in the household, promptly threw it back at him; and the old man, admiring her spunk, smiled forgiveness and they became the best of friends. Doctors were summoned from the mainland, but they found him a strong-minded and difficult patient. As a last desperate measure, an operation was suggested; but the old man reared up in bed and shouted: "No! Were General Washington himself alive and here to join you in advocating it, I would decline!" Strong admirer of Washington that he was, he could say nothing stronger than that.

But the efforts of friends and doctors were in vain. For a few days he rallied a little and walked out under the moss-laden live oaks; but it was the last spark of life. On March 25th he died; and a few days later was buried in the garden by the side of his old commander.

Although his last years had been wretched, he was honored in death by an imposing military funeral. An American fleet was patrolling the South Atlantic coast, and there was a garrison of soldiers at nearby Fernandina under General Gaines. Officers of the Army and Navy had visited with the old hero during his last illness; and when he died they gave him the fullest burial honors, with minute guns booming from the fleet and from the fort at Fernandina.

So young Robert E. Lee was left fatherless at the tender age of eleven years. His father he had not seen since he was six years old; and even during those early years the old general was at home but intermittently. His father was to him, therefore, but a vague kind of memory—but it was a very tender memory, and the valor of Light-Horse Harry Lee was ever very dear to the heart of his youngest son, Robert.

CHAPTER II

Boy and Man

DURING all his father's restless wandering through the West Indies in search of health, Robert E. Lee was growing from infancy to young boyhood in the old brick house on Cameron Street in Alexandria. The War of 1812, which was just getting well under way when his father sailed for the Barbadoes, had surged on and enveloped them in 1814 when Alexandria was captured and occupied by the British troops. Little Robert was then only seven years old; but even a seven-year-old boy could appreciate what it meant when the town was over-run with redcoats. He could listen to the exploits of his elder half-brother, Henry, who was a full-fledged major in the American army; and he could see the red reflection against the night sky when the British captured Washington across the river and burned it.

Robert's position in the Lee household at Alexandria, young as he was, came to be a difficult and trying one. Charles Carter, his eldest brother, went away to Harvard in 1815 and was there until 1819. His other brother, Sydney Smith, entered the Navy as a midshipman in 1816. His elder sister was in very poor health throughout her youth and was away from home most of the time; and his other sister was too young to assist in household affairs.

The net result of this combination of circumstances, coupled with his father's long absence and subsequent death, was that Robert became his mother's principal solace and dependence during the trying years she spent at Alexandria. Mrs. Lee had become a chronic invalid; and although, in her husband's long absence, she was the head of the little household, she leaned on Robert, in spite of his tender years, for help and companionship.

Although any boy is unfortunate who is deprived of a father's directing care during the years of his youth, Robert Lee had the great gift of a mother who was a model of what a mother should be. She was a great-granddaughter of Alexander Spottswood, who came to Virginia as Colonial governor and who had fought under the banners of Marlborough at Blenheim. Through her side of the family Robert Lee was able to trace his lineage to King Robert Bruce of Scotland. One of his Virginia friends once said: "If General Lee owed his greatness to his father's blood, he owed his goodness to his mother's, for through many generations the Carters have been noted for purity and nobility of character." And it might also be added that the circumstances which made him, as a boy, the constant companion and at-

tendant of his invalid mother developed in him that
gentle and considerate manner in which his martial
spirit was so well clothed.

For even in his extreme youth Robert Lee showed
that gentleness of manner which marked his character in adult years: and old residents of Alexandria
used to recall how faithfully he would have the carriage called for his mother's daily drive and how
tenderly he helped lift her in the seat and looked
after her comfort as Nat, the old family coachman,
drove them through the village's quiet streets. The
Lee family carriage in those lean years was growing
shabby and needed repairs. On windy days its worn
curtains flapped in the breeze and gave but little protection to the occupants. But foresighted Robert im-
provised curtains from old newspapers, and gaily
joked with his mother about his handiwork instead of
bewailing the poverty that made it necessary.

But despite the sobering effect of the tragic end of
his father and the constantly failing health of his
mother, despite the frugal living made necessary by
their reduced circumstances, the youthful years passed
pleasantly for Robert Lee in Alexandria; and when
he was an old man and was back there on a visit, one
of his first acts was to go round on Cameron Street
to see if the old snowball bushes were still blooming
in the garden there. And, even though he was but a
small child when he left it, Stratford held tender
memories for him too. Looking at a picture of the

old house, in late years, he said: "It vividly recalls scenes of my earliest recollections and happiest days. Though unseen for years, every feature of the house is familiar to me." And when the fortunes of war had left him homeless, his first thought was to try in some way to re-purchase Stratford and end his days there.

Robert Lee's first schooling in Alexandria was in the private school of Mr. W. B. Leary, described as "an Irish gentleman who was a fine scholar and an excellent teacher." Mr. Leary, like most schoolmasters of his time, attached particular importance to the classics; and the mark of this old tutor's efforts was visible in the pupil throughout his life. His preparatory education was completed in the school of Mr. Benjamin Hallowell of Alexandria who was famous in his time as an instructor in mathematics. Mr. Hallowell said of Lee that the boy was a most exemplary student in every respect, that he was never behind time at his studies, never failed in a single recitation, was perfectly observant of the school's rules and regulations, and was gentlemanly, unobtrusive and respectful in all his deportment to teachers and fellow-students. "Robert's specialty was finishing up," said Mr. Hallowell; and here we have a hint thus early of that thoroughness which played so important a part in his military success in later years.

When Robert was eighteen years old the time had arrived for him to make some choice as to his life's

LEE AS A YOUNG MAN

STRATFORD

Courtesy Miley, Lexington, Virginia

LEE ON TRAVELER

Courtesy Virginia State Chamber of Commerce

ARLINGTON

GENERAL ROBERT E. LEE

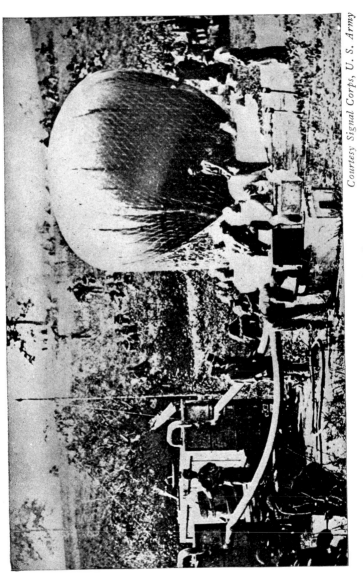

Courtesy Signal Corps, U. S. Army

PROFESSOR LOWE'S GAS GENERATOR

Courtesy Miley, Lexington, Virginia

LEE IN 1865, JUST AFTER SURRENDER

Courtesy Miley, Lexington, Virginia

LAST PHOTOGRAPH OF LEE (1869?)

work; and with the blood of the Lees and the Carters in his veins, it is not strange that his dreams turned in the direction of a military career. At this time Andrew Jackson was representing the state of Tennessee in the United States Senate, and it was through Jackson that Lee received his appointment to the military academy at West Point. His aunt, Mrs. Lewis, took him to Washington in person and introduced him to the old warrior; and her report was that he was much pleased with the young man and immediately pledged himself to arrange for the desired appointment. Robert's elder half-brother, Henry, was an admirer and friend of General Jackson's, and later his private secretary; and probably Henry's influence was helpful in inducing Old Hickory to appoint to the academy the son of the hero of the Revolution whose exploits Jackson must have admired.

Robert Lee's first visit home was two years after his appointment to the military academy; and the erect young cadet, handsome in his uniform of West Point gray with gleaming round metal buttons, made a great impression on the young ladies of Alexandria and the nearby countryside. He had matured in two years under the stern influence of West Point; but he was still full of life and fun. During his furlough there was a round of parties and dances arranged for him; and old ladies in Alexandria long afterward looked back wistfully and talked about the soldierly bearing of the young cadet and how handsome he was.

Near neighbors and old friends of the Lees were the Custis family, living in Arlington, the big house with the big white pillars across the river from Washington and a few miles above Alexandria. George Washington Parke Custis was the grandson of Martha Washington and the adopted son of General Washington himself. He had lived at Mount Vernon until 1802, when he built Arlington and moved there with his wife, and at Arlington his daughter Mary was born. Young Robert had visited at Arlington with his mother frequently during his boyhood, and he and his sister Mildred had been childhood playmates of Mary Custis. It was not until his first visit home from West Point, however, that this childhood acquaintance developed into a mutual affection; and when Cadet Lee returned to the academy in the summer of 1827 it was with the promise of Mary Custis that she would marry him after his graduation.

The four years of hard study and strict discipline at West Point changed the boy into the man. Fitzhugh Lee in his biography says: "He was a model cadet. His clothes looked nice and new; his cross-belts, collar and summer trousers were as white as the driven snow mounting guard upon the mountain top; and his brass breast- and waist-plates were mirrors to reflect the image of the inspector. He conscientiously performed his tours of guard duty, whether the non-commissioned officer of the guard was approaching his post or sleeping in his quarters. He never 'ran the sentinel post,' did not go off the limits to the 'Benny Havens' of his day or put dummies in his bed to deceive the officer in charge as he made his inspection after taps; and at the parades he stood steady in line. It was a pleasure for the inspector to look down the barrel of his gun; it was bright and clean, and its stock was rubbed so as almost to resemble polished mahogany."

No doubt we should discount this eulogy to allow for the natural enthusiasm of an admiring nephew in speaking of a famous uncle; but Robert Lee did have an unusual record at West Point, famous for its strict discipline. He never received a demerit of any kind for anything during his four years there. He was cadet officer of his class; and during his last year in school was honored with the highest distinction available to a cadet, being made adjutant of the corps.

On July 4th, 1829, he graduated from the military academy, second in his class of forty-six, and was given a commission as brevet second lieutenant in the Engineer Corps, appointment to which branch of the army was considered a reward for excellence in a graduating cadet, reserved for those who finished with the highest marks.

The triumphant happiness of his graduation, however, after four years of hard effort, was clouded by the knowledge that the life of his mother was rapidly drawing to an end. He hastened home in July and was able to reach her bedside while she was still alive; but during the same month she died.

The young lieutenant spent his leave of absence in the summer of 1829 visiting the Randolph family in Fauquier County and other friends and connections in Virginia. Mary Custis was visiting at Chatham, a stately old Fitzhugh family mansion on the north bank of the Rappahannock across from Fredericksburg, and Chatham was one of the places Robert Lee visited frequently during that summer. Years later, in 1863, he stood on the hills on the other side of the river and looked through his glasses at Chatham on the farther side. Chatham was then the headquarters of the Federal commander, General Burnside, and the Federal guns were bombarding Fredericksburg. Eagerly the Confederate artillerymen trained their guns on the big old house; but gently General Lee stayed their hand. "I could not bear to see Chatham shelled" he told his artillery chief. "It was under those trees that I courted my wife." Probably Burnside never knew of the tender sentiment to which he owed his immunity.

But in September his furlough was over and he was assigned to duty at Fort Pulaski, on Cockspur Island, in the river below Savannah, Georgia. Old Nat, his mother's old coachman, was in desperately bad health; and since his old mistress had just died and he now had no one to care for him, the young lieu-

tenant bundled up the sick old negro and took him
with him to Savannah, where he cared for him until
Nat died the next year.

At Savannah Lieutenant Lee entered upon the first
duties of his military life. They were not particularly
important duties—the minor engineering problems
incident to keeping the waters of the sea from the
low-lying little island—but Lieutenant Lee gave to
this small, insignificant job all that devotion to duty
that characterized his whole life; and his reports
show his deep concern over the task of keeping up the
embankments which the tides and gales insisted on
destroying. On February 1st, 1830, he won his first
promotion. It was a trivial promotion, merely an appointment from Major Samuel Babcock, in command
at Savannah, as "acting assistant commissary of sub-
sistence of the post"; but it must have been very
gratifying to the young officer—his first recognition
of merit. Here on Cockspur Island Lieutenant Lee
remained until December 1st, 1830—his first tour of
duty in the Army.

From Savannah he was transferred to Fortress
Monroe, across Hampton Roads from Norfolk, and
put to work strengthening the fortifications there.
The coast defenses had been seriously damaged during the War of 1812; and, now that Andrew Jackson
was President, he considered nothing of greater importance than the restoration of these fortifications
all along the Atlantic seaboard.

Lieutenant Lee doubtless welcomed the transfer back to Virginia. For one thing, it was convenient to Arlington and Mary Custis; and so effectively did he improve this opportunity to continue his courtship that within six months of his transfer the wedding was announced.

Mary Custis was one of the outstanding belles of Virginia. She had family distinction, wealth and charm. Robert E. Lee was a personable young man of good family, but he had little of this world's goods, and it was hinted that the proud Mr. Custis would have preferred a wealthier husband for his only daughter. But Mary Custis had eyes for none other than Robert Lee; and the objections of her father, if they existed, soon vanished before her great love for the man of her choice. The wedding at Arlington on June 30th, 1831, was according to all accounts a brilliant affair, as befitted the union of a Custis with a Lee. There was the customary round of social festivities following the wedding; but soon Lieutenant Lee was back with his bride at Fortress Monroe, once more engrossed with his blue-prints and drafting-board, acting as assistant to Captain Andrew Talcott who was in charge of the reconstruction of the fortifications.

In 1834 Lieutenant Lee was transferred to Washington, as assistant to Colonel Gratiot, chief engineer of the Army; and in 1835 he was made assistant astronomer of the commission surveying the boundary line between Ohio and Michigan—a very important work, as the accurate surveying of the line was to determine in which state the city of Toledo was located. In 1836 he was back in Washington assigned to duty again as Colonel Gratiot's assistant, and he served in this capacity for two years.

These were two happy years, since it was possible for him and his wife to live with the Custises at Arlington and enjoy with their two infant children the home life thus made possible. Lieutenant Lee (he was now a full-fledged first lieutenant) rode horseback from Arlington to Washington every morning and back home in the afternoon; and he was a familiar figure, cantering through the streets of Washington and Georgetown those two years, on his way to and from the Chief Engineer's office.

Sometimes the roads or the weather prevented the trip on horseback, or an unusual press of work kept him in town. On those occasions he lived with a "mess" in Washington composed of army officers and several members of President Jackson's cabinet, the Senate and the diplomatic corps. The young army officers, then as now, enjoyed having a good time during their leisure hours; and sometimes some of the elder and more stately members of the mess were slightly shocked at the frolicsome behaviour of the young men.

One day, as Lee was about to start on horseback for Arlington, he saw one of his Army cronies, Lieutenant Macomb, on the sidewalk and, drawing up alongside him, called out: "Come, get up behind me." Macomb, probably to Lee's surprise, promptly accepted the invitation and, placing his foot in the stirrup, vaulted to the horse's back. Lee, carrying the joke through, galloped off up Pennsylvania Avenue before Macomb could dismount. Turning the corner in front of the Treasury they were spied by the dignified Secretary, Levi Woodbury. His eyes nearly popped out at the sight of two supposedly dignified army officers riding double up Washington's main thoroughfare; but they bowed gravely to him and galloped on up by the White House, while he turned into the Treasury slowly shaking his head at such didoes.

Even early in life, Lee was exhibiting that trait of character that was afterwards to be so valuable to him—that close attention to details and care about having everything just exactly right.

Upon first being stationed in Washington in 1835 he was careful to search out a blacksmith who would shoe his horse carefully in accordance with his own directions; and, having found that man in a smith named Schneider who had a shop on Twentieth and G Streets, he patronized him throughout the rest of his life in Washington. As late as the fall of 1860, when Schneider's blacksmith shop had grown into an iron foundry at the corner of Pennsylvania Avenue and Eighteenth, Lee called on him one day and left with him the drawing of a special kind of coulter he wanted made for use in plowing up some new ground at Arlington. The coulter was later delivered at the farm by a market-man, and Lee did not see Schneider again before the breaking out of the war. But he did not forget the transaction with the Washington blacksmith, and late in 1861 while his mind was crowded with other matters he found a way to send to Schneider through the lines two gold dollars wrapped in paper in discharge of the old account, accompanied by a note of apology for the delay.

In 1837 Lieutenant Lee was assigned to work on the Mississippi River, the most immediate problem in connection with his new work being the control of the river's currents at St. Louis where it was threatening to cut a new channel that would leave the young metropolis high and dry. The St. Louis people, naturally enough, were greatly agitated about the matter, and urged the War Department to send out an army engineer who could harness the rebellious river. General Winfield Scott, head of the Army, without hesitation recommended Robert E. Lee for the job. "Lee is young," he said, "but if the work can be done he can do it."

After a preliminary survey at St. Louis and at the rapids at Des Moines, requiring several months of close study, Lee returned to Washington and made his recommendations for the straightening and widening of the river's channels and the building of obstructions to control the currents properly at St. Louis. His recommendations were approved and adopted, Lee himself was sent back to St. Louis and put in charge of the work, and until 1840 the Army engineers were employed in carrying his ideas into execution under his direction.

Lee proceeded with the huge task with painstaking care, and local newspapers and politicians were free and caustic in their criticisms of the engineer sent out from Washington while he was slowly and carefully laying his plans. He didn't work fast enough to suit them, and they didn't hesitate to say so. But then, as in later years, hostile clamor had no effect on him. He knew what he was doing and he kept at it quietly and persistently, without quarreling with his critics; and at length he had the satisfaction of seeing them convinced by the success of his work and added to the growing fold of admirers of his quiet efficiency.

Lee's assistant in this work was Lieutenant Meigs, later quartermaster general of the United States army; and Meigs describes him at the time as being "then in the vigor of youthful strength, with a noble and commanding presence and an admirable, graceful and athletic figure. He was one with whom nobody ever wished or ventured to take a liberty, though kind and generous to his subordinates, admired by all women and respected by all men. He was the model of a soldier and the beau ideal of a Christian man."

But in spite of Lee's rather premature air of gravity and dignity, his letters home and to his army
friends in Washington reveal that playful sense of
humor that his close associates always saw in him.
Writing back to his old friend, Joe Johnston, whom
he playfully called "Colonel," he told of meeting at
Galena, on one of his up-river trips, an old army
friend of theirs who had been with them at Old Point
Comfort, General Brooke. Brooke was just back to
civilization after fighting the Indians; and, running
across an old friend, was inclined to celebrate. "But,"
wrote Lee to Johnston, "it was done temperately and
in a temperance manner, for the general has fore-
sworn strong potations, and our refreshment consisted
of only soda-water and ice-cream, delicacies that had
been untasted by the general for the last nine years;
and four times a day did we pay our respects to the
fountain and freezer." And he goes on to describe
to friend Joe, back in Washington, how another of
their army friends was enjoying himself on the frontier, fraternizing with the Indians, joining in their
dances and flirting with the squaws.

The headquarters of Lee and his crew of army engineers was established for a while on an abandoned
steamboat that had been stranded on one of the
Mississippi's treacherous sand-bars. Here the young
officers found comfortable living quarters; and in the
summer evenings they went in swimming from the

lower deck of the boat, fished in the river's clear water, and otherwise enjoyed life.

While engaged in the work on the Mississippi River, in 1838, Lee was promoted to the rank of Captain; and during the following year his superior officers' confidence in his ability was indicated by the offer to appoint him to a position on the faculty of the military academy at West Point. Lee, however, modestly disclaimed sufficient knowledge of the subject to make a good teacher; and in a letter to a friend he revealed what was probably his real reason for declining the appointment—his unwillingness to exchange active Army service for a professor's chair in the class-room.

In 1841 Captain Lee was placed in charge of the defenses of New York harbor, with his headquarters at Fort Hamilton. Here in the officers' quarters he established his home, bringing along Mrs. Lee and the two boys and two girls from Arlington. Mrs. Lee and the children made frequent visits back home to Virginia from time to time, but here at Fort Hamilton the little family spent five happy years together, with all the ups and downs of family life.

Young Fitzhugh (always called "Rooney" by his father) was a bold and venturesome lad, even in his childhood; and one day when his father was in New York and his mother was out visiting some of the other officers' wives, Rooney strayed off to the big barn, where the cavalry horses were kept, although he had been warned against doing so. Boy-like, he lost no time in investigating the fascinating mysteries of the hay-cutter; and before he knew what was happening had cut off the ends of two of his fingers. The surgeon stationed at the fort was in New York City, and there was a great hue and cry raised before surgical attention could be brought to the captain's little son. Captain Lee took this opportunity to point out to his older son, Custis, the tragic results of disobedience and recklessness; but he could not restrain a note of pride as he told of Rooney's patience and courage while waiting for the doctor.

Captain Lee was now steadily growing in prestige in Army circles. Whatever his hand found to do he was doing well. In 1844 there came official recognition of his high standing in the form of an appointment to the Board of Visitors at West Point, a great honor for a young officer. Late in 1845 there was bestowed on him the further honor of membership on the Board of Engineers for Atlantic Coast Defense. Captain Lee had arrived.

In 1845 Lee was 38 years old. He had been in the Army for 16 years; and, although he had made a good record, it was in the more or less dull and routine work of an Army engineer. There was as yet not the slightest indication that the young man in charge of the New York fortifications was one whose name, within a few years, would be mentioned along with those of Hannibal and Caesar and Napoleon. The country had been at peace since the War of 1812, and there had been no opportunity for American soldiers to try their mettle on the battlefield. But in 1845 there were, away to the southward in Mexico, rumblings of war. The government was talking about increasing the Army's strength in preparation for possible trouble. It was then that Lee wrote to a friend: "In the event of war with any foreign government, I would desire to be brought into active service in the field; and if that could not be accomplished without leaving the Corps of Engineers, I should then desire a transfer to some other branch of the service and would prefer the artillery."

The long-dormant spark of Light-Horse Harry Lee's flaming combativeness was beginning to burn in his quiet son.

CHAPTER III

In the Halls of Montezuma

THE War with Mexico grew out of the boundary dispute which the United States inherited when Texas was annexed. Texas, when it declared its independence and set up as a separate republic in 1836, announced that its southern boundary was the Rio Grande, basing its claim on a treaty made with Santa Anna after Sam Houston had defeated and captured him at San Jacinto. Mexico, however, repudiated this treaty and insisted that the Neuces River was the proper line between them. This dispute was unsettled when Texas was annexed in 1845, but the United States accepted the Texas version of the controversy and when Mexican troops crossed the Rio Grande in 1846 President Polk declared it an act of invasion and notified Congress that a state of war existed.

The Mexican War did not last very long, nor were there many troops engaged in its various battles; but it served as a test and a proving ground for the officers of the United States army, most of whom a few years later were engaged in the War between the States on one side or the other.

[35]

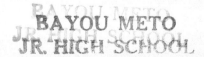

The American advance on Mexico was made by two armies, one marching directly from the north across the Rio Grande under General Taylor, and the other, under General Scott, landing on the Gulf coast near Vera Cruz for the purpose of advancing on Mexico City. Among the officers in Taylor's army were Jefferson Davis, Braxton Bragg and others whose names were later to become well-known. General Scott's officers embraced a surprisingly large number of those who were later to gain prominence in the Union and Confederate armies: Lee, Grant, Joseph E. Johnston, McClellan, Meade, Albert Sidney Johnston, McDowell, Thomas, Hooker, Beauregard, Jackson, Burnside, Sedgwick, Hancock, Ewell, A. P. Hill, Early, Longstreet, Pickett—it was a notable body of military men.

The Mexican War gave to Captain Lee of the Engineers the chance he wanted to serve in the field and get away from the hum-drum monotony of an army engineer's life. It gave him his first actual experience in fighting, and afforded an opportunity to lay the foundation stones of that knowledge of practical strategy and tactics which was later to distinguish him. During the first weeks of the war he was attached to the division commanded by General Wool in General Taylor's army which crossed the Rio Grande, and his first field service under this commander had some amusing aspects but at the same time demonstrated that thoroughness and painstaking care for details which is said to be the germ of success.

Prior to the battle of Buena Vista there was some uncertainty in General Wool's mind as to the movements of the Mexicans, as it was difficult in this hostile country to get accurate information. One night a breathless scout came in with the exciting report that General Santa Anna had crossed the mountains with a tremendous army and was then within a few miles of the American camp. Captain Lee promptly volunteered to reconnoiter and find out whether the report was true; and, obtaining a native guide, he set out cautiously in the direction the enemy was supposed to be.

After proceeding several miles Lee came across a road which, by the light of the moon, he saw to be filled with the tracks of mules and wagons—just the traces that would be left by an army train. This seemed to corroborate the report of the enemy's presence—but "Robert's specialty was always finishing things up," his old schoolmaster said. He wasn't satisfied with this half-way evidence; he decided to move ahead until he came in contact with the Mexican pickets. He therefore proceeded in the darkness, alert for signs of the enemy; but, failing to encounter any pickets, he soon concluded that in some way he must have got by them and placed himself within their lines. This fear was apparently confirmed when he suddenly came in sight of a row of large camp-fires on the side of a hill not far in his front. His Mexican guide was stricken with fear at the sight, saying that he knew that here must be Santa Anna's whole army and that they would be killed or captured unless they fled at once. Lee, however, insisted on a closer view of the Mexican army and rode forward on his horse.

As he approached, he saw looming up on the hillside in the moonlight large clusters of dim white shapes which seemed certainly to be the tents of the soldiers; and as he drew nearer he heard voices and the other noises common to a big army camp. But, drawing still closer, he found to his chagrin that the dim white shapes on the hillside were a flock of sheep, and that the camp was one of a train of wagons and cattle being driven to town to market! He rode boldly into the camp, and by asking questions of the drovers found that Santa Anna had not crossed the mountain; and with this valuable information he galloped back to Wool's headquarters.

The Christmas of 1846 passed when Captain Lee had just reached Mexico; and although this was not the first Christmas he had spent away from home, his thoughts as always turned back to his family at Arlington at the holiday season. "I hope good Santa Claus will fill my Rob's stocking to-night," he wrote in a letter to his two older sons, "that Mildred's, Agnes's, and Annie's may break down with good things. I do not know what he may have for you and

Mary, but if he only leaves for you one-half of what I wish, you will want for nothing. I have frequently thought that if I could have one of you on each side of me riding on ponies, such as I could get you here, I would be comparatively happy."

Shortly after this Captain Lee was transferred to General Scott's army before Vera Cruz; and he served in that campaign in every battle until the Mexican capital was captured. Lee went down to Vera Cruz on the transport "Massachusetts," occupying a state-room with his old friend, Joseph E. Johnston; but he wrote home that "poor Joe was sick all the time" and did not enjoy the trip.

Scott's first step in the investment of Vera Cruz was the construction of earthworks and batteries of naval and siege guns. The naval forces cooperated in the work, and one of Lee's first duties was to superintend the work of a detachment of bluejackets detailed to throw up a line of fortifications. This pick-and-shovel work did not appeal to these sons of the bounding main, and the captain of their vessel lodged with Lee a formal complaint against the outrage of making his men get down and dig ditches. "My boys don't want any dirt to hide behind!" he exclaimed. "When you have finished your dirt banks we won't stay behind them; we'll get up on top where we can fight in the open!" Captain Lee was able to appease the indignant seaman, and the work of entrenchment went on; and, it is recorded, when the fighting began the sailors offered no objection whatever to taking refuge behind the despised banks of dirt. But, even after the battle was over, the ship captain was still only half-convinced. "Well, I reckon you were right," he told Captain Lee. "I suppose the dirt did save some of my boys from being killed or wounded. But the fact is, Captain, I don't like this land fighting anyway. It ain't clean!"

Assisting Captain Lee in placing the batteries was Lieutenant P. G. T. Beauregard of Louisiana; and one of the naval batteries was commanded by Lieutenant Sydney Smith Lee, Robert E. Lee's own brother, who was an officer in the Navy. In his report General Scott made special mention of "Captain R. E. Lee, Engineer," saying that he had "greatly distinguished himself."

As soon as Vera Cruz had been reduced, General Scott started on the march to Mexico City, two hundred miles away through a strange and unfamiliar country; and on this march Lee gave repeated evidences of those budding talents of soldiership which caused General Scott to speak so highly of him for the rest of his life.

The first stand made by the Mexican troops in opposing Scott's forward march was at Cerro Gordo, a high pass in the mountains where Santa Anna had gathered his forces. Santa Anna had chosen his position wisely, with its natural approach along a winding, zigzag mountain road, guarded by heavy batteries. In an effort to find some means of turning the Mexicans' line, Captain Lee and a small body of pioneers were entrusted with the reconnaissance of the formidable position; and at the end of three days he had mapped out a passable way through the mountains, open to light artillery, by means of which it was possible for Scott to gain the victory over Santa Anna. Lee himself guided the storming party that turned the Mexicans' left, cut off their right from retreat and compelled its surrender.

During one of his reconnaissances at Cerro Gordo Lee had a thrilling experience when his daring and unfamiliarity with the country had taken him unawares within the enemy's lines. The only opportunity for escape was by hiding under a fallen tree near a spring where the Mexican soldiers were getting water, and here he took refuge. In this dangerous and cramped position he remained all day, with the soldiers passing all around and about him, some of them at times even sitting on the tree beneath which he was hidden; and it was not until nightfall that he was able to escape from his ticklish situation.

In closing his report of the engagement at Cerro Gordo, General Scott said: "I am compelled to make special mention of Captain R. E. Lee, Engineer. This officer was again indefatigable during these operations in reconnaissance, as daring as laborious, and of the utmost value. Nor was he less conspicuous in planning batteries and in conducting columns to their stations under the heavy fire of the enemy."

This was Lee's first experience in a pitched battle, with musket balls and grape shot whistling through the air, and he was profoundly impressed by it. "You have no idea what a horrible sight a battlefield is," he wrote to his son, Custis, then a student at West Point; and years afterward he spoke with sadness of seeing on the Cerro Gordo field, after the battle, a weeping little Mexican girl, bending over the unconscious form of a wounded drummer-boy. The boy was pinned to the ground by the dead body of a gigantic Mexican trooper who had fallen across him; and Lee removed the dead soldier and helped the sobbing girl get the little boy to a place where his wound could be dressed.

General Twiggs, who commanded the forces actually storming the heights, said in his report: "Although whatever I may say can add little to the good reputation of Captain Lee of the Engineer Corps, yet I must indulge in the pleasure of speaking of the invaluable services which he rendered me. I consulted him with confidence and adopted his suggestions with assurance. His gallantry and good conduct deserve the highest praise." Colonel Riley, whose troops were engaged in the storming, spoke in his report of "the intrepid coolness and gallantry exhibited by Captain Lee of the Engineers, when conducting the advance of my brigade under the heavy flank fire of the enemy."

Captain Lee accompanied the advance division in the forward movement from Cerro Gordo; and he again distinguished himself in the next battle of the campaign, at Contreras.

Contreras was the key to the two highways leading to Mexico City; and the lay of the land was such that it was exceedingly difficult of approach. The American troops in their advance became separated by a peculiarly rugged and difficult piece of ground called "The Pedregal"—a field of volcanic rock, broken into sharp ridges, deep gullies and jagged boulders, having much the appearance of a boiling sea of lava which had been suddenly congealed. After nightfall the brigades on the side of the Pedregal nearest the city of Contreras held a council of war at which it was decided that a concerted attack by the two divided forces was essential. The problem then became one of how to communicate with General Scott.

The rain was falling in tropical torrents, and the night was so intensely dark that it was possible to move only by groping. But Lee without hesitation volunteered to undertake the perilous passage of the Pedregal in the pitch-black darkness in order to arrange for the cooperation of Scott's troops in the morning. It was three miles across this murderous stretch of almost impassable ground; a fall upon the sharp volcanic rock was likely to be dangerously injurious; soldiers who made their way across it in the day-time cut their hands and feet in the passage. To attempt it in the dark and in the midst of a Mexican rain-storm meant that scarcely a step could be taken without danger of death—but Lee attempted it and made it! Earlier in the evening General Scott had sent out in succession seven couriers in an effort to communicate with the troops on the other side and they had all returned reporting the passage impossible. But shortly after midnight Captain Lee stepped into Scott's tent, his clothing torn and dripping wet, his boots in tatters, his hands cut and bleeding, and officially reported the other troops' plan of battle.

General Scott described this as "the greatest feat of physical and moral courage performed by any individual, in my knowledge, pending the campaign"; and it was this dare-devil accomplishment of Lee's that made possible the concerted movement of the American troops at three o'clock in the morning that resulted in the defeat of the Mexicans at Contreras.

The next stand of the Mexicans was at Cherubusco, and here again Captain Lee conducted the reconnaissance and later brought up reinforcements to the left wing when it was hard pressed and victory trembled in the balance.

General Persifer Smith, in his official report of the engagements at Contreras and Cherubusco, said: "I wish to record particularly my admiration of the conduct of Captain Lee of the Engineers. His reconnaissances, though pushed far beyond the bounds of prudence, were conducted with so much skill that their fruits were of the utmost value, the soundness of his judgment and his personal daring being equally conspicuous." General Shields, in his report of the same engagements, made special mention of Captain Lee, "in whose skill and judgment I had the utmost confidence."

The Mexicans were next encountered at Molino del Rey, where they were again defeated; and then followed the last battle and victory of the campaign, the storming of the heights of Chapultepec, in which battle Lee was wounded. In his report General Scott spoke of him in glowing terms, saying that he was "as distinguished for felicitous execution as for science and daring" and further that "Captain Lee, so constantly distinguished, also bore important orders from me, until he fainted from a wound and the loss of two nights' sleep at the batteries."

Following the fall of Chapultepec, the American army entered the City of Mexico; and Lee, as a member of General Scott's staff, was with the squadron that marched across the Grand Plaza and planted the Stars and Stripes triumphantly upon the Halls of the Montezumas.

Captain Lee's exploits in the field were not only recognized and mentioned in the commanding general's reports, but he was rewarded by repeated promotions. After Cerro Gordo he was given the brevet rank of major; after Contreras and Cherubusco he was brevetted lieutenant colonel; and after Chapultepec he was nominated for the brevet rank of colonel.

The news of his distinguished services spread throughout the American forces at the time, and his brother, still at Vera Cruz with the naval flotilla, wrote to him congratulating him on his accomplishments. But Captain Lee replied: "As to myself, your brotherly feelings have made you estimate too highly my small services; and though praise from one I love so dearly is sweet, truth compels me to disclaim it. I did nothing more than others in my place would have done much better. The great cause of our success was in our leader. It was his stout heart that cast us on the shore at Vera Cruz; his bold self-reliance that forced us through the pass at Cerro Gordo; his indomitable courage that, amid all the doubts and difficulties that surrounded us at Puebla, pressed us forward to this capital and finally brought us within its gates."

Later, while he was still in Mexico City, when there was talk among his friends of taking steps to see to it that his conspicuous services were rewarded with promotion, he wrote: "I hope my friends will give themselves no annoyance on my account, or any concern about the distribution of favors. I know how those things are awarded at Washington, and how the President will be besieged by clamorous claimants. I do not wish to be numbered among them. Such as he can conscientiously bestow, I shall gratefully receive, and have no doubt that those will exceed my deserts."

The American army entered Mexico City in September of 1847; and, so far as the actual fighting was concerned, the war ended then and there. Due to political complications, however, there was considerable delay in concluding a treaty of peace; and during the months while the diplomatic negotiations dragged along the Army was quartered in Mexico City and the Engineer Corps was kept busy making maps of the city and its defenses.

Lee, as a member of Scott's staff, was stationed at headquarters, and was frequently the officer in charge of the commanding general's office. One day a dusty, untidy-looking lieutenant came into the office to report to the general on some field work he had just completed. Lee, in his official capacity, hesitated to send him in to the General's presence in his bedraggled, informal attire. "I believe, lieutenant," he suggested mildly, but with the authority of his superior rank, "that you had better go to your tent and change your uniform before reporting to the General." Lieutenant U. S. Grant, without argument, accepted this gentle reproof from Captain Robert E. Lee. Lee probably never thought of it again; but Grant recalled it when the two next met—at Appomattox, Virginia, in April, 1865.

At last the peace treaty with the Mexicans was

signed and the army folded its tents and returned to the States. Captain Lee's last act in Mexico was to buy a little mustang pony (appropriately named Santa Anna) to take home to his youngest boy as a memento of the campaign. Lee sailed from Vera Cruz to New Orleans, took passage in a steamboat up the river; and in June, 1848, he was back at Arlington with his family.

The Mexican War marked a change in Lee's army life. Up until 1846 he had never smelled powder. He had been in the Army for seventeen years, but all these years had been spent in performing the duties of any army engineer. The Mexican campaign changed all that.

Robert E. Lee went to Vera Cruz an engineer; he returned from the Halls of the Montezumas a soldier.

CHAPTER IV

Colonel Lee of the Dragoons

CAPTAIN LEE got back to Arlington during the latter days of June, in time to be present at the celebration of the Fourth of July, an event which was always observed with elaborate ceremonies at Arlington by Mr. Custis.

Mr. Custis felt very keenly the fact that he was the last living link with the spirit of George Washington, and he felt that this relationship placed on him certain peculiar responsibilities to see that the patriotic principles of Washington were kept alive and observed with the proper spirit of veneration. Accordingly, on every Fourth of July, he erected on the lawn at Arlington the tent that had been used by General Washington in his Revolutionary campaigns; and under this tent Mr. Custis sat throughout the day, receiving the visitors who came out from Alexandria and Washington and the surrounding country. The visitors would pay their respects, the Washington family relics were displayed in the house, there were some patriotic speeches and illuminations, and refreshments were served. It was always

[49]

a colorful occasion, enjoyed by everybody—and nobody enjoyed it more than Mr. Custis.

The next day after the Fourth of July festivities, Lee went to visit his sister in Baltimore—his sister Anne, who had married Judge Marshall. His family accompanied him, young Robert in a fever of excitement on account of a "surprise" which his father promised him when they got there. The "surprise" turned out to be the arrival of the ship from Vera Cruz bearing Santa Anna, the little Mexican mustang; and Lee and little Rob went down to the docks to meet the boat, so that the boy could get his first glimpse of the new pony as he walked down the gang-plank.

Santa Anna was a sick-looking pony, after his long ocean voyage; but he was the apple of young Robert's eye from that time until the day the pony died early in 1861. Jim Connally, the Irish army orderly who had accompanied Lee through the Mexican campaign, taught Robert to ride—and accompanied his riding lessons with some tall tales of the fighting in Mexico. "Why, me and Santa Anna was the first men on the walls of Chapultepec!" Jim would solemnly tell the gaping Robert, and the romantic appeal of the little mustang was hugely increased to the little boy, even though he had had enough experience with Army sergeants to take Jim's tales with a grain of salt.

Captain Lee, the war behind him, resumed his

service in the Engineers' Corps; and the first duty assigned him was as a member of a board of Army officers sent to examine the coasts of Florida and its defenses, in January, 1849. In April of that year he was entrusted with the building of Fort Carroll in the Patapsco River, eight miles below Baltimore. The Lee family moved to that city and remained there for three years while the work of building the fort progressed. Young Robert was now old enough to go to school; but his father knew how much interest a boy would find in an enterprise like building a fort, and he took him with him to the fort frequently.

Years later Robert wrote of those happy days: "We would drive to the harbor in a bus, and there take one of the boats of the fort, sent up to meet us, with a crew from among the employees there, and were rowed to Sollers Point. There I was generally left in charge of the people of the place while my father visited the works and the workmen at the fort, a short distance out in the river. Those days were very happy ones. The shipping, the river, the boat and oarsmen, and the country dinner at Sollers Point —all made a strong impression on me. But, above all, I remember my father—his gentle, loving care of me; his bright talk; his stories; his maxims and teachings. I was so proud of him, and of the evident respect for and trust in him that everyone showed. The impressions received at that time have never changed nor left me. When he and my mother went out in the evening to some entertainment, we were allowed to sit up and see them start. My father, as I remember, was in uniform; and always ready, waiting for my mother, who was generally late. He would chide her gently in a playful way, and with his bright smile. After telling us goodbye, I would go to sleep with this beautiful picture in my mind—the golden epaulets and all; always the epaulets!"[1]

While he was stationed in Baltimore Captain Lee was approached by the Junta of Cuban revolutionists in New York who wanted him to take command of the revolutionary forces in Cuba. Jefferson Davis was Secretary of War at that time and Lee went to Washington to discuss with him the propriety of accepting the offer. He had been educated in the service of the United States, and doubted whether it would be proper to accept service in the army of a foreign country, while he held his Army commission. Davis officially reassured him on this point; but, after mature deliberation, Lee declined the attractive offer.

On September 1st, 1852, Lee was honored with the appointment as Superintendent of the Military Academy at West Point, the office carrying with it the temporary rank of Colonel. While he was arranging the details of the transfer from Baltimore to West Point the family went to Arlington for a short

[1] From *Recollections and Letters of Robert E. Lee*, by Captain Robert E. Lee. Copyright, 1904, 1924, by Doubleday, Doran & Company, Inc.

stay, but soon they were all together again in the house at the Point assigned to the Superintendent. This was a delightful place to live—a large stone house, with stables and pasture and garden. The children enjoyed their new home immensely, and Robert particularly enjoyed the long rides he had with his father—he on Santa Anna and his father on Grace Darling, the mare he had ridden throughout the Mexican campaign. Grace Darling had stopped seven Mexican bullets during her service in Mexico, and Robert liked to point out the scars proudly to the other boys.

Robert was just then at the most interesting stage of a young boy's life, and his father encouraged him in all kinds of outdoor sports. He took pains to see that the boy learned to swim, and learned properly. Here Robert got his first sled and his first pair of skates; and the Colonel often came out to see him and the other boys as they coasted down the big hill back of the Academy. At night he helped Robert with his studies—not getting his lessons for him, but showing him how to get them for himself—and the boy had his reward in the gleam in his father's eye whenever he brought home a good report. "He was very patient, very loving, very good to me," said Robert long years afterward.

Robert also mentions, in his recollections, that his father was a scrupulous and punctual attendant at the

Sunday services at the Post Chapel—but, with a touch of mischief, he adds that not infrequently the Superintendent dozed off to sleep during the droning sermon of the Post Chaplain.

Custis Lee at this time was a cadet at West Point, and at the head of his class; but we may be sure he got no special favors by reason of being the Superintendent's son. He lived in the barracks with the other cadets, seeing his father and mother only on the days specified for such relaxation of the discipline. Lee writing to his daughter Annie, who was then visiting in Arlington, spoke of how much he enjoyed these little visits from Custis. "It is the only time we see him except when the Corps come under my view at some of the exercises, when my eye is sure to distinguish him among his comrades and follow him over the plain." In Custis's class was his first cousin, Fitzhugh Lee, later a general in the Confederate army. And there was also in the class another gay young cadet from Virginia of whom the Superintendent was very fond—the popular, laughing, jovial James Ewell Brown Stuart, later famous as the dashing General "Jeb" Stuart, but then called "Beauty" by his classmates, for the same reason that a fat boy is sometimes nicknamed "Skinny."

Lee remained at West Point until April 1, 1855, at which time he was appointed Lieutenant-Colonel of the Second Dragoons, one of the two new regiments of cavalry then being raised for service on the frontier. At first the headquarters of the new regi-

ment was at Louisville, Ky., and here he assumed
his new command on April 20th. Later it was decided
that the new companies should be organized and instructed at Jefferson Barracks, Mo., and Lieutenant-
Colonel Lee was transferred there. Meanwhile the
family returned to Arlington to live with Mr. Custis,
Mrs. Custis having died in 1853.

The task of organizing a new regiment was one
full of difficulties, but Lee greatly enjoyed his new
line of work and got a full measure of enjoyment out
of all the amusing episodes that cropped out. There
was some delay in forwarding uniforms and equipment to the new regiment, and one morning at muster Lee found one of the new recruits in the ranks
dressed in a dirty shirt and pants, worn shoes and
a battered beaver hat. Reproved for his appearance,
he explained that these tattered garments comprised
his entire wardrobe and that he could not even wash
and mend them because he had nothing else to put
on. But Colonel Lee solved that difficulty. "After
muster," he told the ragged recruit, "go down to the
river and wash your clothes, and sit on the bank and
watch the passing steamboats until they dry, and
then mend them." The next morning at inspection
the soldier stood proudly in his place, his solitary
two garments clean, his hat cocked back and his toes
sticking through his shoes. Lee roundly complimented
his improved appearance; and the recruit grinned
happily.

The recruiting work occupied the fall and winter

of 1855-1856; and in the spring of the latter year the regiment marched off to its assignment in western Texas. The Second Cavalry boasted a remarkably fine lot of officers, a surprisingly large number of them attaining to high rank in the Union or Confederate Armies a few years later. Colonel Albert Sidney Johnston, Lieutenant-Colonel Robert E. Lee, First Major W. J. Hardee, Second Major George H. Thomas, Captains Earl Van Dorn, W. H. Whiting and E. Kirby-Smith, and Lieutenants John B. Hood, Fitzhugh Lee, R. W. Johnson, N. G. Evans, and George Stoneman—all of these attained to the rank of General!

The Second Cavalry was entrusted with the difficult duty of patrolling that wild part of western Texas, stretching from the Rio Grande to the Arkansas River and to New Mexico on the west; a country, to use the words of one current historian, "occupied exclusively by wild animals and Comanche Indians" —and in those days there wasn't much difference between the two. The Comanches gave the Second Cavalry by far the most concern. They were unusually active at this time, going on the warpath frequently; and unprotected settlers and emigrants had only the cavalrymen to look to for protection from the savages' murderous attacks.

The headquarters of the regiment was established at Fort Mason, Texas; but the troops were split up into several detachments and stationed at outlying posts. The first and fifth squadrons of the regiment were placed at Camp Cooper on the Brazos under command of Lieutenant-Colonel Lee. This assignment was notable for one thing: It marked the first time that Robert E. Lee had independent command of a body of soldiers in active service.

Lee's first move in his new location was to get in touch with the most accessible Comanche Chief, Catumseh, who was supposed to be partly civilized and semi-friendly. Through an interpreter, Lee and Catumseh had a long pow-wow. The Colonel hailed the Chief as a friend, as long as his conduct and that of his tribe deserved it, but warned him that he would meet him as an enemy the first moment he failed to keep his word. Catumseh received this with a characteristic non-committal grunt. He introduced the cavalry commander to his six wives, bedecked in all their paint and gaudy trinkets, and was visibly disappointed when he found that the white Colonel had only one. The white man could not amount to very much if he had only one wife! Despite all this palaver and all Catumseh's promises of good behaviour, the Comanches gave constant trouble; and there were innumerable small encounters between the troopers and the marauding savages.

In July, 1856, Lee was off on a scouting trip on the Brazos; and when he got back he wrote to Mrs. Lee: "I hope your father continues well and enjoyed his usual celebration of the Fourth of July. Mine was spent, after a march of thirty miles, under my blanket, elevated on four sticks driven in the ground, as a sunshade. The sun was fiery hot, the atmosphere like the blast from a hot-air furnace, the water salt; still my feelings for my country were as ardent, my faith in her future as true, and my hopes for her advancement as unabated as they would have been under better circumstances." Campaigning on those sunbaked, barren plains of the Texas Panhandle was not a pleasant experience for the Virginia gentleman, accustomed to life's comforts and luxuries; but this one letter to his wife is the nearest approach to grumbling in all his correspondence.

During the latter part of 1856 Lieutenant-Colonel Lee and his friend, Major George H. Thomas, later the distinguished Union general, were detailed for service on a court martial sitting at Fort Brown on the Rio Grande; and he was absent on this duty for several months. His first letters home from Fort Brown included messages to Mr. Custis (who had a great fondness for cats) regarding an especially fine cat named Jim Nooks possessed by the wife of Colonel Waite who was present at the court martial. But, alas, before he left there, Jim Nooks was dead. "He died of apoplexy," Lee wrote to his little daughter. "I foretold the end. Coffee and cream for breakfast; pound cake for lunch; turtle and oysters for dinner; buttered toast for tea; and Mexican rats, taken raw, for supper. He grew enormously and ended in a spasm. His beauty could not save him!" Then he went on to tell her of another fine cat he had seen in San Antonio, a snow-white one with a gold chain around his neck and with bows of pink and blue ribbon in holes pierced in his ears; of a Frenchman's cat who drank claret; and of a wildcat kitten somebody had given him. The Comanches and the courts-martial and the cholera in the camp were all forgotten when he sat down to write to the little girl back at Arlington.

Camp life passed tediously and sometimes painfully. On Easter Sunday, 1857, he wrote home: "I hope you have been able to attend the services at church to-day. My own have been performed alone in my tent—I hope with a humble, grateful and penitent heart."

In June an epidemic of sickness swept through the camp, and the little son of one of the soldiers died. Death is a cruel thing at all times; it is doubly dismal in an isolated frontier army camp when an only child is snatched from his loving parents. The father and mother wanted their little boy buried with the formality of Christian rites; but they were far away from any church and minister or even army chaplain. In their extremity they asked Lee to perform the ceremony; "So", he wrote, "for the first time in my life I read the beautiful funeral service of our church over the grave to a large and attentive audience of soldiers." A few weeks later the scourge carried off the infant son of one of the sergeants and he, with the tears flowing down his rough cheeks, asked Lee to officiate at the burial. So, for the second time within a month, he performed this sad service.

Christmas, as usual, reminded him of home; and again we find a trace of home-sickness as he writes, calling up a mental picture of the gathering "around the family hearth at dear Arlington." Deprived of the privilege of ministering to the pleasure of his own family, he derived great delight from his self-appointed task of playing Santa Claus to the children of the garrison at Fort Brown. The stores at the fort were rather barren of suitable Christmas presents for boys and girls, but by searching them carefully he at last found something for all. "Tell Mildred," he wrote, "that I got a beautiful Dutch doll for little Emma Jones—one of those crying babies that can open and shut their eyes, turn their head, etc. For two other little girls, Puss Shirley and Mary Sewell, I found handsome French teapots to match cups given them by Mrs. Waits; then, by means of knives and books, I satisfied the boys. After dispensing my presents I went to church. The discourse was on the birth of our Saviour. It was not as simply or as touchingly told as it is in the Bible. By previous invitation, Major Thomas and I dined with the clergyman, Mr. Passmore, at 2 P.M. on roast turkey and plum pudding. I had provided a pretty singing bird for the little girl, and passed the afternoon in my room. God bless you all."

In July, 1857, Colonel Albert Sidney Johnston was ordered to report in person at Washington for the purpose of leading an expedition overland to Utah; and the command of the regiment was turned over to Lieutenant Colonel Lee who was from then on the actual commander of the Second Cavalry. Lee continued in command at Fort Mason until October 21st, when he received notification of the death of Mr. Custis. He immediately obtained leave of absence and left for Arlington, arriving there on November 11th.

Mr. Custis was a man of considerable wealth and property, and he left a rather complicated will which necessitated careful administration of the estate. His will named Robert E. Lee as his executor; and Lee, securing an extension of his leave of absence, set about the difficult and tedious task of settling the tangled affairs of his father-in-law.

One of the foremost provisions of Mr. Custis's will was that all of his slaves should be set free at the end of five years. The expiration of this five-year period came during the midst of the war, when Lee was submerged in his military problems; but he found time carefully and methodically to arrange for the manumission of the slaves at the proper time.

The Arlington estate was left to Mrs. Lee for her use and occupancy during her lifetime, then to go to her son, Custis. The White House Estate, on the Pamunkey River below Richmond, he left to his grandson, W. H. F. Lee; and the Romancoke plantation was bequeathed to young Robert. The family silver, the Washington relics, all were carefully disposed of in the will, as were his other properties in Virginia.

Custis Lee was at this time in California with his regiment, and as soon as he was notified of his grandfather's bequest to him he, with rare filial affection, drew up a deed transferring to his father all his right in the Arlington estate and sent it to him. Lee was very much touched at this mark of his eldest son's devotion and generosity, but promptly wrote him that he preferred not to accept it. "It would not be right for me to do so," he wrote. "Your dear grandfather distributed his property as he thought best and it is proper that it should remain as he bestowed it." Lee's only suggestion to Custis was that he might consider the propriety of applying for transfer to some War Department work in Washington so that he could live at Arlington and be with his mother there—an arrangement that was finally made.

Administering an estate of this size was a tremendous task; so Robert E. Lee obtained an extension of his leave of absence from the army and stayed on at Arlington until the fall of 1859. Even though the reasons for his home-coming had been of a melancholic nature, he enjoyed the time—nearly two years

—spent at home. He took hold of things on the Arlington farm, rather run down under the careless management of the aging Mr. Custis, and was active in repairing the roofs, rebuilding fences, sowing the fields, making repairs and otherwise improving the appearance and condition of the place. The only cloud in his sky was that Mrs. Lee's health was extremely bad and gave him great concern, and also his daughter Annie was then beginning to show the first signs of that wasting illness which resulted in her early death.

Mrs. Lee and the girls were all at home at this time. Robert was away at a boarding school, but he wrote home frequently telling what a good school it was—they had fried chicken every day—and his father was delighted at his fine spirits. Rooney had graduated from Harvard two years before and, at the special request of General Scott, had been given a commission as lieutenant in the Army. He was arranging to resign and get married when he was ordered to accompany the forces preparing to go to Utah: and, since a Lee could not think of resigning in the face of active service, he postponed his wedding and set out for the West after a short visit with his father and mother at Arlington.

Colonel Lee, during his stay at Arlington, was not entirely out of touch with military life, for the War Department called on him twice for active duty— once to serve on a court martial at Newport Barracks, Kentucky, and once on a court of inquiry at West Point. But all the while his heart and his mind were with his regiment in Texas. The necessity for straightening out the involved Custis estate and the condition of his wife's health were sufficient reasons for staying on at Arlington; but, he wrote, "I feel that I ought to be with my regiment, and this feeling deprives me of half the pleasure I derive from being here."

The months dragged along, and Lee was still at Arlington in October, 1859, when Virginia and the whole United States were suddenly startled by the news that the abolitionist fanatic, John Brown, had gathered about him a small group of deluded followers and, with the hope of inciting an uprising of the Virginia slaves, had seized the armory of the federal government at Harper's Ferry. Brown took a number of the prominent citizens of Harper's Ferry to hold as hostages, barricaded himself in a stout brick building, and successfully resisted the efforts of the local authorities to rout him out.

In this emergency the Virginia authorities appealed to the federal government for aid, and a detachment of marines were immediately sent from Washington to Harper's Ferry to restore order. Colonel Lee was the nearest available officer of his rank, and he was hastily ordered to hurry to the scene of the insurrection and take command. Lieutenant J. E. B. Stuart happened to be spending a furlough in Virginia near

Washington, and when he heard of the trouble he volunteered to act as an aide to Lee.

Lee was standing in a drug-store in Alexandria when the messenger from the War Department found him. He acted promptly and was in Harper's Ferry by midnight. Within two hours he had sized up the state of affairs and laid his plan of campaign —to demand a surrender of "the robbers" (as he called them) and their hostages at daybreak, and if the surrender was not made to batter down the door and charge the inmates with the bayonet. This plan was followed, Lieutenant Stuart conducting the initial parley with Brown in an attempt to get him to surrender without bloodshed; but this effort proved futile. Brown threatened to kill the hostages if attacked. Among them was Colonel Lewis Washington, a relative of George Washington, and when he heard Brown's threat he boldly called out: "Never mind us! Fire!" Colonel Lee, admiring the grit of the brave old man, said: "The old Revolutionary blood does tell!" and ordered the assault. The hostages were rescued unhurt, and all of the insurrectionists were killed except Brown and three of his followers, who were made prisoners. In accordance with his instructions from Washington, Lee turned his prisoners over to the civil authorities and then returned to Arlington.

John Brown was formally indicted and tried in the Virginia courts, convicted and executed. The "John

Brown raid" was a subject of conversation everywhere, and various participants for many months told of how prominently they figured in the affair. One who was present at the raid, disgusted with all this self-seeking, wrote an account of the capture of Brown, in the course of which he said: "Colonel Lee's name has appeared perhaps less in the papers than many others less deserving, owing partly to his well-known unobtrusiveness; but the country and the state are greatly indebted to him for his coolness and sound judgment, and resolution tempered with forbearance, in the various duties he had to perform, such as military, judicial, municipal and even diplomatic."

The John Brown affair created a great furor, with the abolitionists indulging in the most extravagant eulogies of the "martyr" and the outraged Virginians denouncing him as a robber and murderer and insurrectionist. But Lee took no part in the discussion; indeed, seemed not to realize its far-flung significance. Lee had long ago freed his own slaves and was opposed to the institution of slavery; but he believed that it could best be ended by gradual, orderly processes. He could not understand the insane zeal of the abolitionists and their willingness to indulge in violence which, he thought, would defeat the very purpose they sought. He looked upon Brown as a misguided lunatic whose lunacy had led him into the commission of an offense against the peace and dignity of the state. It was merely a coincidence that he, Colonel Lee, was the most convenient army officer available to arrest the offender. Having done his duty in the affair he put it out of his mind; and a few months later he was on his way back to Texas to take command of his regiment again.

Conditions in Texas were about as he had left them, except that the difficulties with the Indians were now complicated by the raids across the border of the then current Mexican bandit, Cortinas. The trouble from this source was such that Lee moved his headquarters to Fort Brown on the Rio Grande. There was some sharp correspondence with the Mexican officials, some threats of invasion of Mexico in pursuit of the banditti; and conditions were in a turbulent state throughout the whole of Lee's stay there.

Meanwhile Rooney Lee had finally resigned from the Army and married Miss Charlotte Wickham in 1859; and in April, 1860, there was a letter from Virginia announcing the birth of their first-born boy, who was named Robert in honor of his grandfather. Rooney was living on his White House Estate, and was succeeding as a farmer. Robert was getting ready to enter the University of Virginia. Custis was stationed in Washington now, and was living at Arlington.

Everything was moving smoothly. To be sure there were, already in 1860, rumblings of trouble between the North and South; but level-headed people considered it unthinkable that hot-heads could ever bring the country actually into a state of war. In the Army the principal topic of conversation was the fact that John B. Floyd, Secretary of War, had promoted his cousin, Lieutenant-Colonel Joseph E. Johnston, to the soft job of Quartermaster-General of the Army, with the rank of Brigadier General, advancing him arbitrarily over the heads of several officers who outranked him—Albert Sidney Johnston, Samuel Cooper, Robert E. Lee, and others. Army officers are touchily jealous of their rights of seniority, and throughout the Army there was much criticism of this display of favoritism; but Lee wrote: "I rejoice in the good fortune that has come to my old friend, Joe Johnston; for while I should not like, of course, that this should be taken as a precedent in the service, yet so far as he is concerned he is in every way worthy of the promotion and I am glad that he has received it."

Late in December, 1860, Colonel Lee returned from the Rio Grande to his old camp at Fort Mason; and in letters written at this time he expressed apprehension at the growing animosities between the Northern and Southern states, hoping that serious trouble could be averted. Far away on the frontier, out of touch with the rapidly moving events, he little realized how closely the country was approaching to the brink of war; and he was probably surprised when, in February, 1861, he received orders from the War Department to "report to the commander-in-chief at Washington."

By that time seven states had seceded and the authorities at Washington knew that war was highly probable. General Scott wanted to have at his right hand the man whom he had frequently described as "the greatest soldier alive." So Robert E. Lee returned from Texas to Washington, to stand on the threshold of immortality.

CHAPTER V

The Great Decision

R OBERT E. LEE returned to Arlington in the latter part of February, 1861, and the next morning rode thoughtfully across the Potomac to Washington and reported at the War Department.

Washington was in a turmoil. The right of a state to secede from the Union was something that had been discussed, theoretically, ever since the Union was formed. Some of the states, including Virginia, explicitly reserved the right of withdrawal when they originally adopted the Constitution. There had been threats of secession before 1860, notably on the part of the New England states.

But now secession was no longer a theory; it was a fact. South Carolina had set the example. She seceded on December 20th, 1860. The other states trembled at her audacity; but no bolt of official lightning flashed down on her from Washington in punishment; and so, one by one, the other Cotton States followed her. On February 8th the representatives of these states—South Carolina, Georgia, Florida, Alabama, Mississippi, Louisiana and Texas—met in

Montgomery and formed the provisional government of the Confederate States of America, with Jefferson Davis of Mississippi as President.

This unprecedented action, of course, brought on the most spirited discussions. Some of the more moderate of the Northern statesmen and newspapers advocated a policy of "Let the erring sisters go in peace." The New York *Tribune* boldly advocated the right of the Southern states to withdraw peaceably, saying: "If the Cotton States shall become satisfied that they can do better out of the Union than in it, we insist on letting them go in peace. The right to secede may be a revolutionary one, but it exists nevertheless." The New York *Herald* said: "Coercion, in any event, is out of the question. A Union held together by the bayonet would be nothing better than a military despotism." On the other hand, there were plenty of people in the North who loudly and insistently demanded that armed force be used to compel the seceded states to resume their relations with the Federal government; and some, like Seward, were muttering darkly about an "irrepressible conflict."

President Buchanan frankly admitted that he was baffled by the situation. He said that he could find nothing in the Constitution which empowered a state to withdraw from the Union; but, on the other hand, he found nothing that authorized the use of force to make a seceded state come back into the Union. Mr.

Buchanan knew, however, that so far as he was concerned the problem would be ended on March 4th when his term of office should expire and Abraham Lincoln would be inaugurated as his successor. So he let things drift along, doing his utmost to prevent open disorder and bloodshed, and letting the future take care of itself. Meanwhile the hotheads, North and South, indulged in some very intemperate talking, which did not serve to pour any oil on the troubled waters.

Robert E. Lee had been taught in his text-books at West Point the political principle that this was a voluntary Union of independent states, and that it logically followed that any state had a right to withdraw from this voluntary compact whenever it might choose to do so. "To deny this right," he was taught, "would be inconsistent with the principle on which all our political systems are founded, which is that the people have in all cases a right to determine how they will be governed."

A surprisingly large number of prominent men in the North, as well as in the South, held to that principle. Horace Greeley said: "The great principle embodied by Jefferson in the Declaration of Independence, that governments derive their just powers from the consent of the governed, is sound and just; and if the Slave States, the Cotton States or the Gulf States choose to form an independent nation, they have a clear moral right to do so." Daniel E. Sickles, later a distinguished Union general, prominent in the Battle of Gettysburg, was in Congress in 1860, and in a speech there he said: "In our federal system the recognized right of secession is a conservative safeguard. It is the highest moral and constitutional guarantee against injustice." Many other Northern people held similar views—secession was not a strictly Southern doctrine, nor was it regarded then as necessarily revolutionary.

Lee, however, although he believed in the legal right of a state to secede, very strongly questioned the wisdom of exercising that right. In January, 1861, he wrote a long letter on this subject to his son, Custis, in which he agreed that the South had been aggrieved by the acts of the North; but, he said: "I can anticipate no greater calamity for the country than a dissolution of the Union. It would be an accumulation of all the evils we complain of, and I am willing to sacrifice everything but honor for its preservation." But, he concluded: "Still, a Union that can be maintained only by swords and bayonets, and in which strife and civil war are to take the place of brotherly love and kindness, has no charm for me. If the Union is dissolved and the government disrupted, I shall return to my native state and share the miseries of my people; and, save in defence, will draw my sword on none."

At the time of Lee's return to Washington the only states which had seceded were the so-called Cotton

States. The border states still remained in the Union, hoping for the best, and unwilling to sever their bonds with the federal government except as a last resort. Abraham Lincoln in his inaugural address seemed to be inclined to a conservative and conciliatory course. He sought to mollify the Southern states by saying that he had no purpose to interfere with the institution of slavery where it already existed and that, in his opinion, he had no right to do such a thing. He, however, firmly denied the right of a state to secede from the Union, and expressed his determination to retain control and possession of all federal property in the states which had announced their secession.

On the basis of this declaration, Fort Sumter in the harbor of Charleston, South Carolina, soon became the great bone of contention, the focusing point of the clashing theories. The new Confederate government sent commissioners to Washington to discuss the matter with President Lincoln; but he did not admit the legal existence of the Confederate States government and would not officially recognize or receive them. Furthermore, in pursuit of his declared policy, early in April he threw down the gauntlet to the Confederates by sending a strong naval squadron to reinforce Fort Sumter. The Confederates, as soon as they learned of this expedition, decided to seize the fort. Major Anderson, in command at Sumter, refused the demand that he surrender peaceably; so the batteries at Charleston opened fire on Fort Sumter, and after a bombardment lasting thirty-two hours, Major Anderson surrendered. This was on the 13th of April.

Two days later President Lincoln, taking advantage of the patriotic frenzy aroused by the fact that the Confederates had actually fired the first shot, issued a call for 75,000 volunteer troops, and the next day issued proclamations ordering the blockade of the Southern ports and suspending the writ of habeas corpus. Thus the die was cast, and thus the hesitating border states were moved to cast their lot with the Southern Confederacy.

A convention to vote on the question of the secession of Virginia was being held in Richmond at this time. The delegates to the convention had been elected in February, and at the time of the election a large majority of the delegates were Union men and opposed to secession. Lincoln's call for troops, however, changed the complexion of the matter. Governor Letcher answered the President's call for troops by saying that Lincoln had started the war and that Virginia would not furnish any troops to coerce the Southern states. On April 18th the Virginia convention passed the ordinance of secession.

The same day that the Virginia convention voted for secession, Lee was confronted with the necessity for making the most serious and far-reaching decision of his whole life. General Scott had not forgotten the brilliant part played by Lee in the Mexican campaign. Repeatedly he referred to him as "the greatest living soldier in America"; and on one occasion he said to the governor of Kentucky: "I tell you that if I were on my death-bed to-morrow, and the President of the United States should tell me that a great battle was to be fought for the liberty or the slavery of the country, and asked my advice as to the ability of a commander, I would say with my dying breath: 'Let it be Robert E. Lee.'" Evidently General Scott had communicated his high opinion of Lee to President Lincoln, for on May 18th the President sent the Honorable Francis P. Blair to see Lee and offer to him the supreme command of the armies of the United States.

Here was a difficult decision for any man to make. Lee's whole adult life had been spent in the United States Army. Only a few weeks before, on March 16th, he had been promoted to the rank of Colonel of his regiment. The uniform and the flag were very dear to him. He knew that the resources of the United States government were limitless. He knew that in the impending war the chances for success must all lean in that direction. In addition to the high rank offered him, materially he had everything to gain by accepting the President's offer. Obviously Virginia was to be the chief battleground; and the best way for him to save the property of himself and his family was to stay with the side which promised to be victorious. But merely material considerations did not influence Lee in making his decision. During the last year of the war he said: "I have never believed we could, against the gigantic combination for our subjugation, make good in the long run our independence, unless foreign powers should, directly or indirectly, assist us. But such considerations really made with me no difference. We had, I was satisfied, sacred principles to maintain and rights to defend, for which we were in duty bound to do our best, even if we perished in the endeavor."

Before Robert E. Lee was born his distinguished father, Henry Lee, had said: "Virginia is my country; her will I obey, however lamentable the fate to which it may subject me." Virginia was Robert E. Lee's country; Virginia was leaving the Union; it was a sad wrench to his feelings, a terrible tug at his heart strings, but Lee knew that he must go with Virginia, for weal or woe.

All of this must have raced through his mind as he sat and listened to the flattering proposal laid before him by Mr. Blair. So easy to say Yes, stay with the strong side and share in the victory and the glory! But Lee, the Virginian, could not say Yes to that proposal. Courteously he thanked Mr. Blair for the tempting offer, told him how he had opposed secession and how it grieved him to view the coming of war; "but I can take no part in an invasion of the Southern States." Mr. Blair regretfully accepted his decision and left to tell President Lincoln. Colonel Lee, still the Army officer loyal to his superior, went straight to General Scott and told him of the offer and his refusal.

General Scott begged him to reconsider; repeated assurances of his esteem and high regard. Deeply rooted as were Lee's affections in the old Army and its life, Scott's appeal seemed for the moment to shake his resolution; and he rode across the river to Arlington, his spirit groaning under the burden of the great crisis in his life. There was still a faint ray of hope: Virginia's secession ordinance had to be submitted to a vote of the people for ratification, and there was thus a bare possibility that the state might stay in the Union. But it was a slender thread. As long as he was in the Army, he was, to use his own words, "liable at any time to be ordered on duty which I could not conscientiously perform. To save me from such a position, and to prevent the necessity of resigning under orders, I had to act at once."

This decision, however, was not reached without due deliberation. He spent long hours in reflection, in trying to find the answer to the only question in his mind: What was the *right* thing for him to do? Down on his knees he went in prayer, seeking guidance from above; and on the morning of the 20th he came down the broad stairs at Arlington and said quietly to his wife: "Well, Mary, the question is settled. Here is my letter of resignation, and a letter I have written to General Scott."

His resignation, addressed to the Secretary of War, had the dignity of simplicity: "Sir: I have the honor to tender the resignation of my commission as colonel of the First Regiment of Cavalry"—that precious commission, the culmination of a lifetime in the army, which he had held only two short months.

His letter to General Scott began: "Since my interview with you on the 18th instant, I have felt that I ought no longer to retain my commission in the Army. I therefore tender my resignation, which I request you will recommend for acceptance. It would have been presented at once, but for the struggle it has cost me to separate myself from a service to which I have devoted all the best years of my life and all the ability I possessed."

To his brother he wrote, explaining his resignation, and concluding: "I am now a private citizen, and have no other desire than to remain at home."

Then he sat down and penned perhaps the hardest letter of all to write, to his sister Anne in Baltimore, who was married to a Northern man who, he knew, would fight on the side of the Union. We can see the tears in his eyes as he concluded his letter to his sister: "With all my devotion to the Union, and the feeling of loyalty and duty of an American citizen, I have not been able to make up my mind to raise up my hand against my relatives, my children, my home . . . I know you will blame me; but you must think as kindly of me as you can, and believe that I have endeavored to do what I thought right."

The war was a peculiarly cruel ordeal to Mrs. Marshall—her son and her husband both were officers in the Union army; her brother a Confederate commander. Day by day, through those four terrible years, she followed the fortunes of the Union army as it fought in Virginia, always breathing a sigh of relief when she learned of the safety of husband and son, always feeling the natural glow of satisfaction at their successes—but always concluding with: "But they can't ever whip Robert!"

Lee's ambition to remain at home, a private citizen, was not gratified for long. Two days later Governor Letcher summoned him to Richmond to accept the position of major-general of the Virginia troops. The state had withdrawn from the Union but had not yet joined the Southern Confederacy, so it was operating for the time being as an independent republic. In the nature of things, troops were being recruited and had to have a commander; and the convention, still in session in Richmond, elected Robert E. Lee to serve in this capacity.

A special session of the convention was held for the purpose of officially notifying Lee of his selection. When he entered the hall of the Capitol he received an ovation. He was then in the prime of life, 54 years old, six feet tall and straight as an arrow, his black hair but slightly shot with gray and his face clean-shaven except for a close-cropped black mustache. He was the picture of a soldier.

The chairman of the convention, Mr. Janney, made an eloquent and florid address, full of flowery metaphors and brilliant figures of speech. Lee's speech of acceptance, his first and last public address, was a model of modest simplicity: "Profoundly impressed with the solemnity of the occasion, I accept the position assigned me by your partiality. I would have much preferred had the choice fallen on an abler man. Trusting in Almighty God, an approving conscience, and the aid of my fellow-citizens, I devote myself to the service of my native state, in whose behalf alone will I ever again draw my sword."

Then he went back to his room and sat down and wrote to his wife, telling her of the events of the day. To his son, Custis, still an officer in the Engineers' Corps at Washington, he sent word that he must consult his own "judgment, reason and conscience" as to whether or not he should resign and cast his lot with Virginia. "I do not wish him to be guided by my wishes or example. If I have done wrong, let him do better." But he was very much exercised over the fact that the War Department had formally accepted his resignation as of April 25th. Scrupulously honest in all things, he insisted that his resignation must be effective the day that he tendered it, April 20th. He was very emphatic in his instructions to Custis, who was winding up his father's affairs in Washington, and he told him to return his whole pay-check to the War Department rather than accept pay beyond the 20th.

To Mrs. Lee he wrote sadly, telling her that war was apparently inevitable and that she must make her preparations to leave Arlington, as it was directly in the path most logically to be taken by an army entering Virginia from Washington. Mrs. Lee, naturally, was reluctant to leave the stately old home where she had been so happy for so many years; but her husband was insistent that she get out of the way of the deluge that was about to descend. "Do not put faith in rumors of adjustment," he wrote to her. "Make your plans for several years of war." Accordingly she packed up the Washington family portraits and some of the more valuable of her personal effects; young Robert and one of the servants buried the Mount Vernon silverware in the woods at night by the light of a lantern; and she and her daughters took refuge at the home of a relative down the Potomac, out of the war's way. On May 24th Arlington was occupied by General Irvin McDowell, who commanded the Union forces advancing into Virginia. General McDowell's first act was to write Mrs. Lee a most courteous letter stating that he was carefully taking care of the property "so that on your return you will find things as little disturbed as possible." Little did the urbane General McDowell and the distracted Mrs. Lee realize that never again would she be permitted to return to her beautiful old home.

Custis Lee did not hesitate long about what he should do. Within a few days he resigned his commission in the United States Army and reported at Richmond. President Davis promptly made him a member of his staff, and later put him in immediate charge of the work of protecting the city of Richmond from attack. Custis Lee was really a capable army officer in his own right, not merely the son of a successful father. He craved active service in the field; but, like a good soldier, served where he was assigned. The more President Davis saw of him the more he admired him: and, late in the war, when there was talk of sending Robert E. Lee to command the disorganized Confederate armies in the West, Davis proposed putting Custis at the head of the Army of Northern Virginia. General Lee, however, promptly vetoed this plan. He was naturally proud at seeing his son so highly regarded by the President; but, he pointed out, Custis had never had an opportunity to command an army in the field, and it would not be right to advance an untried man over commanders of known ability. Not until the last few months of the war did Custis Lee get into active service in the field.

Rooney Lee was living the life of a Virginia farmer on his White House Estate with his wife and baby when the war started. He at once organized a company of cavalry and volunteered for service with the Confederacy.

Young Robert, at the University of Virginia, was frantic to enlist, but his father declined to permit it. "The war may last ten years," he said. "We must save our young men." Robert helped organize a company of University students and they drilled on the campus. He was elected Captain and, boy-like, wrote to his father at Richmond asking him to send him a sword and a sash to wear. Lee had plenty of swords and sent him one; but he had no sash, although a general, and he had to apologize for not being able to supply one.

From the first Lee was impressed with the gravity of the situation confronting Virginia and the South. He knew it would be a long and bitter struggle. He was profoundly vexed at the boastful predictions of some of the leaders, North and South. Secretary Seward proclaimed that he would conquer the South in ninety days. Southern politicians predicted freely that the Yankees would be easy prey. A commonly heard boast in the South was that one Southerner could whip five Yankees. Lee, with some heat, exclaimed: "They do not know what they say. If it comes to a conflict of arms, the war will last at least four years. Northern politicians do not appreciate the determination and pluck of the South; and Southern politicians do not appreciate the numbers, resources and patient perseverance of the North. Both sides forget that we are all Americans, and that it must be a terrible struggle if it comes to war." To his wife at this time he wrote: "I agree with you in thinking that the inflammatory articles in the papers do us much harm. I object particularly to those in the Southern papers, as I wish them to take a firm, dignified course, free from bravado and boasting."

Meantime, while the politicians and editors sputtered and fumed, Lee was working quietly and steadily, trying to whip the raw recruits into an army. As soon as Virginia joined the Southern Confederacy his authority was extended to include all the Confederate troops within the state of Virginia; and this kept him busy. On May 29th the Confederate capital was moved from Montgomery to Richmond; and on June 8th the military and naval forces of the state were turned over to the Confederacy.

Meanwhile Lee had been studying the map of Virginia, and it was at once apparent to him that the most likely approach of the Northern troops would be along the line of the Orange & Alexandria Railroad. The most important strategic point on this railroad was Manassas Junction, where a branch line diverged to the Shenandoah Valley; and here, in Lee's judgment, was the place to meet the enemy. General Beauregard, who had fired the first shot at Fort Sumter and was a popular hero, was put in charge of the troops concentrated at Manassas on June 1st. Other lines of possible attack were not overlooked. General Joseph E. Johnston was placed in command at Harper's Ferry, which controlled the approach to the Valley from that direction; General Huger was stationed at Norfolk; General Magruder was ordered to Yorktown; General Holmes was stationed at Acquia Creek near Fredericksburg; and General Garnett was sent to the mountainous region in the western part of the state.

Thus all the approaches to Virginia and Richmond were effectively guarded—but, much to his chagrin and regret, it left Lee still in the position of a staff officer in Richmond. He was anxious to take up active service at one of the points of possible attack; but President Davis appreciated his services at headquarters, and so the great battle of Bull Run was fought at Manassas on July 21st between the two old West Point classmates, Beauregard and McDowell, with Lee working diligently and obscurely in Richmond, helping organize the Confederate forces, and sharing not at all in the frenzied acclaim for Beauregard and Joe Johnston who had led the gray troops to victory.

Wistfully Lee wrote to his wife: "I wished to partake in the battle and am mortified at my absence. But the President thought it more important that I should be here. I could not have done as well as has been done, but I could have helped and taken part in a struggle for my home and neighbors." But, he added with prophetic vision, "The battle will be repeated there in greater force. I hope God will again smile on us and strengthen our hearts and arms."

CHAPTER VI

The Heavy Weight of Failure

WHILE the Confederates were winning the great victory at Manassas, their fortunes were not progressing so satisfactorily elsewhere in the state of Virginia. In the mountainous region in the north-western part of the state, where the people later seceded from Virginia and set up the new state of West Virginia, the Confederate cause had been floundering.

In the first battle fought in that region, on July 8th, between General McClellan and General Garnett, the latter was killed—the first Confederate general to lose his life in the war. This victory enabled McClellan to occupy and fortify the principal mountain passes—Rich Mountain, Cheat Mountain and Sewell's Mountain. General Loring was sent to take General Garnett's place; and General Rosecrans soon replaced McClellan, who was called to Washington to succeed McDowell.

In one of the skirmishes between McClellan and Garnett disaster overtook the company of college students from Hampden-Sidney University, captained by the president of the university. It was their first engagement—and their last. They knew little of military science and their captain knew less; and the first time they got into a battle they were flanked by the enemy and, after a sharp engagement, were captured in a body. It was a sad and dispirited body of boys that huddled together that night in the Federal prison camp; but General McClellan heard about them, admired their pluck, and within a few days paroled the whole company. They immediately applied for exchange; but General McClellan told them they were too young to be fighting, that they ought to go back to school and complete their studies. And he saw to it that they did that very thing by arranging that they could not be exchanged for a year.

One of the boys of this command was sick with typhoid fever when captured, and before the parole was arranged he was taken to a private home within the Federal lines where he could be nursed back to health. When he got well he escaped and made his way back to Richmond and wanted to get back into the Army; but when he found that his company had been paroled his conscience troubled him because he thought that perhaps he might be technically included in the parole. In his perplexity he appealed to General Lee, and Lee with a characteristic sense of honor and fair dealing told him: "Legally you are not included in the parole. They haven't your name on the parole list, and from a legal standpoint you are at liberty to get back into the army if you want to. But they were kind to you when you were sick, and if I were you I would consider myself morally bound by my company's parole and would refrain from fighting until the company is exchanged."

General Rosecrans was one of the most energetic and talented of the Federal commanders, and when he replaced McClellan he proceeded rapidly to recruit his forces and strengthen his positions. General Loring, although an old army officer, did not distinguish himself in his new command. Other Confederate commanders in this sector were General John B. Floyd, who had been Secretary of War under President Buchanan, and General Henry A. Wise, former governor of Virginia—two typical political brigadier generals who spent most of their time disagreeing with each other.

An amusing story is told of General Wise's nonmilitary point of view in this campaign. On one occasion the Federals were making a demonstration in his front, and were indulging in some heavy musketry fire. The bullets whizzing over the heads of the Confederate raw recruits, who were acting on the defensive, were making them nervous and uneasy, and General Wise determined to do something to restore their confidence. Rushing up to the lieutenant in command of a section of artillery he ordered him to commence firing. The lieutenant suggested that since he could not from his position see any of the enemy he must necessarily fire at random and could do no execution. But General Wise heatedly retorted: "Damn the execution! Start firing; it's noise we want!"

The indecision and delay displayed by General Loring were displeasing to the Richmond authorities, who were at that time convinced that it was very important to hold western Virginia, and they determined to send a man from Richmond to take charge there. General Joseph E. Johnston was the first man selected for the post, but he objected to being side-tracked on such an assignment when apparently the principal theatre of the war would be around Richmond, so President Davis decided to send Robert E. Lee to see if he could restore order out of chaos in the Confederate operations in the mountains.

Meanwhile the Confederate government had created the rank of "General" in the Confederate Army and had assigned this title to five men: Samuel Cooper (who had been adjutant general of the United States Army and held the same position in the Confederate government); Albert Sidney Johnston, Robert E. Lee, Joseph E. Johnston and P. G. T. Beauregard, ranking in the order named, which was the order of their seniority in the old Army.

General Lee faced a difficult situation in western Virginia. The Federal forces had won a number of minor engagements which, though small and relatively unimportant in themselves, had served to strengthen the Union cause in that part of the state, already strongly Union in sentiment. General Loring did not receive General Lee with much enthusiasm, for he had out-ranked him in the old Army and resented finding himself under his command now. Wise and Floyd were bitterly antagonistic to each other, and cooperation between them seemed impossible. As a first command in the field for a newly-appointed General, it was not a pleasant prospect.

Lee left Richmond on July 28th and proceeded to his new command, taking up his first headquarters at Huntersville, where Loring was established. Loring was uncommunicative as to his plans, and Lee spent several days in the pastime he had learned to love in the Mexican War—reconnoitring and scouting to learn the position of the enemy. He soon concluded that the only possibility of dislodging the enemy was by an attack on his flank and rear, and he began to lay his plans for such a plan of procedure.

All the conditions for campaigning were unfavorable. It started to rain early in August, and rained nearly every day. An epidemic of measles and typhoid fever raged among the troops; and although he reported that they were "cheerful and light-hearted," sickness cut down their ranks until some regiments were able to muster only 250 active men. But Lee's difficulties were lessened to some extent, at least, by the fact that Rooney Lee, now a major in command of a cavalry battalion, was attached to Loring's command and he frequently got to see him. And although Rooney now proudly wore a major's star on his collar, the commanding general still saw in him the grown-up figure of the little boy who had cut his fingers at Fort Hamilton; and when it started to rain after Rooney had gone out on a scouting trip, his father worried because he hadn't taken his overcoat with him.

While General Lee was studying the positions of the enemy and trying to discover some means of reaching the rear of Cheat Mountain, he was also busily engaged in restoring the health of the soldiers and getting them in shape to move when the time came. The men who were well and able-bodied had lots of idle time on their hands, and they also had a good deal of curiosity about what was going on. One day a little group of privates from a Tennessee regiment, seeing General Lee and some members of his staff standing, with field-glasses in hand, on a commanding brow of the mountain near the camp, strolled over to see what the General was looking at. This was early in the war, and few of the soldiers had learned that a good private is supposed to keep himself quiet and inconspicuous except when the fighting is going on. Unabashed, they joined the group of officers, and looked out over the valley to see what they could see.

When General Lee observed the uninvited addition to his party, he turned to one of the forward privates and said to him kindly: "What command do you belong to?" "First Tennessee, Maury Grays," proudly replied the soldier. "Are you well-drilled?" asked the General. "Yes, sir!" emphatically. "I'll try you," said General Lee. "Take the position of a soldier"; and when the private had clicked his heels together, head erect and fingers on his pants seams, the General in rapid succession gave him the orders: "About face!" "By the right flank! march!" This headed the bold Tennessean directly towards the camp of his regiment, and the General said: "Double quick, march!" There was no command to halt, so the soldier soon found himself back in camp—and the boys who had accompanied him took the hint. Thus, without any offensive display of authority, the considerate commander taught these inexperienced boys an effective lesson in discipline and military etiquette.

At length a path through the mountains was developed by means of which it was possible to reach the rear of Cheat Mountain pass, and Lee laid plans to surprise the enemy in their position. It was decided to send a regiment of troops to the rear flank to open the attack, the other troops being ordered to advance when they heard the guns of the others' assault. All were placed in position on the morning of September 12th, and Lee had every reason to expect a signal victory. The soldiers in front waited and waited for the sounds of the first shots from the enemy's rear

—but they never came. The colonel in command of the flanking troops turned up the next day with an unsatisfactory explanation of why he had not started the fighting according to schedule—he thought the enemy was too strong in his front for him to cope with, apparently unmindful of the fact that his failure had caused the failure of the whole movement. The only result of all the maneuvering was that the Federals learned of the Confederates' plan of attack and so disposed themselves as to make impossible the surprise planned.

General Lee, writing home to his wife, told of his disappointment at the frustration of his plans; but his chief regret over the day's events grew out of the loss of his volunteer aide, Colonel John Augustine Washington. Colonel Washington was the grand nephew of George Washington and was the last of the name to live at Mount Vernon. He and Rooney Lee had ridden forward to reconnoitre the enemy and before they knew it had ridden into an ambush. Three balls passed through his body, wounding him fatally. Lee felt his loss keenly. Colonel Washington had always been anxious to go on one of these scouting expeditions, but Lee had refused to let him undertake such hazardous duty. At last, on this occasion, he had consented; and the daring Colonel lost his life. "The righteous perisheth," Lee quoted from the Scripture; and added fervently: "May God have mercy on us all!"

The rains continued; the General's tent had not come up from Richmond, being lost on the way. The weather turns cold in the mountains early in September, and he shivered at night as he slept on the ground, dressed in his heaviest clothing and wrapped in his overcoat. But chiefly he worried about the comfort of his men; and, in writing to Custis at Richmond about the sad state of affairs, he urged him to say nothing about it—it might get in the papers, and possibly the enemy might learn of the Confederates' plight.

Following the failure of his coup at Cheat Mountain, and knowing that further advance in that quarter was physically impossible at the time, General Lee went on to Sewell Mountain where the Federals under Rosecrans and the Confederates under Floyd and Wise were confronting each other. Floyd and Wise were still operating independently, refusing to cooperate with each other; and Lee's first move was to insist that their forces be joined so that they might not be attacked and defeated in detail. He also brought up a part of Loring's men, and with his combined forces occupied a range parallel to that occupied by Rosecrans, where the two armies were in sight of each other, looking across the mile-wide valley. Both were in strong defensive positions, and neither wished to hazard the risk of attack under adverse conditions.

After twelve days of glowering at each other,

Rosecrans withdrew, drawing off quietly during the night and being fifteen miles away before his absence was discovered in the morning. The roads were hub-deep in mud, the rains continued to fall, the horses were in bad shape from exposure and lack of nourishment, rations were scarce, the sickness of the men continued—Lee did not take up the pursuit, well aware that a skilful engineer officer like Rosecrans could easily defend himself against attack in the mountain passes. He knew that his failure to pursue Rosecrans would be criticised in the Richmond papers, and in a letter to his wife he said: "I am sorry that the movements of the armies can not keep pace with the expectations of the editors of papers. I know they can regulate matters satisfactorily to themselves on paper. I wish they could do so in the field."

Lee was a remarkably even-tempered man, and it was hard to get under his skin. But the way in which some of the Southern newspapers criticised the conduct of the war seemed to nettle him at all times. Once after the war he remarked to a friend, with a quite unusual tinge of sarcasm, that the Confederacy had made a great mistake at the beginning—"We appointed all our worst generals to command the armies, and all our best generals to edit the newspapers." He said that in planning his campaigns and battles he had frequently found, after fighting them through, that there were defects in his plans which he had overlooked—defects which, after the battles were over, the editor-generals announced they had seen from the start. "But unfortunately," he added, "they did not communicate their knowledge to me until it was too late."

The failure of Lee's West Virginia campaign gave the Richmond newspapers material for many a critical editorial. They ignored the causes of the failure; they looked only at the fact that it had not been a success. The attempted surprise at Cheat Mountain had failed; Rosecrans had been permitted to escape. Sneering epithets were hurled at the commander of the unsuccessful troops. Contemptuously they referred to him as "Evacuating Lee"; and commented that he "Displayed an absurd misconception of the basic principles of mountain warfare." Lee made no reply or explanation. He returned to Richmond bearing, as Jefferson Davis said in later years, "the heavy weight of failure"; but he made no excuses. He did, as a matter of duty, write to Governor Letcher after the frustration of his plans at Cheat Mountain, telling him of his "grievous disappointment" at the failure caused by the troops' failure to attack; but, he added, "This, governor, is for your own eye. Please do not speak of it. We must try again." Back in Richmond he made out his reports and got ready for whatever service should next be assigned him. In his report to President Davis he went fully into the details of the campaign, from which it was apparent that a large part of the failure was attributable to his subordinates' lack of enterprise; but he asked Davis to say nothing about this phase of the matter. "I would rather rest under unjust censure myself," he said, "rather than injure those who are doing what they can for the cause."

The Confederate authorities showed their faith in Lee's ability by abandoning the mountain campaign entirely. If Lee could not do it, they decided, it could not be done; so the troops there were dispersed to other commands, and the mountains abandoned to the Federals.

Lee came out of the mountains with a diminished reputation; but while in that region he made an accession which he cherished to the end of his life—his favorite horse, Traveler. Traveler was General Lee's favorite mount throughout the rest of the war and, indeed, after the war. The form of the stalwart gray horse became as familiar and well-beloved to the Confederate soldiers as the revered commander who rode him.

After the war an artist wrote to General Lee for a description of Traveler, stating that he wished to paint a picture of him, and Lee replied: "If I were an artist like you, I would draw a true picture of Traveler, representing his fine proportions, muscular figure, deep chest and short back, strong haunches, flat legs, small feet and black mane and tail. But I am no artist and can only say that he is Confederate gray. I purchased him in the mountains of Virginia in the autumn of 1861, and he has been my patient follower ever since—to Georgia, the Carolinas and back to Virginia. He carried me through the Seven Days' battle around Richmond, the Second Manassas, at Sharpsburg, Fredericksburg, the last day of Chancellorsville, to Pennsylvania, at Gettysburg, and back to the Rappahannock. From the commencement of the campaign in 1864 at Orange till its close around Petersburg the saddle was scarcely off his back, as he passed through the fire of the Wilderness, Spotsylvania, Cold Harbor and across the James River. He was in almost daily requisition in the winter of 1864-1865 on the long line of defenses from the Chickahominy north of Richmond to Hatcher's Run south of the Appomattox. In the campaign of 1865 he bore me from Petersburg to the final days at Appomattox Court-house."

When General Lee returned to Washington from Texas early in 1861 his baggage, including his saddle, was sent by boat. It did not reach New York until after he had resigned from the army and returned to Virginia, and so the port authorities at New York confiscated it. Lee had had this saddle made to his order in St. Louis when his regiment was organized there years before and he preferred it to all other models; so he promptly wrote to the saddle-maker in St. Louis explaining his trouble and asking him to make and send him a duplicate "if he were willing to risk receiving his pay." The saddle-maker was willing to take the risk, the saddle came through to Richmond, and the money got through to St. Louis; and General Lee rode this contraband saddle all the rest of his life.

Lee did not have long to stay in Richmond after his return from West Virginia. The Federals, with their superior naval forces, were threatening the South Atlantic coast. The Confederate defensive works had been put up hastily and, to a great extent, inexpertly and ineffectively; and the Federals soon gained a foothold on the coast from which they threatened both Charleston and Savannah. The citizens of that region and the governors of the states appealed to Richmond for help; and President Davis, knowing of Lee's outstanding ability as an engineer, ordered him in November to go down and take charge of the defensive work. So successful had been the newspapers' mud-slinging campaign against him, on account of the mountain campaign, that some of the officers on the coast defenses sent up a protest against having him sent there; but Davis coldly replied: "If Lee is not a general, then I have none that I can send you."

Lee proceeded immediately to Charleston, then to Savannah; and promptly put all available forces to work on the construction of the best possible fortifications. In Savannah he was back at the scene of his first service in the United States Army, thirty years before, and it must have caused a twinge in his heart as he saw the Federal gunboats trying to work their way up to Fort Pulaski, the fort which he had helped to build when on his first tour of duty.

This service on the coast was tedious and exacting, and Lee was frequently on the works until late at night; but physically it was a pleasant change from the dismal and unsatisfactory campaign in the mountains. Here the sun shone brightly, the weather was crisp and pleasant throughout the winter. It was possible to work steadily, without interference by the weather; and by the end of February Lee had so strengthened and improved the coast defenses that they successfully withstood attack until the very last days of the war.

CHAPTER VII

Commander—Under the President's Direction

THE curse of the Confederacy during its early days was excessive self-confidence. The firebrand orators told the Southern people that the Yankees wouldn't fight, and the people foolishly believed them. The rout of McDowell's army at Bull Run tended to confirm this belief, and there was a feeling throughout the South after that battle that little then remained but for the Confederacy to dictate its terms of peace.

But there was a sad awakening from this dream. Bull Run was an opiate to the South, lulling it into a false sense of security; but it was a spur to the people of the North, causing them to redouble their efforts. It soon developed that, despite what the orators had said, the Yankees could fight. There was abundant and increasing evidence that they could and would. And, as the Federals began to win victories, questions began to be asked by the Southerners as to the quality of the leadership they were getting.

Criticism centered around Jefferson Davis, President of the Confederate States of America and constitutional commander-in-chief of its army and navy. Davis was a graduate of West Point, had served seven years in the regular army, had commanded a regiment of Mississippi volunteers in the Mexican War, and had been Secretary of War under President Pierce. He was inclined to fancy himself as a military genius, and from the very beginning undertook to direct the Confederate armies' strategy and tactics. He had a Secretary of War in his cabinet, but he was commonly regarded as a mere figure-head. Jefferson Davis was the one-man director of the armies of the Confederate States. As long as the South was winning battles this was all right; but when the tide turned in the other direction, some newspaper editors and public men in the South began boldly to express the belief that Mr. Davis was showing himself incompetent to conduct the war and that there should be an active and able head for all the Southern armies.

The Confederate Congress brought the matter to a head in March, 1862, by passing a bill "to create the office of Commanding General of the Armies of the Confederate States." President Davis promptly vetoed this bill, assigning as his reason that it would vest in the proposed commanding general the power and duties which under the Constitution belonged to the President. Davis was a confirmed and sincere constitutionalist and, aside from any personal pride or vanity, conscientiously resented any invasion of the President's constitutional powers. With his point of view, he could not approve the bill passed by Congress. On the other hand, he had sense enough to recognize the growing surge of dissatisfaction with his single-handed conduct of the war, and he attempted to silence the critics by throwing them a bone. Accordingly, on March 13th, 1862, he issued an order proclaiming that "General Robert E. Lee is assigned to duty at the seat of government, and under the direction of the President is charged with the conduct of military operations of the armies of the Confederacy."

So, Lee was ordered to report at once in Richmond; and he quickly wound up his affairs on the South Atlantic coast and hurried to the capital. Arriving there, he found himself placed in a difficult, not to say impossible, position; but, as was becoming to a soldier, he accepted without complaint the orders of his superiors. That fatal phrase, "under the direction of the President" robbed his appointment of any possible promise of real authority in the conduct of the war. Nor did the newly-created office offer him any increase in rank, as he was already a full General. It was, from any angle, an unattractive prospect for him; and, consulting his personal preferences, he would have much preferred to continue his work as an engineer on the coast defenses. "I do not see either advantage or pleasure in my new duties," he wrote his wife. But without a murmur he went to Richmond and took his place as a sort of glorified rubber-stamp for President Davis.

General Lee was deeply concerned over the state of affairs. In a letter to Custis he said: "The victories of the enemy increase, and consequently the necessity of increased energy and activity on our part. Our men do not seem to realize this, and the same supineness and carelessness of their duty continue. If it will have the effect of arousing them and imparting an earnestness and boldness to their work, it will be beneficial to us. If not, we shall be over-run for a time, and must make up our minds to great suffering."

The duty to which Lee was now assigned was not only foreign to his desires; but the false color of authority carried by his official title has, in latter years, brought upon him some unwarranted criticism from military biographers who, thinking that he was actually in charge of all the armies' operations, have blamed him for not taking a broader view of the war in all its different theatres and for not achieving something like concerted action between the armies in some sort of grant strategy.

Something like this would have been very helpful to the Confederate cause; but the truth is that Lee was never actually the directing head of all the Confederate armies, except for a period of a few weeks in 1865 when, in a last spasm of desperation, Jefferson Davis did at last—too late—bestow such supreme authority on him.

The position to which he was called in 1862 was one of pseudo-authority, under the direction of a President who considered himself an authority on military matters and who possessed and used the power of veto of any of his subordinate's views. And even this limited authority was his for only a few weeks, for the office was abolished after Lee was suddenly called to take the place of the wounded Joe Johnston in May, and after that Lee's only authority was as commander of the Army of Northern Virginia. In this position his strategy was cramped by Davis's insistence that Richmond must be defended at all hazards. Lee on one occasion is quoted as saying in a confidential conversation, displaying a flash of his quizzical humor, that while he was commanding the Army of Northern Virginia he "got a crick in his neck from looking over his shoulder after Richmond." And that very aptly describes the limitations set on the great commander's strategy during his three years of campaigning.

When Lee returned to Richmond in 1862 to accept his new position under President Davis, one of his first steps was to establish there a home for his family, so that they could all live together again. His wife and daughters he had not seen since he entered the Confederate service a year before. They were living with Rooney's wife and child at the White House on the Pamunkey, and he wrote to them and told them to pack up and come to Richmond. Meanwhile he started to look over the town for a suitable residence. This was soon found in a modest brick house of three stories at 707 Franklin Street, which is still preserved and now occupied by the Virginia Historical Society. The house belonged to a friend of the Lees, Mr. John Stewart; and when he learned that the General was looking for a Richmond home he promptly tendered it to him. General Lee immediately took up his residence there, along with his son, Custis; and they gathered a group of young officers around them and established a military mess there while awaiting the arrival of Mrs. Lee and the girls. The house thus came to be known familiarly as "The Mess," and it continued to bear this nickname throughout the war.

Mrs. Lee, after leaving Arlington, had first gone to Cedar Grove, the plantation of a relative on the Potomac River below Washington; but from there she went to the White House and took up her temporary residence there. When she received General Lee's message summoning her to Richmond, the Northern troops had already begun their march up the Peninsula; and she, justly proud of the historic memories clustered about the old house where Martha Washington had lived and been wooed by George Washington, before abandoning it left a note pinned to the door, reading: "Northern soldiers, who profess to reverence Washington, forbear to desecrate the home of his first married life, the property of his wife, now owned by her descendants." This note had its effect, momentarily at least. McClellan established his base of supplies at the White House, and the place was carefully guarded by his troops while the battles around Richmond were raging; but unfortunately its salvation was only temporary, and when McClellan moved his base to Harrison's Landing a few weeks later the White House was burned to the ground.

Mrs. Lee delayed her own departure from the White House a little too long; and, to her chagrin, was taken a prisoner by the rapidly advancing Federal troops. She was held a week, but as soon as she succeeded in making known to General McClellan her desire to go to Richmond, he promptly notified General Lee of his wife's plight and sent her in her carriage to the Confederate lines under a flag of truce. So at last, with a Confederate soldier in the driver's seat, she finally drove up to 707 Franklin Street and established her residence there.

But before the Lees could get their home established again, there came another break in the family circle. Young Robert who, by his father's calm counsel, had been temporarily held in leash when the war broke out the previous spring, could now be restrained no longer. He was a man now—eighteen years old. It was all right for young boys to stay in school at the University, where he had been chafing impatiently for a year, but now Robert just had to get into the army with his father and his brothers. So in March, 1862, he renewed his pleadings; and his father, reluctantly, no doubt, consented that he might volunteer. Robert had already selected the company he wanted to join—the Rockbridge Artillery, under Stonewall Jackson—and he promptly enlisted. Proudly he went down from Charlottesville to Richmond, a full-fledged Confederate soldier, albeit a private, to see his father and outfit himself for service. He took a room at the Spottswood Hotel, proud of his newly attained man's estate; and the next morning the General-in-chief laid aside his duties while he and the new buck private made a tour of Richmond's stores buying his uniform, overcoat, blankets and other essentials of his camp equipment.

Nobody seemed surprised that the commanding general's son was enlisting as a private. His father could have got him some soft job at Richmond, but such a thought never entered anybody's head. Robert did not want that kind of a job; and his father did not want him to have such a job.

That night the young gunner, proudly arrayed in all his new panoply of war, set off for the Valley of Virginia to join the Rockbridge Artillery. "Good-bye, my son," said the General gently. "Be obedient to all authority; do your duty in everything, great or small"; and turned away with shining eyes. That night he wrote to his wife to tell her of their youngest son's enlistment: "God grant it may be for his good. I must be resigned. I hope he will do his duty and make a good soldier."

All three of General Lee's sons were now in the Confederate service—Colonel George Washington Custis Lee; Colonel William Henry Fitzhugh (Rooney) Lee; and Private Robert E. Lee, Jr. Another Lee enlisted under the Confederate banner was General Lee's brother, Sydney Smith, who had graduated from the Naval Academy in 1820 and was a commander when he resigned in April, 1861, to enter the naval service of the Confederate States. Sydney Smith's son, Fitzhugh (better known as "Fitz"), himself a graduate of West Point, was a Confederate cavalry commander throughout the war, being a major-general at the time of his surrender.

When Mrs. Lee took charge of the household at "The Mess" she was filled with a spirit of hopefulness and resignation; and, being still in fairly good health, immediately became active in what was then one of the most popular pastimes in Richmond—doing things for the soldiers in the field and in the hospitals. Her daughters and their young girl friends gathered here every day and industriously worked, knitting and sewing, scraping lint and making bandages for the hospital. Mrs. Lee and the girls were desperately in earnest in their work for the soldiers; and although she was soon stricken into almost total helplessness with rheumatism, she continued from her wheel-chair to direct the work of the young women. Throughout the war "The Mess" was the center of activity for the soldiers' aid workers in Richmond; and the harassed commander of the Army of North Virginia was never too tired or too busy to see to the distribution of the bundles of woolen socks which his wife sent to him for the suffering soldiers of his command.

CHAPTER VIII

Knocking at Richmond's Gates

WHEN Robert E. Lee was called to Richmond in the spring of 1862, the military situation was becoming acute. Repeated reversals had shaken the confidence of the Southern people. The Federals held Nashville, after the fall of Fort Donelson and Fort Henry, and were using it as a base of supplies. New Orleans had been surrendered. Roanoke Island on the coast of North Carolina had also been captured. Joseph E. Johnston clung tenaciously to his position in Centreville, in Virginia, where he had established himself after the victory at Manassas the preceding July. Here he accumulated stores, presumably for an eventual advance on Washington—but the advance never took place. Just at this time Johnston seemed to have his mind occupied principally with the question of his proper rank in relation to the other Confederate generals; and he and President Davis carried on a long and tedious correspondence on the subject. Johnston accused Davis of a deliberate effort to humiliate him, and Davis characterized Johnston as insubordinate; but nothing happened except that the gulf between the two men was widened and their usefulness to the Confederacy correspondingly lessened.

It was taken for granted that the spring of 1862 would see another Federal advance on Richmond; but the Confederates were in doubt as to whether this advance would be by way of the straight overland route from Washington or if the Northern troops would be transported down the Potomac to Fortress Monroe and thence marched up the Peninsula. General George B. McClellan had been put into supreme command of the Federal forces in Virginia following the rout at Bull Run; and, with the unlimited resources of the government behind him, he was gathering and training at Washington an immense army that threatened to be able to crush all opposition.

McClellan was a West Point man, having graduated second in the Class of 1846, in which class Stonewall Jackson ranked seventeenth. He had served with distinction in the Mexican War, being twice promoted for gallantry; and when he was called to Washington to take command of the Union forces in 1861 he was fresh from a "brief and brilliant" campaign in western Virginia that had made him a popular hero. He was a man of real ability, with a personality that aroused the enthusiastic affection of the men in the ranks; and his appointment was hailed with unbounded enthusiasm in the North. He was a man of rather small stature, and his soldiers called him "Little Mac." After his first successes, the Northern newspapers called him "the little Napoleon" and the Southern editors took up the term and used it in derision; but when he took charge of the demoralized Federal troops in Washington in the summer of 1861 he displayed a genuine talent for organization which helped quickly to restore the confidence of the Northern people.

But in the spring of '62 McClellan was having his troubles. Strangely enough, both North and South suffered at the beginning of the war from the handicap of Presidents who insisted on taking an active part in directing military affairs. Both President Lincoln and Secretary Stanton continually meddled with McClellan, volunteering advice and asking endless questions. Lincoln even went so far at one time as to issue orders for a general advance of all the armies in the field without consulting McClellan at all.

All this well-meant interference irritated McClellan very much; and, with the West Pointer's characteristic intolerance of civilian advice, he drifted into a sulky attitude toward his superiors and displayed an inclination to keep them in the dark as to his plans as much as possible.

Furthermore, McClellan was sadly handicapped by the inefficiency and inaccuracies of his Secret Service, and by reason of the misinformation with which they supplied him he gained a vastly exaggerated idea of the size of the Confederate Army. President

Lincoln had put the Secret Service under the direction of the greatest private detective then living, Allen Pinkerton; and although Pinkerton was a genius at tracking down bank robbers and counterfeiters, he had but little talent for his new duties. His agents brought in hair-raising stories of vast levies of Confederate troops being raised, and McClellan's natural caution was intensified by the spies' tall stories of "masked batteries" and mysterious reserves of gray-clad soldiers lurking in the Virginia forests. While Johnston had 40,000 men in his entrenchments at Centreville, McClellan was convinced that he had 150,000; and he shivered every time he looked in that direction.

While training and equipping his army in Washington McClellan worked out a scheme of attack which seemed to promise success. He planned to load his soldiers on all the available transports, slip quietly down to Urbana on the southern bank of the Rappahannock River only 50 miles from Richmond, and dash so swiftly and unexpectedly on the Confederate capital that he would be able to capture it before Johnston could move to its defense. But Johnston had plenty of spies in Washington and through them he got wind of the plan in time to frustrate it by suddenly abandoning Centreville and falling back to previously prepared entrenchments on the Rappahannock, where he was closer to Richmond and still between Richmond and Washington.

McClellan marched his army out to the abandoned Confederate camp at Centreville "to give the troops a little experience on the march and in bivouac, get rid of extra baggage, and test the workings of the staff departments." Having done this, he marched back to Washington; and Johnston, seeing that there was to be no attack from that direction, fell back to the Rapidan where he could still protect Richmond from the North and at the same time watch the Potomac. About the first of April his scouts reported that transports loaded with blue-coats were passing down the Potomac, and Johnston promptly advised the Richmond authorities that they could get ready to resist an advance on the capital by way of the Peninsula.

The Peninsula of Virginia is that neck of land stretching southeastward below Richmond, bounded by the James on the south and by the York and Pamunkey on the north, with Fortress Monroe on its tip overlooking Hampton Roads and the mouth of Chesapeake Bay. From Old Point Comfort to Richmond, on the James, is about 75 miles as the crow flies. Some forty miles above its mouth the York River divides into the Mattapony and the Pamunkey, the latter continuing roughly to parallel the James. The Chickahominy, a sluggish meandering stream with swampy banks, has its headwaters above Richmond and wanders down about midway between the Pamunkey and the James until, about 35 miles below

Richmond, it turns almost at a right angle and flows into the James. Yorktown lies on the south bank of the York River, near its mouth, and about 20 miles in an air line from Fortress Monroe.

The Confederates had a force of 11,000 men at Yorktown under General John Magruder, a veteran of the Mexican War. Magruder was a large man of imposing appearance, with a florid complexion setting off a magnificent set of side-whiskers. He was always dressed to perfection in the showiest uniform permissible, with all the epaulets and gold braid possible; and his grand air and courtly manners had won for him the nickname of "Prince John." On the battle-field and in the ball-room he lived up to his regal nickname; he looked and acted the part to perfection; but there was one slight flaw in his princely make-up—he lisped. Magruder was panic-stricken when McClellan's transports began unloading in his front a vast, well-equipped and well-trained army, out-numbering him about ten to one. He immediately telegraphed Richmond of the developments in his sector, and reported that he had held a council of war which had voted for an immediate retreat; but Lee firmly ordered him to dig in and hold McClellan at bay at all hazards until Johnston could come up from the Rapidan with the main body of the army.

Magruder already had a line of entrenchments stretching from Yorktown on the Warwick River on his right, the basis of his line of defense being the self-same trenches that had been dug there by Cornwallis during the Revolution. He had built dams in the Warwick, and the heavy spring rains soon made that stream a chain of impassable pools; so, fortunately for him, he found it necessary to hold only a stretch of about eight miles from Yorktown to the Warwick. But 11,000 men spread out mighty thin along eight miles of fortifications; and Magruder's men worked night and day, regardless of the continuous rains, to make the works impregnable. Borrowing a leaf from Andrew Jackson's experience at New Orleans, he supplemented his sand-bag breastworks with heavy supports of cotton bales; and, since cotton sold later in the war for $500 a bale, it has been said that these were the most costly fortifications ever built.

When McClellan started out from Washington with his expeditionary force he was relieved of his title of commander-in-chief and his authority was strictly limited to the troops under his immediate command, numbering in excess of 105,000. In the Valley of Virginia and along the Orange & Alexandria Railroad the Federals had 30,000 men under General Banks and General Shields; and on the Potomac, for the immediate defense of Washington, there was left a reserve of 40,000 men under General McDowell. Lincoln and Stanton would not permit McClellan to undertake the Peninsula campaign without leaving a big force to protect the capital; but McClellan, always cautious, insisted all along that McDowell must be sent to reinforce him in the investment of Richmond once the fighting got under way.

As soon as it was recognized by the Confederate authorities that the Peninsula would be the scene of the impending campaign, Johnston was ordered to move his main army there from the Rapidan and prepare to contest McClellan's advance. Johnston was put in charge of all the troops engaged in the defense of Richmond, and he stopped in the capital on his way to the front for a conference with Davis and Lee. When he left for Yorktown there was an affectionate parting between the two old army friends. Lee held the hand of "dear Joe" a long time in telling him good-bye; and, remembering his reckless bravery, urged him to take care of his life. We can well believe that Lee's heart burned with eagerness to go with his old friend to the scene of the fighting; but, tied down by the dictates of duty, he turned back to his office desk as Johnston left for the field.

Opposing McClellan in the Peninsula, Johnston had 53,000 men immediately under him, including Magruder's forces. He had left 8,000 men under General Anderson on the Rapidan to confront McDowell; and there were 18,000 under Huger at Norfolk.

Johnston's first inspection of Magruder's fortifications convinced him that they could not be successfully defended, and he advocated an immediate retreat to the fortifications of Richmond. Here, he suggested, all the available troops of the Confederacy should be quickly gathered and an assault made on McClellan when he appeared before Richmond, staking everything on this one pitched battle. Davis and Lee opposed this plan, and Johnston was ordered to defend the Yorktown line as long as feasible and then retreat slowly towards Richmond, keeping up a rearguard action with the advancing forces of McClellan.

Lee had studied the military situation intently, and he realized that it would be difficult, if not impossible, to cope with the invading Federals on any basis of sheer force. If the armies under Banks and McDowell should be permitted to reinforce McClellan or to cooperate with him by assailing Richmond from the north and west, it would be simply impossible for the Confederates to resist such an over-powering attack. Lee had a strong belief in the power of strategy to offset opposing numbers; and here he had his first opportunity to put it to the test. He sensed the nervousness of the officials at Washington. He knew that McClellan was counting on the reinforcement of 40,000 men from McDowell in attacking Richmond. As he advanced up the Peninsula McClellan kept stretching out his right wing further and further to facilitate the reinforcement, and he kept the Washington wires hot with urgent appeals that McDowell be ordered to march and join him.

But Lee recognized that those 40,000 men under McDowell were the key to the whole campaign. With them, McClellan would undoubtedly crush the Richmond defenses; without them, McClellan's strategy would be upset and his plans necessarily changed. Lee determined that McDowell's men should not be permitted to join McClellan; and his insight told him that the best way to keep them pegged down harmlessly in the neighborhood of Washington was by playing on the fears of Lincoln and Stanton who dreaded, above everything else, the possible loss of their capital.

Early in April Lee was in correspondence with Stonewall Jackson, adroitly suggesting to him how his small force in the Shenandoah Valley could be used to neutralize the armies of Banks and Mc-Dowell; and as McClellan advanced, he kept in touch with Jackson, opening up to him by skilful hints a vista of the great work he could do with his little army. Jackson, that great genius of strategy and tactics, comprehended the vast importance of what Lee had in mind; and when the time came he played his part to perfection.

McClellan, camped in the mud on the tip of the Peninsula with the rain falling in torrents every day, was suffering under the delusion that the Confederates had 200,000 men in the Yorktown trenches;

and he was reluctant to risk a direct assault with his 105,000 men. Accordingly he developed an elaborate plan for besieging Yorktown and shelling Johnston out of his position with long-range guns, the mud making it impossible to bring up the field artillery. Accordingly he sent to Washington for siege guns and heavy trench mortars; and, despite the tremendous work involved in such a plan, he fell to work in the mud and rain.

The siege of Yorktown, it should be mentioned incidentally, marked the first use of aircraft in military activities, the alert McClellan having enlisted the services of Prof. T. S. C. Lowe, then America's leading authority in the new art of ballooning. Prof. Lowe had little trouble in demonstrating to McClellan the great advantages to be gained by the use of captive observation balloons, and he not only went up himself, with a telegraph line trailing back to the ground, but he took up with him from time to time some of the more venturesome of the Federal generals and gave them a birdseye view of the Confederate works. Incidentally, one of the foreign military observers attached to McClellan's army at this time was Count Zeppelin, representing the Prussian government; and it was probably right there in the Peninsula of Virginia that he gained his first idea of dirigible balloons.

As soon as they saw the big bags rising up over the Federal lines, the Confederates realized the great value of this new adjunct to the military art, and they immediately laid plans to make use of this new device for themselves. Even thus early in the war silk was coming to be a scarce article in the Confederacy, and an appeal was sent out to patriotic Confederate women to donate their silk dresses for use in making a balloon. The silk dresses were promptly forthcoming; and the balloon, looking like a flying crazy-quilt, was soon stitched together in Savannah and sent to Richmond. In lieu of the waterproof paint needed to make it airtight and water-tight, the resourceful makers dissolved gutta-percha car springs in benzine and smeared the outside of the bag with this makeshift rubber paint.

The Confederates had no such facilities as the portable chemical plants used by Professor Lowe in the field, and they had to resort to the expedient of filling their balloons in Richmond at the city gas works and then hauling it down to Yorktown moored to a flat car on the railroad. On one of its first ascents it broke from its moorings and was swept by the winds far over the enemy's lines. Later a change in the wind brought it back towards the Confederates who, deceived by its approach from a hostile quarter, started to firing at it. The Confederate artillery had evolved an ingenious system of anti-aircraft fire which had been successful in bringing down one of the Federal balloons; but fortunately their own balloon escaped their fire and finally came to ground in a nearby orchard. It was patched up for duty during the Seven Days, and when McClellan had reached Harrison's Landing it was carried down the James moored to the deck of a small armed tug and made observations there. But the tug went aground on a flow tide, and the balloon was captured. "Thus," wrote General Longstreet sadly, "perished the last silk dress left in the Southern Confederacy."

It took McClellan about two weeks to get his emplacements prepared and his siege guns in place; and then when everything was ready for the bombardment, Johnston forced an anti-climax to his adversaries' carefully laid plans by quietly withdrawing on the night of May 3rd and leaving McClellan his empty trenches. It was Professor Lowe in his balloon, making an ascent by moonlight, who discovered the evacuation of the Yorktown fortifications during the night; and by reason of the knowledge thus gained the Federals were able to take up the pursuit of the retreating Confederates more promptly than would otherwise have been possible.

Both the retreat and the pursuit were made exceedingly difficult by the rains and the mud. Horses sank to their flanks in the sticky Virginia clay; guns and wagons were mired to their axles. The lower Peninsula was one great mud-hole; the roads were long stretches of quagmire. Reminiscing of the retreat, a Confederate artilleryman said: "We carried our guns by the order: 'Right shoulder, *shove!*'" On one occasion, when a bogged-down gun was blocking a road, General Johnston himself got down from his horse and, seizing a mud-covered wheel-spoke in his hands, helped the struggling men release their gun and clear the way.

There was some sharp fighting when McClellan overtook the retreating Confederates at Williamsburg, and Jeb Stuart's cavalry had their hands full for several hours: but Johnston was at his best in a slow, deliberate retreat, and it was May 20th before he finally took a position in front of Richmond. His right was on the James River, near Drewry's Bluff, where impregnable forts blocked the passage of the river: and his left rested on the Chickahominy about New Bridge. Here he stood his ground, with about 50,000 men, to defend the Confederate capital against the attack of the slowly advancing McClellan.

McClellan, as he crept up on Richmond, was clamorously calling on Washington to send McDowell's 40,000 men to his aid. Finally, in response to his appeals, McDowell's troops on May 26th were started on the march to effect a junction with McClellan's extended right flank. But the junction was never made. Stonewall Jackson, with perfect timing, struck a sudden and vicious blow at Banks in the Valley and sent him reeling back on Washington. Blow followed blow, and as Jackson's brilliant and bewildering campaign developed itself, Washington officials trembled for the safety of the city. McClellan would have to look out for himself. It was Banks who needed reinforcements. Accordingly McDowell's march was hastily stopped. Ten thousand of his men were detached and hurried to the Valley to stop the meteoric Jackson; and the remaining 30,000 were planted firmly in front of Washington to defend it from attack.

Lee's strategic foresight and Jackson's brilliance in the field had neutralized 70,000 Federal troops.

During the siege of Yorktown and Johnston's retreat up the Peninsula, General Lee had been occupying himself largely with the work of constructing a line of emergency fortifications around the outskirts of Richmond to defend the city itself against the entry of the enemy. It was no part of Lee's plan to withdraw into these fortifications and permit McClellan to lay siege to the Confederate capital. His idea was to meet the advancing Federals somewhere outside the city and give them battle on ground selected by the Confederates; but he gave particular attention to the inner works as a means of a last-ditch defense; and the formidable nature of these defenses contributed greatly to the improvement of the morale of the citizens of Richmond.

Meanwhile, General Johnston had so maneuvered that he had all his army on the south side of the Chickahominy River with his center near Fair Oaks station and a farmhouse known as Seven Pines. Mc-

Clellan, in his effort to stretch out to meet Mc-
Dowell, had divided his forces so that he had part
of them on the north side of the Chickahominy and
part on the south side. Federal outposts were within
five miles of Richmond; and Prof. Lowe in his balloon, to use his own words, "was looking into the
windows of Richmond houses."

Under such circumstances, naturally enough, the
citizens of Richmond were in a state of high nervous
tension closely bordering on panic. They could see
the invading army's balloons in the sky, sometimes as
many as three at a time. The thunder of guns was
plainly heard in the city as the Federal gunboats tried
to force a passage of Drewry's Bluff and as the opposing artillerists of the land forces practiced marks-
manship on each other. Not only the citizens, but the
government officials themselves, were terrified by the
close approach of the enemy. It was feared that nothing could save the city, and plans were made for its
evacuation. The official papers were packed in trunks,
ready for flight. Planking was laid on the railroad
bridge to expedite the movement of artillery and
wagons. A special locomotive and cars, with steam
up, were held in readiness for the Secretary of the
Treasury to fly with the government's bullion and
specie.

Lee was working feverishly, bringing in regiments
of reinforcements from every available point; and
as these troops arrived in the city every effort was

made to cover their movements with secrecy on account of the Federal spies that infested the city. McClellan boasted that he got the Richmond newspapers every day as regularly and promptly as the subscribers in the city; and the Confederate War Department's plans were generally an open secret.

President Davis and Johnston were still at loggerheads, and Johnston took a keen delight in telling Davis as little as possible about his plans for defending the capital. Davis made a practice of riding out on the field, accompanied by members of his staff and generally followed by a lot of noncombatant hangers-on; and this habit on the part of the Confederate President kept Johnston in a constant state of irritation. General Lee, in this unpleasant state of affairs, acted as an intermediary between the two antagonistic leaders; and although he was never able to bring them to an understanding of each other, he handled the difficult situation so tactfully that he retained the respect and friendship of both.

Finally, on May 31st, Johnston decided that the time had come to attack McClellan's left wing, south of the Chickahominy, which stream was now so swollen by the rains as to have the two wings of the Federal army completely separated. With a battle impending on the city's very doorstep, Lee's martial spirit rebelled at the idea of staying in an office, but he knew how sensitive his friend Joe Johnston was and he was careful not to offend him by forcing his help on him. He did send word to Johnston that he would be glad to participate in the battle—that he had no desire to interfere with his command, but wished to aid him in the field to the best of his ability and in any manner in which his services would be of most value. Johnston thanked him for his message and expressed the hope that Lee would ride out to the field and observe the progress of the battle. Lee, therefore, at Seven Pines was simply a spectator; Johnston was jealous of even his old friend's help.

The Confederate attack was sadly botched. Longstreet, who was supposed to command the main attack, misunderstood his orders; and the assault ordered for daybreak did not begin until late in the afternoon. The muddy roads and swollen creeks impeded the movements of both armies, and the day closed without any decisive result from the fighting. Late in the afternoon President Davis came riding out on the battlefield to lend the aid of his advice and counsel; and when Johnston saw him coming he promptly mounted his horse and galloped off to a distant part of the field. It was here that he was severely wounded, when the day's fighting was almost ended; and Johnston's friends always insisted that it was the officious interference of Davis that forced Johnston to expose himself unnecessarily.

Incidentally, Johnston might have kept Davis in the dark as to his plans; but, in some mysterious way, it was understood throughout Richmond that May

31st would see a great battle. On the morning of that day, thousands of men, women and children gathered on the hills to watch the fighting; and, like an audience at a circus, they were very critical when the battle did not start on schedule time.

General G. W. Smith, one of Johnston's division commanders, was appointed to succeed him, and on the next day he continued the battle of Seven Pines (or Fair Oaks, as it is also called). General Smith acquitted himself creditably in this sudden emergency, but the contest was at best a drawn battle, with no advantage resting on either side. General Smith's health was very bad, and the excitement and exertion of the battle brought on a stroke of paralysis; so on the evening of June 1st President Davis appointed Robert E. Lee commander of the forces then defending Richmond.

Lee's star was rising, at last.

CHAPTER IX

Richmond Delivered

THE appointment of General Lee as commander of the Army of Northern Virginia, with McClellan's host of blue-coats in Richmond's very backyard, did not give universal satisfaction by any means. Richmond newspapers did not hesitate to criticize the wisdom of the choice, and referred to Lee contemptuously as "the President's pet." The unsuccessful campaign in West Virginia had not been forgotten, and critics emphasized the fact that the army was being turned over to a general who had never fought a battle. There were sneers about his timidity, as evidenced by the trenches he had dug around Richmond. There were doubts as to whether he would get out in the open and fight. Joe Johnston had behind him the prestige of the great victory at Manassas the previous summer; and regrets were openly expressed that there was not available some really capable man to take Johnston's place in this great emergency.

Ambulances and carriages and wagons were pouring into Richmond with the thousands of mangled

dead and wounded from the field of Seven Pines.
Churches, warehouses, vacant stores and residences
were converted into hospitals. The walking wounded
crowded the streets. The cemeteries were dotted with
fresh mounds of red clay. The war was a reality now
to the people of Richmond. The situation was serious. They needed a man of real military genius in
such a crisis—and a man was appointed who spent
his time digging trenches.

Even the army officers were dubious as to Lee's
suitability. General Longstreet, who seldom found
anybody entirely to his liking, did not hesitate to
question the wisdom of the appointment. He conceded that Lee was a capable military engineer; but
he was doubtful as to his power and skill for field
service. "Officers of the line," he said, "are not apt
to look to the staff in choosing leaders of soldiers,
either in tactics or strategy." In general, the infantry
officers had the traditional feeling that an engineer
officer, at best, was a defensive fighter, weak on offensive tactics.

Colonel E. P. Alexander was one of the Confederate officers who had misgivings as to the new commander's qualifications for his job; and he made so
bold as to ask questions, unofficially, of Colonel Ives
of President Davis's staff.

"We are here fortifying our lines," said Alexander
to Ives, "but apparently leaving the enemy all the
time he needs to accumulate his superior forces, and

then to move on us in the way he thinks best. Has General Lee the audacity that is going to be required for our inferior force to meet the enemy's superior force—to take the aggressive, and to run risks and stand chances?"

They were riding along the works together, and when Alexander asked this pointed question Ives reined up his horse, stopped in the road and replied: "Alexander, if there is one man in either army, Confederate or Federal, head and shoulders above every other in audacity, it is General Lee! His name might be Audacity! He will take more desperate chances and take them quicker than any other general in this country, North or South; and you will live to see it, too."

Recalling the conversation, years later, Alexander said: "It is needless to say that I did live to see it many times over. But it seems, even yet, a mystery how at that time Ives or President Davis or any other living man had divined it. No one could meet Lee and fail to be impressed with his dignity of character, his intellectual power and his calm self-reliance; but all those qualities might be recognized without deducing from them also the existence of such phenomenal audacity, except by an inspiration of genius."

Lee's first act after assuming command of the armies in the field was to call a council of his subordinate generals. He realized, of course, that they knew him only as a staff officer, a commander who had never actually fought an engagement. He knew also that the spirits of the men in the ranks were somewhat shaken by the botching of the Seven Pines battle, which was now being recognized in its true light after the first reports of a signal victory. The morale of both officers and men was sadly in need of strengthening.

The principal question discussed at this, his first, council of war was whether the Confederate army should maintain its position in the field or retire to the inner works and wait for McClellan to invest the city. Most of the officers were despondent, and the opinion prevailed that the line then occupied should be abandoned and the army withdrawn to the comparative safety of the inner fortifications. After listening to what they all had to say, however, Lee gave the first evidence to them of his self-reliance and confidence. Boldly over-ruling their objections, born of timidity, he announced that the advanced line would be maintained; and he gave orders for all hands to fall to work throwing up entrenchments.

Lee well knew that this order did not add to his popularity. In a letter to President Davis he wrote: "Our people are opposed to work—our troops, officers, community and press. All ridicule and resent it. It is the very means by which McClellan has advanced and is advancing. Why should we leave to him the whole advantage of labour? Combined with valour, fortitude and boldness, of which we have our fair proportion, it should lead us to success. There is nothing so military as labour—and nothing so important to an army as to save the lives of its soldiers."

Personally General Lee conducted a reconnaissance of the whole front, and established the position to be fortified. The army he reorganized on the basis of six divisions, commanded by Generals Longstreet, Huger, D. H. Hill, Magruder, Whiting and A. P. Hill, occupying the line in the order named from right to left. Each division commander was made responsible for the duty of constructing the breastworks in his front; and soon a continuous line of entrenchments was established, raising the spirits of the men for whose defense they were built. "The sullen silence with which their labor began gave place to jokes and laughter," wrote one of Lee's aides. Lee daily appeared on the lines, and the magnetism of his quiet confidence inspired the men with renewed hope and enthusiasm. By contagion, the alarm of the citizens of Richmond was to some extent quieted. The government officials ceased to flutter uneasily. The archives were unpacked, and business in the departments went on as usual.

But there was one thing that was not as usual. Lee promptly and effectively put a stop to the steady trickle of information that was leaking through to McClellan. He threw a veil of secrecy about the army and about his plans. Even the Adjutant General did not know how many regiments were in Virginia nor where they were stationed. Officers returning from furlough were sent directly to Lee's headquarters and there told the location of their commands. Lee was planning a desperate and decisive movement; and he took no chances on having information about it leak out.

He established his headquarters at a house in the suburbs near the front line, and here he lived with his staff and his military household. The army was speedily put on a business-like basis. Work on the trenches was kept up at fever heat; and brigade and division commanders were strongly impressed with the necessity for improving the discipline of their commands. The general had his meals with his officers' mess, and they commented on the fact that despite the grave crisis confronting him he was always cheerful and agreeable at meals and frequently hurled a pleasant jest at some member of his staff. High officials from Richmond were frequent visitors at headquarters, although their visits were often impelled apparently more by curiosity than anything else. But Lee was free from Johnston's petulance. "The general bears interruption with equanimity," wrote his aide in his journal.

Within one short year Lee's personal appearance had changed greatly. In the spring of 1861, when he returned to Richmond to offer his sword to Virginia, he excited comment by his handsome appearance— clean-shaven except for a black moustache and with his black hair only slightly touched with gray streaks. But in June, 1862, writing one of his characteristic playful and loving letters to his daughter-in-law, Rooney's young wife, in reply to her questions he gave this description of himself: "My habiliments are not suited to this hot weather, but they are the best I have. My coat is of gray, of the regulation style and pattern, and my pants of dark blue, as is also prescribed, partly hid by my long boots. I have the same handsome hat, which surmounts my gray head (the latter is not prescribed in the regulations), and shields my ugly face which is marked by a white beard as stiff and wiry as the teeth of a card. In fact, an uglier person you have never seen, and so unattractive is it to our enemies that they shoot at it whenever visible to them."

While the Confederates were working feverishly on their defenses, McClellan was strangely inactive. On June 2nd he reported to Washington that he was only four miles from Richmond and that he intended to advance the next day—but it rained the next day. Every few days during the next few weeks he sent in optimistic reports, always promising a movement to-morrow, or next week, or as soon as the roads were dry—and always insisting on reinforcements. Lincoln and Stanton and Halleck bombarded him with urgent suggestions that he get into action. He was profuse in explanations of his delay, and his explanations sounded plausible—but he did not advance.

Stanton and Lincoln, poring over their map in Washington, were losing patience with "the little Napoleon." After one of his appeals for reinforcements, Stanton said with disgust: "If he had a million men he'd swear the enemy had two million, and then he'd sit down in the mud and cry for three million!"

About the middle of June McClellan had a sudden and chilling intimation that the quiet inactivity of the new commander opposing him might conceal some unexpected movement. On June 11th Lee sent Jeb Stuart's cavalry trotting out the road leading northward from Richmond. There was a rumor that he was being sent to the Valley to reinforce Jackson —but it was no unusual thing for misleading rumors to get out about Lee's movements. About twenty miles out from Richmond Stuart turned suddenly to the east and without warning swept brilliantly around McClellan's right flank, on down the Pamunkey, then across the Peninsula and back to the Confederate lines in a sweeping dash around the enemy's left wing. In four days of hard riding he had circumnavigated the opposing army, had gained complete information as to McClellan's position, had captured and destroyed millions of dollars worth of stores, and had left dismay and terror behind him.

The whole country, North and South, was electrified by this audacious sortie. Cavalry raids were familiar movements; but for a cavalry troop to ride completely around an opposing army was a new and spectacular thing. The South was elated and derisive; the North was chagrined. Lee learned from this movement, what he already suspected, that the enemy's right flank was unsupported and fluttering in the air and therefore weak; but McClellan was aroused also to his own weakness, and he laid plans for the prompt evacuation of his base at the White House if later necessity demanded it.

After Stuart's sensational raid the Confederate lines were quiet again; but it was the traditional quiet that precedes the storm. Lee, following the raid, again made a personal reconnaissance of the Federal position. "Now how can we get at those people?" he remarked musingly to his aide who accompanied him as they looked across at the Union lines of trenches. Lee, of course, knew Napoleon's maxim: "The fundamental law of war is that the greater force always overcomes the lesser"; but he also knew Napoleon's qualifying maxim: "It is only the force brought into action which avails in battles and campaigns—the rest does not count." McClellan, as Lee well knew, had the advantage of superior numbers. Lee's problem was to keep him from bringing his force into action effectively. He must get the Federal army out of its protecting trenches piecemeal, and so concentrate his own forces that he could out-number them at the point of attack. It was a nice problem in military strategy; but, great strategist that he was, he found the answer. Turning the matter over and over in his mind he evolved a plan of campaign that was novel and daring.

From Georgia and the Carolinas he drew 17,000 fresh troops. Two divisions of these, as soon as they arrived, were not moved into the front-line trenches at Richmond but were ostentatiously loaded on trains and without concealment started off to reinforce Stonewall Jackson. The vigilance against spies was momentarily relaxed and this information was permitted to get through to McClellan, who accepted it as substantiating his idea that the Confederates had more troops than they knew what to do with. He also deduced that the next activity would be in the Shenandoah Valley, and so warned Washington. But Lee had a dark plot on foot. The "reinforcements" sent to Jackson merely had a good long ride; for no sooner had they arrived at their destination than Jackson, acting on Lee's previous orders, secretly and swiftly disappeared with his entire army out of the Valley and moved them by forced marches, assisted by the railroad, to Ashland, just sixteen miles north of Richmond and thirteen miles from Mechanicsville, where Lee planned to strike his blow. A handful of troops were left in the Valley to keep up a show of force there, and "deserters" and "prisoners" told the Federals alarming stories of Jackson's alleged plans to sweep up the Valley and capture Washington.

Jackson hurried on ahead of his command and on

the afternoon of June 23rd reported at Lee's headquarters after a long ride in a freight car and a hard
ride of fifty miles on horseback. It was the first meeting of the two great soldiers since the war started.
Longstreet and the two Hills were present at the
conference, at which exact plans for the coming battle
were laid and written orders issued to the division
commanders so that all might act in unison.

The plan was simple, and there was every reason
to expect its success. McClellan's right wing, under
General Porter, was stationed at Mechanicsville, with
its flank unprotected. Jackson was to march from
Ashland at 3 A.M. on the 26th and fall on Porter's
right and rear. A. P. Hill, as soon as he heard Jackson's guns that morning, was to attack Porter from
the front; and the natural expectation was that the
unsuspecting Federal commander would be crushed
by the closing in of the two simultaneous attacks.

But the plan failed—and from a cause no one
would have expected. Stonewall Jackson, the usually
infallible, did not carry out his part of the program.
Although he himself set the day and hour for the advance, apparently more was expected of his exhausted
troops than flesh and blood could stand. At any rate,
they were delayed in their advance; and the 26th
wore on with no sound of firing from Porter's rear.
Finally A. P. Hill, unable to control his impatience,
disregarded his orders to wait for Jackson's attack
and decided to make the frontal assault on Porter's

lines on his own responsibility. Lee, when Jackson's men failed to show up on time, had decided to postpone the engagement until the next day and sent orders to Hill, to this effect, but the orders arrived too late. Hill's attack dislodged Porter from his advanced position, where Lee had hoped to trap him, and he fell back to an entrenched rise of ground on Beaver Dam Creek so strongly situated that a frontal assault could be easily thrown back. The Confederates rashly charged this position, but they suffered a bloody repulse and so the fighting ended for that day.

During the night McClellan became aware of his great peril, with Jackson's troops up in force and ready to attack the next day; so at down of the 27th Porter withdrew from the Beaver Dam position and retreated down the Chickahominy towards Gaines Mill, with a strong rear-guard replying to the Confederates' opening artillery fire. Jackson had got into position on Porter's right during the night, and when he moved forward in the morning he collided with the advance guard of A. P. Hill's division moving in pursuit of Porter, and the two Confederate armies fired into each other before it was discovered that Porter had cleverly slipped out of the closing jaws of Lee's nut-cracker.

Meanwhile Longstreet and D. H. Hill had crossed to the north side of the Chickahominy, leaving only Magruder and Huger between Richmond and Mc-

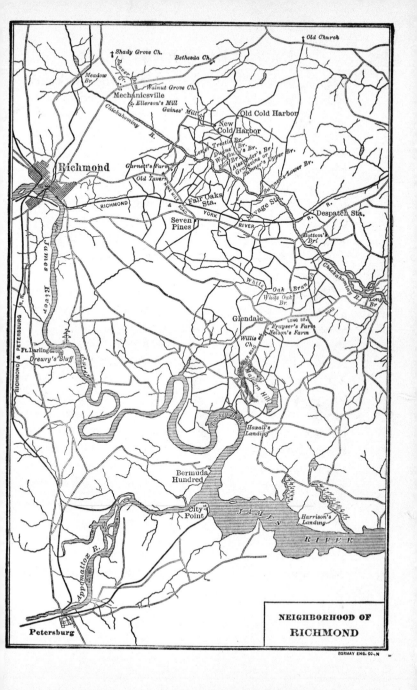

NEIGHBORHOOD OF
RICHMOND

BORMAY ENG. CO., N

Clellan's main force; and the four divisions now on the north side of the river deployed to attack Porter, now in position at Gaines Mill where he had been reinforced with 14,000 fresh men, giving him a total effective force of 40,000. Lee had ordered a demonstration on his extreme right by Magruder and Huger, and this deceived McClellan into believing that it would be unsafe to withdraw more men from that side of his line.

The Confederate divisions assailing Porter became confused in the attack; some of them lost the way; Jackson was late again; and it was not until the close of the day that it was possible to order a charge of the whole line at the same time. When finally the charge was made it swept all before it, and the Federals retreated in disorder from the field of Gaines Mill. Lee was master of the field.

Here was a complete and convincing answer to those who had doubted Lee's daring and audacity. Not only had he fallen on McClellan's weak side with the swiftness of a thunderbolt, but he had boldly moved the greater part of his army to the north side of the Chickahominy in order to strike with as great a force as possible at the point of attack. McClellan's center and left on the south side of the river were opposed only by two weak divisions; but so successfully had Lee concealed his true strength and the disposition of his forces that McClellan had no suspicion of the great opportunity he had to march into the city almost unopposed. Lee knew McClellan; knew his timidity. Such a division of his strength might have been inexcusable in the face of a bolder opponent; but Lee knew that McClellan could be bluffed, and he bluffed him.

On the first day of the Seven Days' fighting, General Lee had a little brush with Jefferson Davis which resulted in his being relieved of that Presidential interference which Joe Johnston had found so galling. President Davis rode out on the field at Mechanicsville, accompanied by several staff officers, Cabinet members and other non-combatants and sight-seers. Lee was obviously annoyed at this, and he greeted Davis politely but with visible reserve. Then, making no effort to conceal his irritation, he turned toward the large group accompanying the President and said: "Who are all this army of people, and what are they doing here?" Davis was somewhat surprised at this greeting, but he knew as well as anybody that Lee's annoyance was justified, and he twisted in his saddle as he met the general's look of severity. Then feebly he said: "It is not my army, general." "Well," retorted Lee sharply, "it is certainly not *my* army, Mr. President, and this is no place for it." Davis had not been accustomed to such plain speaking from his subordinates, but he recognized the right of Lee's position in the matter and said: "Well, general, if I withdraw, perhaps they will follow"; and so the little cavalcade of non-combatants left the field. And General Lee had no further battlefield visits from President Davis.

On the morning of the day following the fighting at Gaines Mill, General Lee, making the rounds of his lines, came upon the camp of the Rockbridge Artillery where Stonewall Jackson's men were resting, awaiting orders for the day. They had had a hard week of it, with their swift movement from the Valley to the environs of Richmond in the heat of a Virginia summer, on short rations and with little time for sleep. Most of the men were lying down this morning, glad of a chance to rest. One dirty, ragged unkempt cannoneer had stretched himself in the shade under a caisson and was snatching a few winks of sleep. He was aroused by a companion vigorously poking him in the ribs with a sponge-staff and shouting to him to wake up and come out and meet some visitors. Still rubbing his eyes, and only half-way awake, young Bob Lee stumbled out from under the caisson to meet the smiling face of his father. "It took me a moment or two to realize what it all meant," he said, "but when I saw my father's loving eyes and smile it became clear to me that he had ridden by to see if I was safe." The great commander had just won a great victory; rapidly he was maturing plans for the pursuit of the flying enemy; but, for a few brief moments, the preoccupied general of a victorious army became simply a fond father, concerned about the safety of his son in the ranks.

During the night of the 27th the Federals fell back from Gaines Mill in comparatively good order, although thoroughly beaten, and crossed the Chickahominy under cover of their superior artillery. McClellan was now thoroughly alarmed for the safety of his army. Over-night he abandoned his original idea of capturing Richmond. He was now definitely on the defensive, concerned primarily with the problem of saving his great army from capture or destruction. Quickly he ordered a general retreat to a new base, Harrison's Landing on the James where a fleet of Federal gunboats lay at anchor. Following Stuart's raid, the supplies at the White House had been loaded on the transports there, in preparation for such a movement; and although Stuart, following the engagement at Gaines Mill, again raided down the Pamunkey, McClellan was able to make off with most of his supplies.

Lee, on the 28th, was uncertain what the enemy would do, and paused while his cavalry was reconnoitring to see whether McClellan would retreat down the Peninsula to his old base at the White House or would undertake to establish a new base on the James. The day was spent burying the dead, caring for the wounded and consolidating the scattered detachments. On the morning of the 29th it was definitely established that McClellan was retiring in the direction of the James, the troops having been withdrawn during the night from the trenches before

Richmond; and Lee immediately issued orders for a vigorous pursuit by the whole army, Magruder and Huger marching out from their breastworks where they had been holding McClellan's left in check.

Military experts and critics for seventy years have been discussing what happened, and what did not happen, during the next few days. For various reasons the pursuit of the retreating Federal army did not work out according to Lee's plans and expectations. The great Stonewall Jackson, always at all other times a model of dependability, was strangely ineffective during the whole of the Seven Days fighting. Again on the 29th he moved slowly and weakly. Magruder and Huger, realizing their numerical inferiority, proceeded with excessive caution, afraid that McClellan might turn on them with his superior numbers. If Lee's orders had been promptly and properly carried out, McClellan's army would probably have been destroyed that day. As it was, there was a brisk engagement at Savage Station, which the Confederates properly considered a victory; but McClellan withdrew in safety, and the next day had his army in fairly good shape within sixteen miles of his goal on the James.

On the 30th Lee managed to mass 44,000 men on McClellan's flank near Frayser's Farm; and, with Jackson close in the rear of the retreating blue columns with a force of 25,000 men, Lee had every reason to believe that despite previous disappointments he would this day give McClellan the death stroke. But Jackson and Huger again failed to strike when expected. The piecemeal attack delivered late in the day by Longstreet and A. P. Hill was just strong enough to drive McClellan off the field with heavy losses; and on the morning of the 1st of July he was strongly entrenched on the top of Malvern Hill where his own artillery was supported by the gunboats on the James close by.

The escape of McClellan from the trap into which he had been forced was a bitter disappointment to Lee, a frustration of all his skilful strategy: but in his report of the battle he manfully concealed the vexation he must have felt at the miscarriage of his plans and spoke with mildness and restraint of the failure of his subordinates to cooperate properly.

Malvern Hill is a high plateau about a mile wide, rising from the low banks of the James and on its northern side stretching in a rolling slope for two miles to a heavy forest. On its crest McClellan had planted his 350 guns, tier above tier, sweeping the surrounding plain in every direction; and his troops were massed behind the guns. Lee recognized the strength of the position and hesitated about making a direct assault. Efforts were made to effect a concentrated artillery fire on the hill, but this was not sufficient to dislodge the enemy, and in the late afternoon an infantry attack was ordered. The fighting waged furiously until after dark, and the Confederates were slaughtered in great numbers as they charged across the open meadows in a desperate effort to capture the works on the top of the hill. Night at last stopped the fighting; and when morning arrived McClellan had withdrawn and had his army safely under the gunboats' protection at Harrison's Landing. Huddled on the bank of the river, his army was safe; but he had suffered staggering losses in men and equipment. Sadly he wrote to Stanton: "I doubt whether there are to-day more than 50,000 men with their colors"—and he had come up to Richmond with 115,000 men under arms.

McClellan's efforts to disguise the week of shattering defeats as a series of simple tactical maneuvers, a "change of base," deceived nobody. It is due him to say that he did manage his retreat most skilfully, and showed talent in extricating himself from the predicament in which he found himself after his disaster at Gaines Mill; but there was no escaping the fact that he had suffered a decisive defeat.

Lee, unavoidably, felt disappointed at the week's work. He had cunningly maneuvered his enemy into a position where he hoped to crush him; and his prospective victim had eluded him. But the army which, a week before, had had its fingers on Richmond's throat had been thrust reeling and staggering back to its new base, where it was content to rest and bind up its wounds without thought of counter-attack. The threat against the Confederate capital was relieved; and in Richmond there was rejoicing.

Lee was the hero of the hour. There was now no longer any question raised as to his ability or his audacity. From thence on, he was the hope of the Confederacy—in a military sense, he *was* the Confederacy.

CHAPTER X

A Braggart Punished

WITH McClellan pushed back in disorder to the shelter of his gunboats on the James, Richmond was safe from invasion, temporarily at least; but Lee's problems were by no means ended. One of his chief difficulties was that he could not know what McClellan would do next. For that matter, neither did McClellan. In his reports he put the best possible face on his recent "change of base"; but the authorities at Washington clearly recognized the fact that the campaign was a failure. McClellan told them that he would capture Richmond if they would send him 100,000 more troops; but they said they didn't have that many troops to send. He suggested crossing to the south side of the James and approaching Richmond by way of Petersburg. They dismissed that suggestion with the comment that it was impracticable—although three years later General Grant demonstrated that it was Richmond's most vulnerable avenue of approach.

While McClellan was arguing with Stanton and Lincoln, Lee spread his troops out in a crescent around Richmond, with the northern point of the arc resting at Mechanicsville, and entered a period of watchful waiting. Now he had not only the army of McClellan to occupy his attention—there was another new Federal army threatening Richmond from the north, and he was keeping his eye on them too.

General John Pope, who had achieved some fame by the capture of Island Number Ten in the Mississippi River, had been called to Washington and had been given the duty of consolidating into one army, "The Army of Virginia," the demoralized and scattered troops making up the commands of Banks, Fremont and McDowell.

What General Pope lacked in military knowledge he made up in the most unbecoming brag and bluster. When asked by Stanton if he could take Richmond if given 200,000 troops he airily replied: "Oh, yes; and then march right on through to New Orleans!" After being assigned to the new army he issued an official address which breathed the same spirit of vanity, and was a perfect model of what such documents ought not to be. It must have been especially irritating to the troops making up his command. Soldiers who have been taking the hard knocks of battle for a year don't like to be patronized by an arrogant newcomer.

"I have come to you," he told them, "from the West, where we have always seen the backs of our enemies; from an army whose business it has been to seek the adversary and beat him when found;

where our policy has been attack and not defence. I presume I have been called here to pursue the same system. I desire you to dismiss from your minds certain phrases which I am sorry to find much in vogue among you. I hear constantly of 'taking strong positions and holding them,' of 'lines of retreat' and 'bases of supplies.' Let us discard such ideas. The strongest position which a soldier should desire is the one from which he can most easily advance upon the enemy. Let us study the probable line of retreat of our opponents, and leave our own to take care of itself. Let us look before and not behind. Disaster and shame lurk in the rear."

In the light of events of the next few weeks, these bombastic words proved to be peculiarly ill-advised.

General Lee had enough knowledge of human nature to know that a boasting general is seldom a good fighter. He was not particularly worried over the new commander's vain words; but Pope had 47,000 veteran troops massed on the Rappahannock, evidently preparing to advance, and something had to be done about that. Pope's objective was Gordonsville, a small town northwest of Richmond through which passed the railroad upon which the Confederacy depended for communication with the southwest; and when he moved forward and began to concentrate his forces at Culpeper Court-house, Lee on July 13th detached Jackson and Ewell from his army before Richmond and sent them post-haste to

Gordonsville. This movement checked Pope's advance; and, aside from some cavalry clashes, there was little fighting for nearly a month.

Meanwhile, General Halleck who was now in Washington acting in the capacity of chief-of-staff, on August 4th had ordered McClellan to withdraw from his camp at Westover on the James and move his troops to the line of the Rappahannock to operate in conjunction with Pope. McClellan disliked to leave his position, and particularly disliked the prospect of a clash in authority with Pope, so he began writing letters to Halleck and Stanton trying to show them the wisdom of staying where he was.

Affairs were brought to a climax on August 9th when Jackson started to move in force on Pope's advanced forces under General Banks massed at Culpeper and Banks moved out to meet him at Cedar Run at the base of Slaughter Mountain—a well-named place for a battle. The encounter was a brisk and bloody one; but it resulted in nothing. Neither side could claim much advantage—although Jackson's men did manage to pick up some 1500 new rifles on the field with which to displace their ancient muskets; and this in itself was enough to make the Confederates look on it as a successful day. In addition, they captured a train of twelve wagons, loaded with precious ammunition, and six wagon-loads of clothing. Jackson's men again had cause to thank "Commissary" Banks for supplies.

After the battle there was brought to Lee's head-quarters a letter found on a captured Federal colonel giving important military information. Lee promptly forwarded the letter to President Davis; but, with characteristic kindliness and consideration for others, suggested that the name of the indiscreet Federal officer should be held confidential so as not to get him into any trouble.

The principal outcome of this battle was that it provoked a positive order from Halleck to McClellan to move from the James to the Rappahannock without more parley; and the minute McClellan left Westover, Lee started the remainder of his troops, under Longstreet, to join Jackson.

With his army assembled again and facing Pope, who was now advanced to the Rapidan, Lee realized that he must act promptly to avoid being over-whelmed. Pope was being reinforced steadily, and although he now had only 50,000 men, he soon would have three times that many. Lee had about 55,000, with little prospect of getting any more; and he knew that the wisest thing for him to do was to strike while he had the temporary advantage of slightly superior numbers.

Accordingly he evolved a plan to throw his forces across the Rapidan, turn Pope's left flank and attack him front and rear, a plan which gave every promise of success. But Fitz Lee's cavalry was a day late getting into position—and a swift cavalry movement was the key to the whole attack. Meanwhile, Lee's letter to General Stuart outlining the plan of attack was captured on the person of one of Stuart's officers; and the next morning the Confederate lookouts on the top of Clark's Mountain saw in the Federal camp at Culpeper the unmistakable signs of a general retreat. Pope, warned by the captured letter, was already thinking about the "line of retreat" for which he had expressed so much disdain, and was falling back to the safety of the Rappahannock. Once again Lee's plans were spoiled by his subordinates' carelessness; but he silently swallowed his chagrin. Although foiled, through no fault of his own, in a well-planned attack which might have changed the course of the war, he simply said in his official report: "The movement was appointed for August 18th, but the necessary preparations not being completed its execution was postponed to the 20th"— and on the 20th it was too late.

General Stuart was exasperated over the capture of his staff officer bearing the valuable despatch from General Lee; but he was almost equally as much embarrassed by a personal misadventure which befell him at about the same time. While on a scouting trip between the lines, he and several members of his staff asleep on the porch of a farm-house were surprised by a party of Federal raiders and barely escaped capture. Stuart's famous hat, with its flowing plume, fell into the hands of the Federals; and this stung his pride. "I must pay them back for that!" he said repeatedly; and his chance for repayment came sooner than he expected.

When Lee's columns, following the retreating Pope, reached the south bank of the Rappahannock it was found that the Federals were strongly placed on the other side of the flooded stream, making a direct assault impracticable. Every day of delay added strength to the Federals and lessened the Confederates' chances of success. Lee was worried, and justly so. In these circumstances he sent General Stuart to make a raid on Pope's rear, to see what information or other results might be developed; and this raid, successfully carried out, brought military results of great importance to Lee—and, incidentally, a large measure of personal satisfaction to Stuart.

The raid was conducted in the midst of a driving rainstorm on a pitch-black night, and Stuart was able to reach Pope's headquarters at Catlett's Station where he pounced suddenly on the unsuspecting guard before warning could be given. Pope himself was not there; but Rooney Lee's regiment, dripping wet amid the flashing lightning and booming thunder, captured Pope's tent and its contents, including his staff officer. Stuart proudly brought back to Lee the Federal commander's despatch box, containing the fullest possible information about his plans and his expected reinforcements. And, to Stuart's great delight, he also brought back General Pope's own

hat and uniform coat with its insignia of a major-
general.

While the cavalrymen were skylarking with
Pope's captured wearing apparel, Lee was busily examining the captured despatches. They showed
clearly how rapidly Pope was being reinforced. Already he had 80,000 men; soon he would have 150,-
000, if permitted to concentrate. Whatever Lee was
going to do must be done quickly—and with 55,000
men against 80,000 it would have to be done boldly
and skilfully.

Confronted with such a state of affairs, Lee decided to make a maneuver said to be the most difficult and dangerous known to military strategy—
dividing an army and reuniting it on a chosen field
of battle. Calling Stonewall Jackson to his headquarters, the two of them discussed the proposed plan in
all its details. Jackson with the toe of his boot marked
out a crude map in the dust, and the two great strate-
gists noted on it the important points of the impending movement. It was a flank attack, but one of
magnificent proportions. Jackson with 22,000 men
was to swing far around Pope's right on a march of
56 miles, cross the mountains and strike his base of
supplies at Manassas Junction, 24 miles in his rear.
Lee, with Longstreet's less than 30,000 men, was to
be left in the perilous position facing Pope's steadily
increasing forces; but Lee knew he could depend on
Jackson to carry out his part of the program, and he

felt that the ensuing demoralization of Pope would probably make the rest easy.

Accordingly, as the sun came up on the morning of August 25th, Jackson's tattered veterans, in light marching order, struck out on the road leading to the northwest. The cavalry and Longstreet's infantry kept up a brisk show of activity on Pope's front; and although Pope's lookouts saw Jackson's men marching away and reported it, he seems to have had no realization of what it might mean to him and displayed the most complete indifference to it.

Jackson's men were called "foot cavalry," they made so much speed on the march, and they lived up to their name on this movement. It was far on in the night of that blistering hot day when the column reached Salem, 26 miles away, and the exhausted, sweating men stacked their muskets and dropped beside them instantly asleep without stopping to unroll their blankets. Long before sun-up they were roused by the never-tiring Jackson and stumbled off in the darkness of dawn. There was the shuffling of the tired men's feet in the deep dust of the road, the rumble of the artillery wheels, and the creak and rattle of harness, punctuated by the officers' ceaseless "Close up! Close up, men!" The weary soldiers, half asleep, plodded on.

Jackson confided in nobody. When the men started out the first morning they had no idea where they were going. But when they marched eastward out of

Salem and crossed the Bull Run mountains at Thoroughfare Gap, not a man in the ranks but knew that they were on their way to fall like a bolt of lightning on Pope's rear. Early in the afternoon they reached Gainesville, and there they were joined by Stuart's cavalry who had been following swiftly, riding night and day.

Steady marching brought the foot cavalry and the mounted cavalry before midnight to Manassas Junction—back to the scene of the war's first great battle, the place where Stonewall Jackson had won his immortal nickname. There was a small force guarding the supplies there, but they were swept aside by the superior Confederate force; and when the sun rose on the morning of August 27th it found Jackson's men completely in charge of Pope's base of supplies, far in his rear.

The next day was like a Confederate soldier's dream come true. Jackson's boys were hungry and tired. When the army left Gordonsville a week before they had left all knapsacks behind. Their rolled blankets were carried on their shoulders; they had a little hard-tack in their haversacks, but their principal baggage was ammunition—eighty rounds of cartridges stuffed into their pockets and cartridge boxes. "They must expect us to eat cartridges," grumbled the hungry men. They had been on short rations for weeks, and during the past two days had had nothing to eat but hard-tack and the corn and

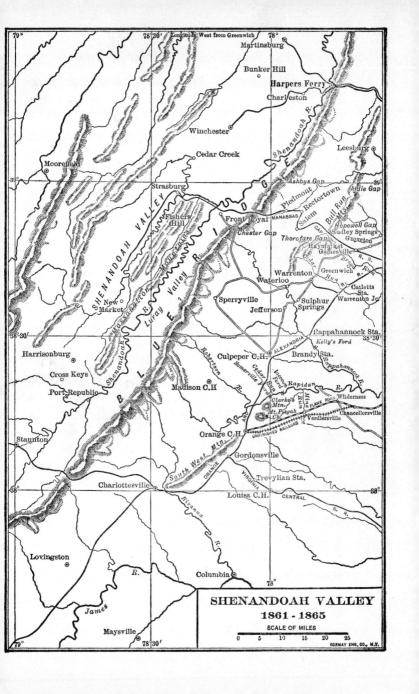

SHENANDOAH VALLEY
1861 - 1865

SCALE OF MILES

0   5   10   15   20   25

SORNAY ENG. CO., N.Y.

apples they were able to gather along the road. Their clothing was in tatters, and many of them were actually bare-footed. Suddenly then they were turned loose on one of the greatest accumulations of army supplies ever gathered together on this continent.

The United States government took good care of its troops, and for Pope's officers and men there was assembled at Manassas Junction an almost unbelievable supply of food and clothing. There were literally acres of ware-houses filled with goods; an over-flow of supplies were piled on the ground covered with canvas. Loaded box cars stood on two miles of side track. No greater blow could be dealt Pope than by the destruction of these stores—but before they were destroyed every one of Jackson's men had a full day in which to equip himself with new shoes, new underwear, new shirts and new pants, and to fill himself and his new knapsack with the fanciest array of food that ever graced the inside of a Confederate soldier's knapsack or stomach. The cavalrymen were the luckiest, for they could carry the most; and they had their horses loaded down with sacks of coffee and loaf-sugar and other luxuries. The infantrymen had their pockets crammed full. They gorged themselves on the luxuries intended for the Federal officers—sardines, cheese, Rhine wine, coffee. And then, when night came on, Jackson ordered that everything be burned.

It was a bitter sight to Jackson and to every soldier

there to see the flames licking up millions of dollars worth of flour, salt pork and corned beef—the very things that the Confederate army needed so sorely; but there was no way to get the stuff to where it was most wanted, and he could no longer linger at Manassas. Already warning had reached Pope of the disaster that had overtaken his base of supplies: and though he at first regarded it as nothing more serious than another cavalry raid, it soon dawned on him that a considerable portion of the Confederate army had got in his rear and then panic seized him. Immediately he started a backward movement of his whole army, ordering a concentration at Manassas.

Lee meanwhile, with his characteristic boldness, had been standing steadily in front of Pope on the Rappahannock. The Federal general, had he realized the truth, could have crushed him by an attack in force. But Pope had no idea how many men faced him, and he hesitated—with fatal results. On the 26th, while Jackson was still on the march, Lee started Longstreet off with his corps to follow in Jackson's path; and he himself stayed on the Rappahannock with a few thousand men to keep up the appearance of opposition in that quarter. On the 27th Pope was in full retreat, and then Lee set out to overtake Longstreet.

It was on this march that Lee had his most narrow escape from capture during the whole war. Riding ahead of the column, accompanied by his staff, as

they neared Thoroughfare Gap they were suddenly
surprised by a squad of Federal cavalry. The ten or
twelve men accompanying him hastily formed in line
across the road and prepared to protect the General
with their lives; but the Federals, apparently fear-
ing that they were in contact with the head of a large
force, after hesitating a moment wheeled and galloped off.

Jackson, knowing that the main body of the army
was coming to his support, did not have any idea of
risking a general engagement with Pope. But the
Federal commander conceived the brilliant idea of
capturing Jackson's corps. "We shall bag the whole
crowd!" he predicted boastfully, as he ordered Mc-
Dowell to fall back from Thoroughfare Gap, where
he might have done some real good by staying and
contesting Lee's advance.

While Pope was puffing and blowing and ordering his divisions around more or less at random, Jackson withdrew from Manassas, marching his men off
in three separate groups in three different directions,
but all converging in the woods north of the Warrenton Pike, where he hid himself to await the coming of Longstreet and Lee. He selected a strong
position, his left being behind a railroad cut and his
right and center on a commanding ridge. Pope had
no idea where Jackson was, but fancied he might
have marched to Centreville, and so changed his orders so as to provide for a concentration there. In

carrying out this movement, General King's division moved down the Warrenton Pike late in the afternoon of the 28th, and the temptation was too much for Jackson—he poured a sudden and galling fire into them as they marched in front of his line, and although he almost annihilated them he also thereby disclosed his presence and brought down upon himself a lot of trouble.

Pope immediately ordered a concentration of his bewildered and confused divisions at Groveton, so as to place as many men as possible in Jackson's front; and early on the 29th he let loose on him with all his power. Jackson's men put up an almost superhuman defense against great odds and, aided by their strong position, somehow or other managed to repel the attack. Longstreet's advance had been slowed down by a force left by McDowell at Thoroughfare Gap to contest his passage there, and he and Lee did not arrive on the field until the afternoon of the 29th. Longstreet's men were deployed into position so as to join and support Jackson's right, and on the morning of the 30th the whole Confederate army was in position and strongly placed.

Young Rob Lee was in the thick of all this fighting. His battery had been with Jackson's hard-pressed forces during the terrific struggle of the 28th and 29th; and when Longstreet moved into position on Jackson's right, his gun happened to be one of those detached and sent to strengthen Longstreet's artillery, as it moved into action. The Rockbridge battery advanced rapidly to its new position, firing as fast as possible; and as they took their last emplacement and were ordered to cease firing, General Lee and his staff galloped up to the hill where the guns were placed. Lee, his field glasses in hand, was studying the movement of the troops, all unaware of his son's presence. But the young man advanced and made himself known to one of the members of the staff, Captain Mason. His face and hands were blackened with powder and sweat, and the few garments he had on were ragged and stained with the red soil of Virginia. Captain Mason said: "General, here is someone who wants to speak to you." "Well, my man, what can I do for you?" asked the General as he turned to greet the newcomer; and then, when he recognized his youngest son in the sweaty, grimy gunner before him, there was an impromptu little family reunion right there in the midst of the battle.

The deluded Pope, confused by some of the counter-marching of the Confederates as they straightened their line on the night of the 29th, thought that he had won the engagement and telegraphed Halleck that the enemy was retreating towards the mountains; but he soon discovered his mistake. August 30th saw some of the bloodiest fighting of the war. During the morning there was a continuous artillery duel; and then in the afternoon the fighting began in earnest. Pope's divisions were hurled bravely against the front of Jackson and Longstreet again and again; and again and again they were thrust back. Some of Jackson's men ran out of ammunition during the day and repelled one charge with rocks picked up off the railroad cut. By four o'clock Pope's men, dismayed by their repeated repulses, were beginning to tire; and at this critical moment Lee's whole army came surging out of their position for a violent and unexpected counter-stroke, supported by a barrage of artillery fire that literally shook the ground. Pope's broken ranks could stand no more. Under this sudden onslaught they broke and fled, down the pike across the Stone Bridge and over the fields that had been the scene of the Bull Run rout of the year before.

When darkness came the Federals were in full flight and Lee held the field. And the rain started falling in torrents—as it frequently did following great battles.

The rains hampered the pursuit of the retreating Federals, although the cavalry and such of the infantry as could get up to the front kept up a running engagement with the rear-guard. A force of 25,000 fresh troops marched out from Washington to Fairfax Court-house and held that position while Pope's shattered brigades dragged themselves into Washington. By September 2nd Pope and what was left of his army were safely across the Potomac, and he asked to be relieved of his command. Nobody seemed to object, and so he was assigned to duty on the Minnesota frontier to fight the Indians.

Lee had not only driven the invading troops out of Virginia, but he had abundant other results from his campaign. No less than 20,000 rifles were captured, and 30 pieces of artillery. There were also scores and scores of wagons and other much-needed equipment, including some priceless medical supplies captured at Centreville. Pope's loss in killed, wounded and prisoners was about 17,000; the Confederates' loss was about 8,000.

Lee had been called to the command of the Confederate army two months before to attempt what seemed to be a desperate if not impossible task—to save Richmond from capture. In eight weeks, with inferior numbers, he had not only done that, but had turned the tables and assumed the aggressive. By swift, bold strokes he had driven both McClellan's and Pope's armies entirely out of the state; and stood so threateningly close at Washington's gate that the populace and officials trembled, and a gunboat with steam up stood in the Potomac convenient to the White House.

CHAPTER XI

The General's Cigars

H AVING driven the Federal troops out of Virginia and into the fortifications of Washington, General Lee on September 3rd was confronted with the serious problem of what to do next. Should he try to settle down and stay where he was; should he fall back to the environs of Richmond; or should he take the offensive and advance? Either of the three possible courses of action had its objections, but he had to do something.

It was, in fact, virtually impossible for him to stay where he was. His line of communications to Richmond, his base of supplies, was 150 miles long and he was almost totally cut off from it by reason of the fact that Pope in his retreat had burned the railroad bridges over the Rapidan and Rappahannock. The immediate vicinity of Centreville, where Lee's army was camped, had been fought over and foraged by two armies for a week, and was stripped of provisions.

To go back to a position closer to Richmond had no advantage except to make it easier to supply the army. Such a movement would surrender the gains of the campaign just completed, and would make it easy for the Federals to invade Virginia again just as soon as they could pull themselves together.

To advance directly against Washington was out of the question; as the city was well fortified and lay on the farther side of a deep, wide river.

In these circumstances, Lee decided to move up the Potomac a few miles above Washington and then cross the river into Maryland. There were many reasons which seemed to make this a wise course to pursue. In the first place, it would immediately get the troops into a region where they could live off the country—a very important consideration to a worn-out, hungry army. Then, too, Lee felt sure that such a movement must necessarily draw the Federal army out of Washington northward in pursuit of him, and thereby relieve Virginia of the threat of another invasion. From the political standpoint, taking the Confederate army into Maryland, still considered a doubtful state, might possibly have the effect of causing the hesitating Marylanders to rally to the Confederate cause. Also, the very presence of a Confederate army north of the Potomac was expected to have a demoralizing influence on the Northern people by reason of the threat it would bring to bear on Washington and Baltimore. And, furthermore, there was the possibility that a successful lodgment on Northern soil might bring recognition from Europe

—and European recognition would probably mean Southern independence.

When General Lee advised President Davis of his decision to invade Maryland, the President was seized with a recurrence of his military ambitions and suggested that he would come to the front and ride at the head of the troops as they advanced across the Potomac. Lee promptly wrote to him, politely but firmly urging upon him the inadvisability of his doing any such thing; and to make sure that he would be spared the handicap of the President's assistance he sent one of his aides in person to Richmond to see Davis and impress upon him that it would not be wise for him to join the army. Davis took the hint and stayed at home.

Lee, in his despatch to President Davis, admitted that his army was in poor condition for an invasion, lacking shoes, clothing, wagons and material; but he thought that if he could establish himself in western Maryland he might so threaten Pennsylvania as to keep the Federal army occupied until the coming of winter would probably stop active campaigning. It was not his idea to seek a battle; although he always had in mind the possibility of forcing the enemy into an unfavorable position where they might be given a decisive defeat. It was generally conceded that a Confederate victory north of the Potomac would be of great moral advantage to the Southern cause, and might possibly be a deciding factor in bringing victory to the Confederacy.

So, on September 4th, hardly giving the tired soldiers time to catch their breath after the marching and fighting of the past few days, the Army of Northern Virginia started to cross the Potomac at the fords near Leesburg, and by the 7th the whole army was on the north side of the river—the first movement of a Confederate army into Northern territory. Before starting the advance it was announced that the barefooted men would not be required to make the march, and this reduced the army by thousands, although large numbers of the shoeless men declined the proffered exemption. The lack of shoes was one of Lee's most serious problems. Half of the men in the army, it is said, were barefooted. Many were lame and forced to fall back to the rear; others bravely hobbled along and managed to keep up. The diet of corn and apples had undermined the health of the army, and it was a sick, lame, limping outfit. And, to add to all its other troubles, it was infested with "graybacks," the Confederate soldiers' name for what the World War doughboys called "cooties."

Stonewall Jackson's corps was the first to cross the river, and they rolled up their pants legs and plunged into the shallow waters of the upper Potomac in columns of fours, laughing and singing, shouting the ribald jests of the army at each other, while the bands played "Maryland, My Maryland!" The water was two or three feet deep at the fords, and much deeper at the edge of the crossing; and any soldier who wandered a few feet to the right or left got a ducking for his carelessness. One of the bands stepped off into deep water, and the soldiers laughed and yelled as the big bass drum went bobbing off down the Potomac.

The movement started out with two minor misfortunes which might have been taken as evil omens of the further troubles ahead.

On September 2nd, as the last drive on Pope's retreating army was being made, General Lee had suffered a most painful and troublesome accident. He and several members of his staff had dismounted and Lee was sitting on a log with his arm through Traveler's reins. The horse became frightened at something and plunged suddenly, throwing the General heavily to the ground, spraining both his wrists and breaking a bone in his right hand. As a result of this he had to put his right hand in splints and was forced to carry both arms in slings for several days. It was, of course, impossible for him to control a horse; and so he spent the first few days of the advance riding in an ambulance.

Then the first day the army was in Maryland, some Southern sympathizer, an admirer of Stonewall Jackson, presented him with a gigantic gray horse of great spirit and mettle. Jackson was well satisfied with Old Sorrell, his mongrel mount, but out of deference to his friend he mounted the gift horse to show his appreciation. The horse promptly became alarmed at the sudden music of a band and reared up so erectly that he fell over backwards, falling on Jackson in such a way as to crush and stun him. Fortunately no permanent injury was suffered, but Jackson was unconscious for several hours, and he too had to take to an ambulance until the next day.

Then, too, on the first day of the march there had been a little spat between Jackson and A. P. Hill. Jackson had ordered the troops of his corps to march five minutes and rest five minutes, alternately. Hill decided to march ten minutes and rest ten minutes; and when Jackson discovered this unauthorized change in his orders he promptly put him under arrest and ordered him to the rear of the column. Hill was furious, but Jackson was an iron disciplinarian. When he said five minutes he meant five minutes!

But the army was in no humor to be worried by minor difficulties or evil omens. They were exhilarated by their recent successes and by their advance into the enemy's country, and by the 9th they were concentrated around the city of Frederick. Here General Lee issued an address to the people of Maryland, inviting them to support the Confederate cause and especially urging recruits to come and join the ranks fighting under the Stars and Bars. But this part of Maryland was strongly Union in sympathy. Also the Confederate soldiers, despite the glory of their recent record of victories, were not an attractive looking lot of individuals. They had been marching and fighting steadily, without rest and with insufficient food, for two weeks. They were gaunt and ragged and dirty. Their dilapidated appearance told a story of hardship; and a total of only eight hundred Marylanders chose to cast their lot with the invaders.

A resident of Frederick, in a letter written at the time, expressed surprise at the appearance of Lee's army: "I could scarcely believe my eyes. Was this body of men, moving so smoothly along, with no order, their guns carried in every fashion, no two dressed alike, their officers hardly distinguishable from the privates—were these, I asked myself in amazement, were these dirty, lank, ugly specimens of humanity, with shocks of hair sticking through the holes in their hats, and the dust thick on their dirty faces, the men that had encountered successfully and driven back again and again our splendid legions with their fine discipline, their martial show and colors, their solid battalions keeping such perfect time to the inspiring bands of music? I must confess that I felt humiliated at the thought that this horde of ragamuffins could set our grand army of the Union at defiance. It seems as if a single regiment of our gallant boys in blue could drive this dirty crew in the river without any trouble. But I wish you could see how they behaved—a crowd of boys on a holiday don't seem happier. They are on the broad grin all the time!"

When he planned his invasion of Maryland, of one thing General Lee was very positive: There should be no pillaging of private property by the Confederate soldiers. He was determined to see this rule enforced strictly; the good name and reputation of the Confederacy was at stake; and he issued very positive orders on the subject. Therefore he was aroused to the point of righteous anger when, riding along with the advancing columns, he came up with one of Jackson's hungry men who had stolen a pig and was making off to the rear with him. Sternly Lee had the offender placed under arrest and sent to Jackson with orders that he be executed for deliberate violation of orders in the face of the enemy. Jackson, however, valued soldiers too highly to shoot one of his own men right on the eve of a battle; so he compromised with his military duty by sparing the culprit's life, at the same time placing him in the front rank where he would stand the fullest chance of stopping an enemy's bullet. The pork-fancier came through this ordeal by battle unscathed; and it was not until long afterward that Lee learned how his subordinate had dared countermand his orders.

The famished soldiers seemed to have an especial weakness for pork; and, despite all the orders and regulations, more than one Maryland shoat went to make a Confederate feast. A civilian visitor eating with an artillery mess one day expressed some surprise at being served with a fine roast pig. The soldiers solemnly explained that this porker, while stealing corn, had been killed by being kicked by one of the battery horses. The visitor about this time had his faith in the truth of this story shaken by biting down on a pistol bullet embedded in the meat; but his host gravely assured him that it must be the head of a horseshoe nail.

Lee did not linger long at Frederick. He planned to shift his line of communications to the Shenandoah Valley, by way of Winchester; and in order to do this he had to control Harper's Ferry. Harper's Ferry was occupied by a garrison of more than 10,-000 men, and Lee had confidently expected that it would be abandoned when he advanced into Maryland. Ordinary prudence would have dictated its abandonment and McClellan advised it, but Halleck refused. The position was one that was difficult to defend, so Lee sent Jackson to invest and capture this important strategic point, so that he might establish his communications to the Valley. So Jackson marched on through Frederick (without seeing anything of Barbara Frietchie, who was sick in bed at the time); and Lee, with the remainder of the troops, marched across the Blue Ridge to Hagerstown to wait until Jackson could complete his work at Harper's Ferry and rejoin him. D. H. Hill was left with a small force, as a precautionary measure, to guard the pass through the Blue Ridge at South Mountain.

Meanwhile the Federal army under McClellan, who had been restored to command of the Army of the Potomac, was moving slowly and cautiously northward on Lee's flank. Stuart's cavalry was keeping between McClellan and Lee, screening the latter's movements; and McClellan advanced only twenty-four miles in four days. He was completely in the dark. He did not know where Lee was going nor how many men he had with him nor anything about his plans. The only wise thing for him to do was to proceed with great caution, and this he was doing. But at Frederick he was the beneficiary of an almost incredible piece of luck.

When Lee broke camp at Frederick on the 9th he issued a detailed plan of operations—"Special Orders No. 191"—outlining the movements he had planned for the next few days and issuing specific instructions for the location of each division. When McClellan marched into Frederick on September 13th, still all unaware of Lee's plans and exact whereabouts, a Federal private soldier picked up off the ground at the Confederates' late camp-site a bunch of three cigars wrapped in a piece of paper. The soldier was interested principally in the cigars, but he glanced at the piece of paper in which they were wrapped before tossing it aside—and, lo and behold, it was the official copy of Special Orders No.

191 addressed to General D. H. Hill. The all-revealing order was quickly placed in McClellan's hands; and he, thus made aware of all his opponent's plans, hastily set out to overtake Lee and interpose himself between the two separated parts of the Confederate army before Jackson could get back from Harper's Ferry.

Lee, in his disposition of his troops, was counting on McClellan's well-known caution, bordering on timidity; and on the basis of McClellan's past performances Lee had every reason to believe that he had ample time to capture Harper's Ferry and get his army reassembled at Hagerstown before McClellan could overtake him. But McClellan, with an outline of Lee's plans in his hands, now marched with unwonted rapidity and certainty and got to South Mountain in force on September 14th, before Lee was expecting him. Longstreet was hurriedly sent back from Hagerstown to help D. H. Hill hold the mountain pass, which together they did successfully, although they suffered a heavy loss of men. McClellan still had an exaggerated idea of the numbers facing him, and did not attack as boldly and forcefully as he might have done. The Confederates on the night of the 14th were glad to fall back on the western side of the mountain and retire to Sharpsburg, a small town south of Antietam Creek, there to await the coming of Jackson.

Antietam Creek flows into the Potomac River, and

Lee established a line running along a high ridge before the town of Sharpsburg, with the Antietam in his front and the Potomac at his back. Here he waited for Jackson—and for McClellan.

Jackson, unaware of any necessity for hurry, proceeded carefully to invest Harper's Ferry, and on September 15th the garrison surrendered. It was a red-letter day for the Confederates, the capture amounting to 12,000 men, 13,000 stand of arms, 75 cannon, and many wagon-loads of much-needed ammunition and clothing. Hardly had the surrender been effected than Jackson received imperative orders from Lee to rejoin him at once at Sharpsburg; and so he hurried off on the march of 17 miles to that town, leaving the paroling of the prisoners to the division of A. P. Hill, who had been restored to his command.

McClellan appeared on the Antietam in Lee's front on the afternoon of the 15th; but, proceeding with his customary caution, did not get all his men into position until the 16th. Hooker's division made a half-hearted attack on the afternoon of the 16th, but was beaten off, and there was no more fighting until the morning of the 17th.

Jackson's men had come up and got in line on the 16th and they bore the brunt of McClellan's first attack on the morning of the 17th. Lee had selected for his personal headquarters a rocky hill on the outskirts of the town, from which the whole battlefield

was plainly visible, and from this point he directed
the movement of the troops. The battle raged fiercely
all day; but the force of McClellan's attack was diminished by the fact that it was delivered piecemeal.
Never at any time did he attack all along the line
at once; and Lee, although he had vastly inferior
numbers, was able to shift his men about so as to
put up a stubborn resistance at every point of assault.

General Lee had only partially recovered from
the injuries to his hands, and was still unable to hold
his horse's reins; but, despite his disability, he
mounted Traveler and had an orderly lead him about
—an unsatisfactory way to conduct a battle, but the
best he could do under the circumstances.

While thus seated on his horse, during the hottest
part of the battle, three of the guns of the Rockbridge Artillery which had been disabled and ordered to the rear passed close by where he sat. The
captain in charge of the guns, being without specific
orders, stopped to ask what he should do; and General Lee instructed him to take the most serviceable
of the men and horses, man the only one of the guns
that was uninjured, and go back to the front and
report for duty. One of the gunners on this piece
was young Rob Lee, and while the horses were being
changed he stepped up and made himself known
to his father, who greeted him affectionately and
congratulated him on being uninjured. Young Robert,
apparently, had had pretty nearly enough fighting

for one day, for he made bold to ask his father during the brief interlude: "Are you going to send us in again?" "Yes, my son," replied the General, firmly but with a smile, "you all must do all you can to help drive those people back." So, mounting to his place on the limber, the general's son rode back into the carnage.

Late in the afternoon McClellan massed his men on Lee's right for one more grand effort. The assault was strongly made, with great courage and perseverance, and the tired Confederates were showing signs of weakening when suddenly, much to their delight, the division of A. P. Hill marched up, fresh from Harper's Ferry, and was double-quicked into the firing line just in time to stem the Federal attack. Hill's men were dressed in the new blue breeches they had just captured at Harper's Ferry, and when they first came into view the harried Confederates in the front line thought that they had been flanked and taken in the rear. But quickly they perceived the Saint Andrew's cross of the Confederate battle-flag flying through the smoke; and, although Hill's men were almost exhausted by their long march on that hot September day, they plunged into the battle in the very nick of time to throw McClellan back and put an end to the fighting for that day.

It was a terrible, bloody day; and when it was over and the subordinate generals rode in from the lines to Lee's headquarters he eagerly asked each of them their opinion as to whether the army should stand its ground or should immediately retreat into Virginia. Without exception the generals counseled retreat—even the lion-hearted Jackson pointed out the heavy losses already sustained, the exhaustion of the men, the overwhelming numbers of the enemy. But Lee, daring to be audacious in the face of the counsels of safety, rose erect in his stirrups and said quietly: "Gentlemen, we will not cross the Potomac to-night. You will go to your respective commands and strengthen your lines. Send two officers from each brigade to collect your stragglers. If McClellan wants to fight in the morning, I will give him battle again."

But McClellan did not want to fight in the morning. Dawn of the 18th brought no opening roar of artillery or musketry. Not a gun fired along that long line on either side. More than a hundred thousand hostile soldiers faced each other over a line of four miles, their forces separated by but a few hundred yards. But there was no attack from either side. Both armies were exhausted from the terrific struggle of the preceding day, and both seemed glad enough to rest. During the day there was no sign on either side of renewing the battle, and that night Lee withdrew to the south side of the Potomac.

Although it could not be described as a victory for either side, the battle of Sharpsburg (or Antietam) was a masterly exhibition of Lee's genius. His total forces were only 35,000 men, and they were so thinly spread out and so hotly engaged that he was not able to spare any men at all for a reserve. McClellan had 87,000 men on the field—about 20,000 used as a reserve, and the remainder actively engaged in the battle. But Lee's great generalship made it possible for these 35,000 to fight 87,000 to a standstill; and when he stood there all day on the 18th and defiantly challenged his opponent to renew the battle, he strengthened the morale of his troops and saved the prestige of his army.

The losses in killed and wounded on both sides were terrible—the greatest in any battle of the war up to that time.

Lee has been criticised for fighting at all at Sharpsburg. The critics have said that he had everything to lose and nothing to gain by fighting there. But is this so? McClellan did not think so. McClellan was fully aware of the disastrous results to the North that would have ensued if Lee had won a victory there. Explaining his unwillingness to renew the battle on the morning of the 18th, he wrote to Stanton saying that he did not think the great risk was justified. If Lee had defeated him, he wrote, the Southern army "might then have marched as it pleased on Washington, Baltimore, Philadelphia or New York. It could have levied its supplies from a fertile and undevastated country, extorted tribute from wealthy and populous cities, and nowhere east of the Alleghenies was there another organized force able to arrest its march."

That was a true statement of the existing facts, and Lee knew it as well as McClellan. He was fully aware of the risk he was taking in standing and fighting at Sharpsburg; but a decisive victory there might well have ended the war quickly in the South's favor. It was perhaps a desperate chance that Lee took; but it was a chance worth taking.

The withdrawal into Virginia was made in an orderly and unhurried manner, and not a piece of artillery nor a wagon was left on the field. McClellan feebly threatened pursuit, but A. P. Hill's division left at the ford at Shepherdstown stoutly threw back the first Federals who crossed the river, and McClellan promptly abandoned any effort to pursue Lee into Virginia. He had had enough of the Army of Northern Virginia, for the time being.

After Sharpsburg Lee drew off into the lower Shenandoah Valley and encamped his men on the banks of the Opequon near Winchester. When the camp was established there a member of the General's staff accepted the invitation of a Virginia farmer who lived nearby and pitched the headquarters tents in the yard of the house under the shade of the trees. But Lee made it an invariable rule not to intrude on private homes, and he ordered that the headquarters be moved. His aide, in a spirit of exasperation, set up the tents in the rockiest field he could find, alongside the soldiers' camping ground, where the boulders were strewn so thickly that it was hard to find space for the tents; but Lee made no objection. "This is better than the yard," he said. "We shall not now disturb those good people."

The headquarters consisted of seven or eight ordinary pole tents, set up with their backs to a rail fence. In front of the tents were the wagons in which the baggage was carried, and in these wagons lolled the couriers and cooks. All of the wagons and tents had been captured from the Federals, and most of them were stencilled with the Army's familiar "U. S." The tent occupied by General Lee was prominently marked with the insignia of a New Jersey regiment. There were no guards or sentries around the commander's headquarters, and no particular marks of distinction were visible. The general himself, caring nothing for pomp or panoply, wore a plain gray uniform with only the three stars on the collar to indicate his rank; and his camp was marked by the simplicity which always characterized him and his actions.

Here General Lee was visited in his camp by Colonel Garnet Wolseley of the British Army, who was on a visit of inspection to the Confederacy. Colonel Wolseley arrived immediately after the return of the troops from Maryland and, accustomed to the smart appearance of the British regiments, was astonished at the unkempt appearance of the soldiers under Lee, the soldiers of whose prowess he had heard so much. He wrote, in amazement, of "the men, gaunt and hollow-eyed, worn with marching and lack of proper food, until they did not carry an ounce of superfluous flesh; powdered thick with dust until their clothing and accoutrement were all one uniform dirty gray, except where the commingled grime and sweat had streaked and crusted the skin on face and head; the jaded, unkempt horses and dull mud-spattered gun-carriages and caissons of the artillery." Colonel Wolseley even made so bold as to mention his impressions to General Lee, and he quietly replied: "No, my men don't show to advantage in camp; and, to tell the truth, I am a little ashamed to show them to visitors. But, sir," he added, with flashing eyes, "you should see them when they are fighting! Then I would not mind if the whole world were looking on!"

Here on the banks of the Opequon the Army of Northern Virginia was able to rest and refresh itself. The thousands of barefooted men who had not marched into Maryland rejoined the army. Stragglers came back to their commands. Lee sent the most urgent messages to Richmond, insisting that the men be supplied with shoes and blankets; but supplies were scarce and many of the men remained barefoot. But the genial Valley of Virginia supplied them with food, and during the golden autumn days they rested there and filled out some of the hollows in their cheeks.

McClellan's army remained encamped in the neighborhood of Sharpsburg, and Lee for a while considered the possibility of marching back into Maryland again. He sent Stuart on another raid around McClellan, a ride that took him as far into the enemy's country as Chambersburg, Pennsylvania. Stuart had another gala ride. He remounted all his men and in addition brought back a great store of captured supplies loaded on the backs of 600 horses —fat horses that had been bought from the Pennsylvania farmers, bought and paid for with Confederate money.

After due consideration, Lee decided to stay where he was and let McClellan make the next move. He had hopes that perhaps it might be possible to lure the Federal army across the Potomac, in which event he planned to draw off up the Shenandoah Valley far enough to be able to fight the Federals on a field of his own choosing. But McClellan stayed where he was, although Lincoln and Stanton peppered him with suggestions that he cross the Potomac and engage the Confederates in battle.

While camped at Winchester, during the month of October, General Lee sustained a stunning blow in the death of his young daughter, Annie, of whom he was very fond; but in these difficult circumstances he displayed that self-control and strength of character that were always so prominently his. His aide, Colonel Taylor, tells of how the first news reached him that his daughter was dangerously ill, and of how apprehensive he was as the days went by. Then "one morning," Colonel Taylor relates, "the mail was received and the private letters were distributed as was the custom, but no one knew whether any home news had been received by the General. At the usual hour he summoned me to his presence to know if there were any matters of army routine upon which his judgment and action were desired. The papers containing a few such cases were presented to him; he reviewed them and gave his orders in regard to them. I then left him, but for some cause returned in a few moments and, with my accustomed freedom, entered his tent without announcement or ceremony, when I was startled and shocked to see him, overcome with grief, an open letter in his hands. That letter contained the sad intelligence of his daughter's death. His army demanded his first thought and care; to his men, to their needs, he must first attend, and then he would surrender himself to his private, personal affairs."

In a family letter at this time General Lee wrote: "In the hours of night, when there is nothing to lighten the full weight of my grief, I feel as if I should be overwhelmed. But the Lord gave, and the Lord has taken away. Blessed be the name of the Lord."

But, heart-broken as he was, General Lee could not take time to indulge in the luxury of grief. His army must be reorganized, re-fitted and fed back into health. So the work went on. New recruits were drilled daily. Veterans of the season's campaigns enjoyed the luxury of regular rations and exchanged their tattered rags for new uniforms. The forces were formally reorganized into two corps under Jackson and Longstreet. By the end of October the army was one in whose appearance any general might take pride—even if some of them were barefooted.

Meanwhile the authorities at Washington were continuing to devil McClellan about advancing into Virginia; so finally on October 23rd he started cautiously to cross the Potomac, south of Harper's Ferry at Berlin, with Warrenton as his apparent objective.

As soon as McClellan's men started across the river, Lee's scouts informed him of the movement and he got into action. Longstreet's corps, with most of the cavalry, were swiftly moved eastward to the neighborhood of Culpeper Court-house, with the cavalry closely watching the Rappahannock. After arranging this movement Lee went to Richmond, where he was hardly recognized at the War Department so white had his beard become; but he soon returned to the front and established his headquarters with Longstreet's corps. Jackson was left, temporarily, in the neighborhood of Winchester with about 30,000 men to guard that area until McClellan's plans could be fully developed.

McClellan after crossing the river evolved a plan for striking in between Longstreet and Jackson, a plan of attack for which Lee was prepared and for which he had planned a defense; but it was a plan McClellan never got to carry out. On November 8th a special messenger from Washington walked into his tent and handed him a sealed envelope from President Lincoln relieving him from command of the army and appointing General Burnside to take his place.

"I hate to see McClellan go," Lee wrote to his wife. "He and I have grown to understand each other so well."

CHAPTER XII

The Picture-Book Battle

G ENERAL BURNSIDE knew that he had been placed in command of the Army of the Potomac for one reason—to get action. He also knew of McClellan's unpopularity with the administration in Washington, and he probably considered that the wisest course for him to pursue was to do something entirely different from what McClellan had seemed to have in mind.

Accordingly, a few days after he had assumed command of the army, Burnside submitted to Halleck a plan to march on Richmond by way of Fredericksburg. It is said that Halleck and Lincoln both doubted the wisdom of the plan and consented to it with reluctance. On the other hand, Burnside later claimed that the scheme was forced on him by the authorities at Washington. At any rate, it was agreed to try it; and so Burnside started his army in motion by the left flank.

Lee had his scouts watching Burnside closely, and as soon as the Federals started to move he divined the destination of the marching troops and started

Longstreet's corps in the same direction, to keep between Burnside and Richmond. Jackson and his corps were left in the neighborhood of Winchester to guard against the possibility of a surprise movement in that direction.

Fredericksburg is located on the south bank of the Rappahannock, the northern bank of the river being crowned with a range of high hills known as Stafford Heights. Immediately south of the city is an open plain, crossed by a deep ravine, and then there is another row of hills, roughly parallel to Stafford Heights but somewhat lower. Burnside's 117,000 men occupied the northern hills, with headquarters at Falmouth, the little town across the river from Fredericksburg; but when they arrived there they discovered that Lee had anticipated their movement and temporarily checkmated them. Longstreet was waiting on the southern ridge, the city being left unoccupied. The city, however, was in the unpleasant position of being covered by the guns of both armies, and the citizens were nervous and frightened.

As soon as it became evident that Burnside's whole army was to be concentrated here, Lee ordered Jackson's corps brought up from the Shenandoah Valley; and when he thus got his army reunited he carefully placed his men in a strong defensive position on the crescent of hills south of the city. He established his personal headquarters on a high hill in the center of the line, since known as Lee's Hill, from which he could watch the whole scene. Longstreet he placed on the left, immediately behind the city of Fredericksburg. The artillery, under Alexander, was skilfully placed so as to command all the open space between the hills and the river, Alexander proudly saying that: "A chicken couldn't live on that field when we open on it." Stonewall Jackson's corps was placed on the Confederate right, on the range of hills below the city, his right being guarded by the cavalry under Stuart.

The cavalry was now of increased interest to General Lee. Not only was Rooney's regiment there under Stuart, but Rob Lee was now serving on Rooney's staff as a second lieutenant. The appointment had been offered him while the army was in camp at Winchester, and Rob promptly asked his father's advice about it. He had been hearing Stuart's rollicking riders singing "If you want to have a good time, jine the cavalry," and he wanted to try a taste of it. The general gave his consent, and presented him with a sword and a horse and enough money to buy him a new uniform and outfit. Furthermore, he gave him an even greater honor: He permitted him to ride Traveler down to Fredericksburg as the army was changing its location. General Lee's injured hands were still not quite well, and he was unable to handle the mettlesome Traveler, but rode on a quiet, well-behaved sorrel mare named Lucy Long which General Stuart had bought for the purpose in Winchester and presented to General Lee. Rob's service in the artillery had not given him much opportunity for horseback riding lately, and the jaunt to Fredericksburg on the spirited horse gave him such a painful hammering that he said in later years that he would have suffered less fatigue had he walked. But that day, regardless of the rough riding, he was mighty proud to be riding along on the famous horse beside his famous father; and General Lee, cantering along on his docile mount, had many a sly smile that day at his son's expense.

The two opposing armies were in position by the last day of November, but it was not until the 11th of December that Burnside showed any signs of advancing. The armies were close together in plain sight of each other, separated only by the river, and occasionally the Federal regimental bands in the evening would follow up "Yankee Doodle" and "Hail Columbia" by playing Dixie, which the Southern boys would always acknowledge with their celebrated "rebel yell." It was a fierce and bloody war, but there was no actual hard feeling between the soldiers. The boys who were doing the fighting never were really mad at each other when a pitched battle wasn't actually in progress.

The Rappahannock at Fredericksburg is not wide, but it is too deep to be forded; and Burnside was waiting for his wagons to come up from his base of supplies with the pontoons needed for the building of the necessary bridges. At length the pontoons arrived, and on the 11th the Federals began the work of putting them in place.

A pontoon is simply an over-sized row-boat, and a pontoon bridge is constructed by floating a string of them across a stream and connecting them with wooden stringers upon which a plank floor is built. It makes a wobbly but serviceable bridge.

Burnside planned to cross the river with five bridges at two places—three at Fredericksburg and two a short distance below the town opposite to where Jackson was waiting and watching. Under the protection of artillery fire the lower bridges were built without much trouble, but Lee had placed Confederate sharpshooters in the houses along the river bank in Fredericksburg and the resistance they offered to the bridge builders caused Burnside at length to order the bombardment of the town. Citizens fled as the shells came screeching into town, bursting in the streets and yards of the houses. To this day one of the cannon-balls may be seen imbedded high up in one of the tall white columns of the Presbyterian Church. Under this fire the sharpshooters soon retired, and the bridges were finally completed.

That evening and the next morning the Federals crossed the river in force; and the movement had hardly started before it was threatened with disaster from an unusual cause. It is a well-known law of physics that a bridge can be destroyed by regular vibration, and troops are invariably ordered to break step before crossing a bridge. On this occasion, however, an over-zealous colonel at the head of the leading regiment ordered his band to start playing a lively march; the men instinctively fell into step; and soon the bridges were swaying at a rate which threatened their destruction. A quick-witted Federal staff officer, realizing the danger, spurred his horse straight through the mass of marching men on the bridge, knocking them aside like ten-pins until he reached the head of the column and stopped the music—and averted a disaster.

The 12th was a foggy day, with mists too heavy to permit an advance; but the Confederates in their position could hear the muffled noises made by Burnside's men getting into position on the south bank of the river, and by the evening of that day 100,000 men had crossed. The men's knapsacks had been loaded with rations for twelve days, and they were told that the next issue of rations would be when they reached Richmond. Burnside went so far as to announce that he would eat his Christmas dinner in the Confederate capital.

The 13th also dawned foggy, but about 10 o'clock in the morning the mists lifted like a theater curtain from the plain in front of Jackson's wing, and then the Confederates on the hills above saw spread out before them in that natural amphitheater such a panorama of martial grandeur as has seldom been witnessed by man.

The ground was covered with a light snowfall, and the rays of the sun glittered on the snow and on the bright bayonets of the marching men as they maneuvered into position. Officers on prancing horses dashed up and down the line giving orders, the men wrapped in their blue overcoats moved with precision as though on parade, the bright regimental colors were snapping in the winter wind, there was the rumble of field artillery being hurried into supporting position—even the Confederates were thrilled at the splendid sight and could hardly repress a cheer of admiration! When everything was ready the adjutants came to the front and read the orders of the day to the troops and the advance began, with flags flying, bands playing and a thunder of fire from the 147 guns on the hills north of the river.

Burnside's men were in excellent condition and in fine spirits, laughing and joking as they prepared for the charge. The Federal government had recently started the system of paying $100 in cash to new recruits, and these new soldiers, contemptuously called "bounty men" by the veteran volunteers, were put in the front ranks as shock troops, leaving the veterans lying on the ground in reserve. As the wounded bounty men were being carried to the rear after the first charge, the veterans, with the rough wit of the army, called out to the stretcher-bearers: "Be careful with them men; they cost the government a lot of money." A low-flying Confederate shell neatly cut the knapsack off the back of one of the men lying on the ground and threw it and its contents high into the air. As a deck of playing-cards came fluttering down, one of the irrepressible veterans called out: "Hey, there! Deal me a hand."

But soon the fighting got far too hot for any laughing and joking. Jackson's corps had at first been stationed further down the Rappahannock at a point where it was thought Burnside might try to cross, and he had been in his present location too short a time to throw up breastworks. His men were carefully placed, however, in the edge of a woods; and when the assault against him was launched he was ready for it.

Jackson himself astonished his men by appearing that morning in a brand-new uniform and new cap, a gift from General Stuart; and his men jokingly said that they were afraid Old Jack might not get down to hard work while dressed up in his new clothes. But Old Jack showed them. He was everywhere at once, encouraging the men, shifting his forces, strengthening the weak places at critical moments. Lee, now mounted on Traveler, galloped up and down the line, watching all developments and directing the movements of the men.

The Federal charge was made with desperate courage and for a while seemed likely to break Jackson's line; but when it appeared that a foothold was about to be gained in Hill's part of the line, Lee quickly sent reinforcements from Jubal Early's division, and Early's fresh men rushed into the breach with irresistible enthusiasm, yelling "Here comes Old Jubal!" and "Old Jubal is always getting Hill's men out of trouble." By the middle of the afternoon the Federals gave up their effort to crack Jackson's line, and fell back to the river.

Meanwhile the Federals who had crossed at Fredericksburg had remained concealed in the town, and it was not until 11 o'clock that they filed out of the city's streets and formed into line of battle for the attack on the Confederate left under Longstreet. The center of Longstreet's position was an elevation known as Marye's Hill, and here the Federal attack was aimed. In front of Marye's Hill ran a sunken road, with a rock wall along its northern side, forming a practically impregnable position for defense—a wide, ready-made rifle pit, with a wall rising four feet in its front. Four lines of South Carolina infantrymen were massed in this road, and the four ranks fired regularly in order, one line advancing to the wall to fire while the others fell back to load. By this arrangement they were able to keep up a stream of bullets almost as continuous as a modern machine gun. They withheld their fire until the charging Federals were within 100 paces of the wall. Then they unloosed a withering torrent of musketry that threw the advancing troops into confusion, while the guns on Marye's Hill literally mowed great lanes in their ranks.

In the face of this devastating fire the Federals were shattered and fell back; but in the shelter of the ravine they re-formed and renewed the attack with unabated fury. Again they were sent reeling backward by the sheets of flame that leaped from the sunken road; and again they were reorganized and came back for more. Six times this assault was repeated—one of the greatest exhibitions of dogged courage ever seen in any battle—until at last the coming of night put an end to the suicidal attack. The open field between the sunken road and the ravine was almost covered with the Federal dead; and the night was one of great suffering for the wounded as the temperature sank below the freezing point.

The struggle that day had been a veritable picture-book battle. The commanding generals from their positions on the heights could see every move as though they were looking down on an animated panorama; and it was while Burnside's men were making one of their insanely brave advances against the cruel rain of lead that poured from the sunken road that Lee put his hand on Longstreet's shoulder and murmured: "It is well that war is so terrible, or we would grow to like it too much."

That night Burnside held a conference with his corps commanders. Tears stood in his eyes as he pointed out towards the snow-covered battlefield and in a voice choked with emotion spoke of "My poor boys out there." He proposed another charge on the Confederate works the next morning; said he would lead the advance in person. But he alone favored a renewal of the fight. His subordinates had advised against the attack in the first place, regarding it as certain to result in defeat and slaughter; and there were some blunt words spoken that night in Burnside's headquarters as his generals told him what they thought about hurling their men again at those murderous hills across the river.

There was no renewal of the fight the next morning, but there was a truce for the removal of the wounded in Jackson's front. The next night, under cover of a blinding rain-storm, the Federal forces re-crossed the Rappahannock and abandoned the idea of forcing their way to Richmond across the commanding positions so skilfully selected and bravely defended by General Lee.

Burnside's unexpected retreat was a disappointment to Lee. He had been bringing up an additional supply of ammunition from Richmond and had strengthened his defense, feeling sure that the assault would be repeated in view of all Burnside's elaborate preparations. He felt no doubt of his ability to hold his position, even against the vastly superior forces of the enemy; and it was with regret that he discovered on the morning of the 16th that all the blue-coats had returned to the north side of the river.

The New York *Herald* the next day said in disgust: "The finest and best appointed army the world ever saw has been beaten by a batch of Southern raga-muffins."

It has been suggested by military critics that Lee was at fault in not following up his repulse of Burnside's charge by a counter-attack. With Lee's inferior numbers, however, the wisest thing for him to do was to remain on the defensive in his strong position. An advance against the enemy would have necessitated his taking his men across the open field, raked by the artillery on the hills across the river, and would certainly have resulted in a slaughter of his men similar to that experienced by Burnside's troops as a result of their brave but ill-advised charge against Marye's Hill. Having won the battle decisively, it would have been foolhardy for Lee to risk losing the benefits of his victory by needlessly exposing his men to possible destruction.

Following Burnside's retreat across the river, Lee went to Richmond to discuss with the War Department a plan of campaign against the enemy. He found in Richmond, however, a strange sense of elation. He was assured there that the war was practically over, and that he need not harass his men by any more marching and exposure to hardships. Within 30 or 40 days, he was told, the Confederacy would be recognized by Europe, and peace would be declared. Lee did not share this belief; but, in the face of it, there was nothing for him to do but go back to Fredericksburg and establish himself in winter quarters and watch Burnside.

That was a long, cold and disagreeable winter for Lee and the Army of Northern Virginia, there on the bleak hills looking down on Fredericksburg. The weather was bitter cold, and the supply of clothing, food and shelter was still painfully insufficient. General Lee and his staff were established in a small group of tents on the edge of an open field, near a little forest of pine trees from which they drew a supply of wood to keep their fires roaring.

In spite of his splendid constitution and physical strength, the exposure was too much for Lee, and late in the winter he contracted a severe cold which kept him in bed for a considerable part of the time. In his letters to his family he made light of his illness, telling how the doctors would come and thump his chest "like an old worn-out boiler." He also wrote to one of his daughters that he was tempted to stay in bed, the people of the countryside brought him so many nice things to eat while he was sick. But the illness was more serious than he admitted, and he suffered from the effects of it for a long time.

Shelter for the men was a problem. Tents were scarce, and the army was huddled up in a strange hodge-podge of roughly-built log huts and shelters

[203]

made from the limbs of trees. A regiment of new recruits from Florida were dismayed to find the ground covered with ice and snow—the first they had ever seen—and, in the absence of tents, they dug burrows in the ground like woodchucks in which to live until they could build cabins. Many of the men were still without shoes, and there was real suffering in the ranks. General Lee wrote bitterly about the neglect of the men's needs, insisting that the government take steps to seize the shoes held by Richmond profiteers. But it was not until the Richmond people were shocked by seeing barefooted Confederate soldiers walking through the streets in the snow that the shoes were officially seized.

Food was also scarce. The Confederate commissary was always inefficiently managed, and the daily rations for the army in winter quarters consisted of a pound of raw flour and a quarter of a pound of meat —no bread, no vegetables. That was before the day of vitamins; but General Lee knew that scurvy followed in the track of a diet of plain meat and bread. So he ordered the soldiers to dig sassafras roots to make tea, and to eat the green buds of the sassafras together with other edible leaves and young shoots.

But the soldiers in camp at Fredericksburg, despite their hardships, managed to have a pretty good time. The ground was covered with snow, and there were elaborately arranged snowball-battles between the boys of Jackson's and Longstreet's corps. These were hotly contested fights, in which even the officers took part; and a general commanding a division, reporting at Lee's headquarters one morning with a black eye, sheepishly admitted that he was a casualty of the preceding day's snowball fight. Also there were dances in the homes in the neighborhood; and all the cold weather could not chill the ardor of the boys in courting the Virginia girls.

Aside from his trying military duties in connection with the army at this time, Lee was kept busy a good part of the winter in completing all the tedious details in connection with the freeing of the 1300 slaves of the Custis estate, in accordance with the terms of Mr. Custis's will. Carefully he made out the papers freeing each of them, taking pains to see that each was notified of his freedom. One of the old Arlington servants, Perry, was attending him as a body-servant; and he carefully explained to Perry his new status and on the day of his freedom began paying him a regular monthly stipend. He wrote letters trying to find employment for some of the old Custis servants and tried his best to help them accustom themselves to their new condition. Lincoln's emancipation proclamation, admittedly a war measure, did not affect Lee personally at all. His own slaves he had voluntarily freed long ago; and the Custis slaves were all free before January 1st, when Lincoln's proclamation became effective. This proclamation, by the way, applied only to the Confederate states. It did not attempt to free slaves held in the states which had not seceded, which accounts for the fact that when Lee surrendered at Appomattox, General Grant's wife was still the owner of slaves she had inherited.

Although there was no fighting during the winter months, there was a continuous stream of official correspondence, and this was the kind of work that Lee hated. It was the one thing that occasionally broke down his customary poise and amiability and brought out flashes of that flaming temper which he generally kept so well under control. In a letter to his daughter during this winter he said playfully: "I am so cross now that I am not worth seeing"—and this was not entirely an exaggeration. His military secretary relates that one day during that winter, when the day's correspondence had been unusually heavy and vexatious, General Lee spoke irritably to him and he, in a burst of fretfulness, threw a batch of papers down on the table with some display of heat. Whereupon General Lee said to him in a calm and quiet voice: "Colonel, just because I get angry, don't let it cause you to lose your temper."

But more often the General showed evidence of that humorous turn of mind that has been lost sight of by most of his biographers. While the army was encamped on the Opequon after Sharpsburg there had been much visiting back and forth, and frequently General Stuart and his famous banjo-playing orderly, Sweeney, came to Lee's headquarters and stirred up some of the liveliness that followed him wherever he went. Both General Lee and General Stuart were total abstainers, but on one of Stuart's visits some of the young officers of Lee's staff produced a jug of apple-jack, and the music and laughter were at a high pitch when Lee came out of his tent to see the cause of all the merriment. Although a tee-totaler himself, there was no reproof from him when he saw the jug sitting on a convenient stump; but with twinkling eyes he said: "Gentlemen, am I to thank General Stuart or the jug for all this fine music?"

Now while camped out on the snow-covered hills of Fredericksburg he was probably thinking of that gay scene when he bethought himself to play a little joke on the young men of his staff. One cold evening he invited them into his tent where there was prominently displayed on a table a large two-gallon jug. The general told them it had been sent in by a friend who lived nearby and that it was said to be "very fine stuff." He invited them all to have a drink, and when they sent out and got their cups he ceremoniously removed the corn-cob stopper from the jug and filled their cups with—buttermilk. The general said nothing to indicate that he realized the disappointment of the young officers whose imaginations had led them to expect something stronger; but there was a dancing light in his eyes as they drained their cups.

There were flashes of Lee's humor in nearly all his family letters. General Hooker had been nicknamed "Fighting Joe" by the Northern newspapers, and Lee in his letters to his wife referred to him as "Mr. F. J. Hooker." In one letter he spoke of the arrival in his camp of a young French officer "full of vivacity and ardent for service with me." But, he added, "I think the appearance of things will cool him. If not, the night will, for he brought no blankets."

Because he was naturally a man of much dignity, quiet and reserved in his manner, many people have believed that Lee was a cold, austere man. That this was not true nobody was in better position to know than the members of his headquarters staff, the men who lived with him, day by day, among all the irritations and hardships of army life. They testify that in the companionship of the camp, where men really get to know each other, he showed that warm geniality of nature which removed all restraint and invited the closer fellowship of those around him. When the staff were gathered around the table at meals there was a complete absence of formality and ceremony. The younger men of the staff were naturally deferential in their manner to their elder and superior officer; but the conversation was free and unreserved as between equals, spiced with wit and laughter. General Lee was always fond of a joke, and enjoyed a little mild teasing of the young officers whenever he thought he had a joke on any of them; but there was never any sting or suggestion of unkindness in any of his jesting.

Christmas came and went in the Confederate camp. Stuart's cavalry was brought up from the right flank to cross the Rappahannock above Fredericksburg and make a raid in the Federal rear, and the cavalry column passed Lee's headquarters on Christmas Day. Rooney and Rob were riding with their regiment, and they stopped for a brief visit with their father. That night, hovering over his tiny stove, and with the cold wind blowing the snow through the flaps of his army tent, he sat down and wrote his wife a Christmas letter, telling her of the visit of the boys and concluding: "What a cruel thing is war, to separate and destroy families and friends and mar the purest joys and happiness God has granted us in this world; to fill our hearts with hatred instead of love for our neighbors, and to devastate the face of this beautiful world. I pray on this day, when only peace and good will are preached to mankind, that better thoughts may fill the hearts of our enemies and turn them to peace."

The Lee boys rode gaily off with the gray horsemen, and the next day they were deep in the enemy's territory, laughing at the irrepressible Stuart's prank of capturing a Union telegraph operator and sending a message to Quartermaster-General Meigs of the United States army: "General Meigs will in future please furnish better mules. Those you have furnished me recently are very inferior. (Signed) J. E. B. Stuart."

Early in January General Burnside made one more effort to advance. This time he planned to go up the river a few miles, cross at the fords and descend on Lee's left flank. But the rains came and the roads were transformed into long ribbons of deep, gooey mud. There was mud everywhere. The artillery and wagons stuck in mud up over their hubs. The weary soldiers, splashed with the red Virginia clay and drenched to the skin, could not advance. The Northern newspapers poked fun at what they called "The Mud March." Lee's cavalrymen, sent to guard the fords at the first signs of Burnside's movement, sat on their horses on their side of the river and laughed at the floundering bluecoats. Some of them put up big signs reading "This Way to Richmond" and other taunting comments. Finally Burnside gave up the effort and went back to Stafford Heights, everybody feeling wretched.

By this time Burnside's subordinate generals were frank and open in their criticism of his generalship, and he sat down and wrote to Secretary Stanton demanding that these generals be removed from command or that his resignation be accepted. Lincoln promptly chose to accept his resignation, and General Hooker, "Fighting Joe," was placed in command of the Army of the Potomac—the fifth Federal commander to oppose Lee since he took command of the Army of Northern Virginia.

CHAPTER XIII

"I Have Lost My Right Arm"

WHILE the winter days were passing by, General Hooker was not idle. "Give us victories," President Lincoln had instructed him in his letter elevating him to the command of the army, and "Fighting Joe" was determined to give his chief what he wanted. He had reorganized the scattered, dispirited army he had inherited from Burnside, and he now had a force of 130,000 well-trained, well-equipped men—"the finest army on the planet" he called it, and he had ample grounds for feeling that way about it. Lee had a bare 60,000, having sent Longstreet off with Pickett's and Hood's divisions to Suffolk south of Richmond early in January so that they could live off the country there.

Hooker was one of those who had most strongly opposed Burnside's foolhardy frontal attack on Lee, so he did not repeat that error. He determined to bring strategy into play, and so devised what seemed to be an air-tight plan to encompass the defeat of his opponent. As soon as the roads became passable late in April he was ready to move.

Hooker's plan was really a good one. First he sent

a column of cavalry, 10,000 well-mounted men under General Stoneman, down around Culpeper
Court-house to cut off the railroad and prevent Lee's
possible retreat by that route. As a feint—and a
strong feint it was—he sent General Sedgwick down
three miles below Fredericksburg with 40,000 men
to cross the river and make a demonstration there.
Meanwhile Hooker moved with the main body of his
army, about 90,000 men, up the river and crossed
quickly at the several fords and on pontoon bridges.
So, on April 29th, by swift and well-conceived movements, he had succeeded in virtually surrounding
Lee and his army. It is small wonder that in such
circumstances General Hooker felt justified in boasting that "The rebel army is now the legitimate property of the Army of the Potomac"; or that, feeling
thus elated, he announced that he had so maneuvered
his forces that "the enemy must either ingloriously
fly, or come out from behind his defenses and give
us battle on our own ground where certain destruction awaits him." From his point of view this must
have seemed to be a fair statement of the facts; but
developments proved that he would have been wiser
to postpone his boasting.

Here was indeed a situation that was a serious test
for Lee's generalship. He was faced by greatly superior numbers, and Hooker had so adroitly managed his movements as to create the greatest possible

confusion as to just what he intended to do or where he planned to strike.

The cavalry raid in Lee's rear was a brilliant affair, and the blue riders went surging down through the heart of Virginia to the very outskirts of Richmond, cutting telegraph wires, tearing up railroad tracks, burning stores—but Lee did not make the mistake Hooker thought he would make of sending all his own cavalry off after them. On the contrary, the main force of Stuart's horsemen stuck closely to their work along the banks of the Rappahannock; and when it developed that the main body of the army was crossing in force above Fredericksburg, Lee was promptly notified. Jackson as promptly advised him of Sedgwick's movement in his front. Lee received Jackson's courier genially with "Well, I thought I heard firing and I was beginning to think it was time some of you young fellows were coming to tell me what it was all about. Tell your good general that I am sure he knows what to do. I will meet him at the front very soon." Then he proceeded swiftly to make his dispositions to meet Hooker's well-planned attack.

It did not take Lee long to decide that Sedgwick's movement was a feint, and so he boldly resorted to that most daring and dangerous of military maneuvers—he divided his army in the face of the enemy. Leaving only Early's division on the Marye Heights to hold Sedgwick as long as possible—10,000 men against 40,000—he started the main body of his army marching in the direction of Chancellorsville, where Hooker had concentrated the forces directly under him.

Chancellorsville was not, as the name might indicate, a town or village. It was simply a large brick farm-house, the home of a Mr. Chancellor, located in a cultivated clearing of a few hundred acres near the edge of what was known as "The Wilderness"— a tangled area about ten or twelve miles square, overgrown densely with scrub oak and second-growth pine and vines and underbrush, almost impassable to either infantry or cavalry.

Hooker's first mistake was in selecting this as a battlefield, where the difficulty of movement reduced the advantage of his superior numbers and almost eliminated his artillery. But the big house was about twelve miles from Fredericksburg, directly on the road to Orange, and it was also the point where the roads to the fords joined the big road. It appeared to be a point of greater strategic advantage than it was, and here Hooker established his headquarters.

Lee's advance in the direction of Chancellorsville was checked on the outskirts of the Wilderness by the outposts of Hooker's advancing army on the morning of May 1st, and there was fighting all day as a result of which Hooker fell back to Chancellorsville. The fighting had really not been decisive in its nature and the sudden retreat caused Lee to fear a trap, so he followed slowly; but he encountered no more opposition that day.

The next day Lee spent in arranging his men in position and in pushing forward his skirmishers so as to find out exactly the location of the Federal line. Hooker was building up breastworks of logs and cutting down trees in front of his line to make the approach almost impossible.

Confronted with these impregnable works in his front, Lee was forced to evolve some form of attack other than a frontal assault. Naturally his mind turned to his favorite movement—a turning of the enemy's flank—and he had with him the best man in the world to execute that kind of movement, Stonewall Jackson.

Lee and Jackson, seated on cracker boxes left behind by the retreating Federals, sat about their camp-fire late that night with a map spread out before them. Scouts from the cavalry forces came to tell of the location and condition of Hooker's right wing; natives of the region told of old and little-used wagon roads, twisting through the tangled mazes of the Wilderness, by means of which that unprotected right wing could be reached. The two great generals sat there and talked over the movement in great detail after the others had gone. "I shall move my men at day-break" said Jackson; and then the two friends wrapped themselves in their blankets, stretched on the ground with their saddles for pillows, and fell asleep, little thinking that it was their last time together.

During the night one of the young officers who had been sent to examine the front on the Confederate right flank came up to report. Lee had already determined to make his attack on the other wing, but he greeted the young man pleasantly when awakened by one of his aides, calling out to him: "Come here and tell me what you have learned on our right." And when the lieutenant came over to him he drew him down to a seat on the ground beside him, putting his arm around him in a fatherly way that told of his warm and kindly heart. When the officer had finished making his report, Lee thanked him and then began to joke him about an incident that had occurred during the afternoon; and as the visitor departed he could hear the General's merry laugh ringing out in the dark quiet of the tangled Wilderness.

Before four o'clock the next morning Jackson had his 26,000 men on the march, leaving Lee with less than 20,000 on Hooker's front to keep up an appearance of activity and conceal the flank movement. Jackson's marching men did not escape the notice of the Federal cavalry, and Hooker was notified. He, however, for some strange reason jumped to the conclusion that it was a retreat of the Confederate forces, and paid no further attention to it other than to send a small force of Federals to harass them! Late in the afternoon he sent a message to Sedgwick instructing him to "capture Fredericksburg and vigorously pursue the enemy," stating that on his part of the field the "enemy is fleeing, trying to save his trains."

By six o'clock Jackson had completed his long and laborious march, and had his men formed in line of battle across the highway, ready to fall on the unsuspecting Federal troops forming the right wing. The bluecoats were at rest, their guns stacked in neat pyramids, as they lolled about in small groups, laughing, talking, playing cards or cooking supper. Jackson's men, pushing through the Wilderness close at hand, were invisible to them, but the advancing Confederates were unconsciously driving all the wild life out of the thickets before them; and the first intimation that Hooker's men had of approaching danger was when the alarmed deer and rabbits and squirrels and wild turkeys started running through the Federal lines.

The warning, however, did not come soon enough. Close behind the rabbits and partridges came the swift rush of Jackson's men, their clothing torn to tatters by the dense thorny underbrush, whooping the "Rebel yell" and firing rapidly. Hooker's right wing, thus taken completely by surprise, crumpled up and fled pell-mell down the road and through the woods—a disorderly riot of men, horses and wagons. Meanwhile, perfectly timed with Jackson's onslaught, Lee had boldly attacked with his men on the Federal front and left; and soon there was a general engagement all along the line. The fighting continued until dark, by which time the attacking and victorious Confederates were in almost as much confusion and disorder as the demoralized and defeated Federals; and in an effort to straighten out his lines, Jackson ordered a cessation of firing and rode out in the woods to reconnoitre. Returning to his lines, he and his party were mistaken for Federal cavalry. There was a volley of musketry from a North Carolina regiment; and Jackson, pierced by three Confederate balls, fell from his saddle and was hurried to the rear. A. P. Hill, next in command, succeeded Jackson, but he too was wounded within a short while; and then Stuart temporarily assumed command, but there was no more fighting that night.

The attack on Hooker's right was renewed by Stuart the next morning early, with Lee assailing the left and center again. The Confederate attack was so successful that soon the separated commands were able to join forces; and then Lee advanced the whole line and soon had possession of Chancellorsville, the Federals falling back to a defensive line near the river established during the night by the engineers.

One of Lee's aids, Colonel Marshall, has left a thrilling description of his appearance at the head of his victorious men on that eventful day: "General Lee accompanied the troops in person, and as they emerged from the fierce combat they had waged in the depths of that tangled wilderness, driving the superior forces of the enemy before them across the open ground, he rode into their midst. The scene is one that can never be effaced from the minds of those who witnessed it. The troops were pressing forward with all the ardor and enthusiasm of combat. The white smoke of musketry fringed the front of the line of battle, while the artillery on the hills in the rear of the infantry shook the earth with its thunder and filled the air with the wild shrieks of the shells that plunged into the masses of the retreating foe. To add greater horror to the sublimity of the scene, the Chancellorsville house and the woods surrounding it were wrapped in flames.

"In the midst of this awful scene General Lee, mounted upon that horse which we all remember so well, rode to the front of his advancing battalions. His presence was the signal for one of those uncontrollable outbursts of enthusiasm which none can appreciate who have not witnessed them. The fierce soldiers, with their faces blackened by the smoke of battle; the wounded, crawling with feeble limbs from the fury of the devouring flames; all seemed possessed with a common impulse. One long, unbroken cheer, in which the feeble cry of those who lay helpless on the earth blended with the strong voices of those who still fought, rose high above the roar of battle and hailed the presence of the victorious chief.

"He sat in the full realization of all that soldiers dream of—triumph; and as I looked on him in the complete fruition of the success which his genius, courage and confidence in his army had won, I thought that it must have been from some such scene that men in ancient days ascended to the dignity of gods."

The forces immediately under Lee's command had been signally successful, thanks largely to Jackson's swift and crushing turning movement; but Early at Fredericksburg was having trouble. His little force was able to put up but little real resistance to Sedgwick's 40,000 men; and just as Lee was about to follow up his smashing blow at Hooker, he received word that Early's shattered division was in full retreat and that Sedgwick was advancing from Fredericksburg without serious opposition, hoping to fall on Lee's rear.

Sedgwick and Lee had been close friends in the old army. One of Early's chaplains rode furiously from Fredericksburg, as a sort of volunteer messenger of defeat, and he clattered up to Lee's headquarters in great excitement to tell of the disaster there. Lee had already received Early's courier and was making plans to move to meet the advancing Federals; and he calmed the excited chaplain with his quiet smile. "I am very much obliged to you," he said calmly. "The major is a nice gentleman. I don't think he would hurt us very badly, but we are going to see about him at once. I have just sent General McLaws to make a special call upon him."

In spite of Lee's cheerful calm, however, this was a desperate situation and one that called for prompt and decisive action. But he did not hesitate. Feeling sure that the shock of two days' desperate fighting had temporarily paralyzed Hooker, Lee boldly turned his back on him and marched with McLaws to meet Sedgwick. He was joined by Early at Salem Church, and the combined forces fell on Lee's old friend "Major" Sedgwick violently and after some sharp fighting drove him across the river in complete retreat.

This necessary diversion accomplished, Lee then turned again to Hooker; but the next morning, when Lee was in position to attack, Hooker's entrenchments were empty. He had quietly stolen off during the night and re-crossed the river to the safety of the northern bank. With great audacity he attempted to claim that his campaign had been a success; but the world knew it was not so.

Gloom and despondency prevailed in Washington when the facts of Hooker's crushing defeat were received. People in the North were beginning to feel that perhaps the South could not be subdued. At a Cabinet meeting Lincoln said bitterly that the army might have been successful if Hooker had been killed by the cannon-ball that knocked over a porch column of the Chancellor house and stunned him. One pious Cabinet member expressed the opinion that Hooker's defeat was the natural reward for a "blasphemous wretch" who had exclaimed when he arrived at Chancellorsville: "The enemy are in my power, and God Almighty can not deprive me of them!"

A war correspondent of one of the Northern newspapers sent back to his paper this comment on the battle: "We had men enough, well enough equipped and well enough posted to have devoured the ragged, imperfectly armed and equipped host of our enemies from off the face of the earth. Their artillery horses are poor, starved frames of beasts, tied to their carriages and caissons with odds and ends of rope and strips of rawhide. Their supply and ammunition trains look like a congregation of all the crippled California emigrant trains that ever escaped off the desert out of the clutches of the rampaging Comanche Indians. The men are ill-dressed, ill-equipped and ill-provided—a set of ragamuffins that a man is ashamed to be seen among, even when he is a prisoner and can't help it. And yet they have beaten us fairly, beaten us all to pieces, beaten us so easily that we are objects of contempt even to their commonest private soldiers, with no shirts to hang out of the holes in their pantaloons, and cartridge boxes tied round their waists with strands of rope."

Chancellorsville added new laurels to General Lee's reputation, North and South. General Schurz of the Union army said: "Never did Lee's genius shine more brightly," going on to say that in this engagement "he proved himself a perfect master of the supreme art of the military leader—to oppose with superior forces at every point of decisive importance."

The outcome of the battle even tempered to some extent General Hooker's contemptuous opinion of the Army of Northern Virginia. When he was elevated to the command of the Federal army he issued a general order in which he stated that "in equipment, intelligence and valor, the enemy is our inferior. Let us never hesitate to give him battle wherever we can find him." But the shock of his contact with that "inferior" army left him in a different mood; and when he testified before the Committee on the Conduct of the War he said: "With a rank and file vastly inferior to our own, intellectually and physically, Lee's army has by discipline alone acquired a character for steadiness and efficiency unsurpassed, in my judgment, in ancient or modern times."

But the victory was a dearly bought one for the Confederacy, for on May 10th Stonewall Jackson died as a result of his wounds. At first it was thought that his condition was not dangerous. His left arm was amputated when he was removed from the battlefield; and then it was that Lee said: "He is more fortunate than I am. He has lost only his left arm. I have lost my right." Jackson sent a message to Lee congratulating him on his great victory, and Lee generously sent back word that "the victory is yours." At first it was thought that Jackson's absence from the battle-line would be but temporary; but within a week there came a turn for the worse. Delirium set in, and the watchers around his bedside felt that the end was approaching as they heard him, as in fancy he fought over his old battles, call out his ringing military commands. But even as he said: "Tell A. P. Hill—" he fell back on his pillow. There was a moment of quiet, and then the watchers heard him say gently: "Let us cross over the river and rest in the shade of the trees," and his flashing eyes closed forever.

Chancellorsville was followed by several weeks of inaction on both sides. Hooker's men were temporarily demoralized and there was little danger of any attempted Federal advance for the present at least. Lee could not attack him in his strong position across from Fredericksburg, but he returned to his old line on the hills south of the town and awaited developments. It soon became evident that Hooker had no idea of taking the offensive, so Lee began to maneuver his army into position for a forward movement. Longstreet had brought up the divisions of Pickett and Hood from before Suffolk—the men Lee had asked Davis to send him in time to take part in opposing Hooker's advance—and Lee's army was now stronger in numbers than it had been for several months. The army had been reorganized into three corps, under Longstreet, Ewell and A. P. Hill; and on June 5th he secretly moved the corps of Longstreet and Ewell to Culpeper Court-house, leaving Hill's men spread out thinly in the fortifications to cover the movement of the other two corps.

General Lee was not given to indulgence in much pomp and ceremony in army affairs; but early in June, at General Stuart's earnest request, there was held a grand review of the cavalry near Culpeper. Lee and his staff, mounted on their horses, stood on a little hill; and the Confederate troopers, their horses freshly groomed, their uniforms patched and brushed, their sabres brightly polished with wood ashes, passed twice before their commander, once at a walk and once at a trot. Stuart was in all his glory as he dashed back and forth, his black plume waving in the breeze, his sabre flashing in the sun. Lee wrote to his wife about it, telling her that all the Lees in the cavalry—her two sons and three nephews—all "looked well and flourishing."

The review was quickly followed by real action. Hooker was beginning to suspect that part of Lee's army had slipped away from his front at Fredericksburg, and he sent out his cavalry to see what they could learn. The very next day after the big review Pleasonton's riders swooped down on Stuart at Brandy Station, and there ensued one of the greatest cavalry engagements of the war. Stuart's forces were roughly handled, but at length Pleasonton retired across the river. The battle, though a spirited one lasting all day, was without decisive military result; but, so far as General Lee's personal feelings were concerned, it was an affair of the greatest interest, for Rooney Lee was severely wounded and had to be sent to the rear disabled.

The day after the battle he was carried to the home of his father-in-law, Mr. W. F. Wickham, about twenty miles from Richmond; and Robert was sent along with him to take care of him until he should recover. The trip was made without event; and, under the surgeons' care, Rooney's wound soon began to heal. At Mr. Wickham's he was joined by his wife, his mother and his sisters; so he did not lack for nursing and for tender care.

The Wickham home place was thought to be far enough in the rear to be entirely safe; but the Federals heard about the presence of General Lee's wounded son there, and decided to capture him and hold him as a hostage. Suddenly one bright morning, late in May, there was heard the sound of firing in the road near the house; and Rob, going to reconnoitre, discovered a squad of blue-coated riders approaching the house. Quickly he ran back to notify Rooney, whose helpless condition made it impossible for him to move. He promptly ordered Rob, however, to leave him and make good his own escape, convincing him that it would do nobody any good for him to stay and be captured; so Rob quickly hid himself in the old garden back of the house. From his hiding-place under a low-hanging box-bush he saw his brother brought out from the house on a mattress, placed in the Wickham carriage and carried off, surrounded by a mounted guard. Rob then sadly made his way back to the army; Rooney was carried down to Fortress Monroe and locked up.

General Lee, of course, was deeply troubled by his son's fate; but he wrote a comforting letter to Rooney's wife, who was ill, urging her not to grieve over him or grow sad. "I feel sure that he will be well attended to," he said. "He will be in the hands of old army officers and surgeons, most of whom are men of principle and humanity. So cheer up and prove your fortitude and patriotism."

While Stuart was having his noisy and showy brush with Pleasonton at Brandy Station, Ewell's corps was marching from Culpeper to Winchester, where it fell upon the Federal forces under General Milroy and captured the town along with the greater part of Milroy's men, guns and supplies.

It now became evident to Hooker that Lee was contemplating a forward movement into Northern territory; so he hastily abandoned Fredericksburg and started moving in parallel to Lee, putting his army into position at Manassas and Centreville to await developments. President Lincoln telegraphed Hooker from Washington asking for information as to the whereabouts of the Rebel army. Hooker replied that the advance was at the fords of the Potomac and the rear at Culpeper Court-house, whereupon Lincoln testily wired him: "If the head of the animal is at the Potomac fords and the tail at Culpeper Court-house it must be very thin somewhere. Why don't you strike it?" But Hooker had a wholesome respect for Lee's army now, and he waited to see what would turn up. Meanwhile Lee brought up the corps of Longstreet and Hill to join Ewell, and was then ready for his second invasion of the North. The Confederates had been too weak to drive Hooker out of his strong position on the Rappahannock; but Lee, by this flank movement, accomplished the same result by maneuvering.

In moving into Pennsylvania General Lee was not attempting an invasion in the ordinary military sense of the word. On the contrary, he was adopting apparently offensive strategy as a part of his plan of defense. His principal idea was to get the Federal army out of Virginia and lessen the pressure on Richmond; while, at the same time, he would be able to live off the enemy's stores and provisions. There was also still the political advantage of having the Confederate army in a threatening position. As he expressed it, his movement north of the Potomac started the Federals to thinking about Washington instead of Richmond. He had no idea of trying to stay in Pennsylvania, nor did he expect to provoke a general battle with the superior numbers of his opponent. In the words of his aide: "He expected to move about, maneuver, and alarm the enemy, threaten their cities, hit any blows he might be able to deliver without risking a general battle and then, towards fall, return and recover his base." Back of it all, he had the idea that if he could have any considerable military success it would force the Federals to withdraw troops from other points in the South, notably Vicksburg, which was then being besieged.

Before undertaking his northward movement, General Lee sat down and wrote to President Davis a candid letter about conditions affecting the Confederate cause and the outlook for eventual success. It was not optimistic in tone. He pointed out to Mr. Davis that the North had superiority in "numbers, resources and all the means and appliances for carrying on the war" and that without deliverance by the mercy of Heaven "we have no right to look for exemption from the military consequences of the vigorous use of those advantages." In other words, he might have said: "The North has more men and more money than the South; they will beat us in the long run—unless there is a miracle." To offset this gloomy military outlook, he pointed out to Davis that there was then in the North an active element of people who were tired of the war and wanted peace—peace at any price; and he urged that every effort be made to encourage this feeling in the North. "We should," he said, "neglect no honorable means of dividing and weakening our enemies"; and he suggested that the Confederates should give all possible encouragement to the rising peace party of the North. Lee, even this early, was conscious of the fact that the Confederate armies had been raised to just about the highest possible peak of numbers and effectiveness; and he felt that the aims of the Confederacy could best be attained by inducing the North to propose peace. And he felt that a Confederate victory on Northern soil would do as much as anything to bring such an offering of peace.

With these ideas in view, after the capture of Winchester, Lee ordered his three corps across the Potomac at the fords west of the Blue Ridge and concentrated his army at Hagerstown. Hooker, of course, did not know what Lee's plans were; so he moved his army into a defensive position where he could protect both Washington and Baltimore. Lee's cavalry brigades rode on into Pennsylvania, and the presence of the gray riders in that Northern state spread quick panic before them.

Lee, after he left Winchester, was ignorant of the whereabouts of the Federal army. Stuart had been left to guard the mountain passes and observe the enemy's movements when the army moved northward, being strictly ordered to let Lee know when Hooker crossed the Potomac. But Lee made the fatal mistake of giving Stuart instructions which were capable of being misunderstood; and Stuart could not withstand the temptation to stage another of his dramatic raids around the other army. So he galloped off around the Federal rear, and Lee heard nothing more from him until he rode up on the evening of July 2nd at Gettysburg—when the battle was half over. The cavalry has been called the eyes of the army; and so it might be said that Lee proceeded into Pennsylvania blind-folded.

It was Lee's hope to keep the Federals so confused about his intentions as to make them afraid to send their whole army into Pennsylvania after him. He wrote to President Davis suggesting that General Beauregard be brought up to Richmond along with all the available reserve troops from the Southeast, creating "an army in effigy" with which to threaten Washington so as to hold some of the Federal army there. Davis wrote Lee that he did not think this idea practicable—and, unfortunately, his courier bearing this message to Lee was captured, so Hooker knew that he had nothing to fear in his rear and accordingly moved with boldness.

Hooker, however, was not much longer in command of the army. He complained that Halleck persisted in interfering with the management of his army and asked to be relieved. Lincoln and Stanton did not think he was showing the proper enterprise in opposing Lee's advance and they were glad enough to get rid of him. So, while the army was in motion, General Meade was put in his place. General Meade's first act, so it was reported at the time, was to cut the telegraph wires to Washington so that he would not have to worry with meddling from that source.

Lee did not receive the news of Meade's appointment with any great satisfaction. He had known Meade when they were in the old army together and had the highest respect for him. When the news of the change in Federal commanders was received at Lee's headquarters some of his staff congratulated him on having "a mediocre man like Meade" to oppose him; but Lee sharply disagreed with this view. "Meade," he said, "is the most dangerous man who has as yet been opposed to us. He is not only a soldier of intelligence and ability, but he is also a conscientious, careful, thorough and painstaking man. He will make no such mistakes in my front as some of his predecessors have made; and if I make any mistake in his front he will certainly take advantage of it."

CHAPTER XIV

"It Is All My Fault"

THE battle of Gettysburg was an accident. Neither army had planned to fight there. They just happened to blunder into each other; and then a fight was unavoidable.

Lee was really moving in the dark as he marched up into Pennsylvania through the Cumberland Valley west of the Blue Ridge. Every day he expected to hear something from Stuart, who had been charged with the duty of keeping him informed of the Federal army's movements; and as the days went by without any news from his cavalry leader his anxiety increased, but he felt sure that the Federals could not be anywhere close at hand else Stuart would warn him.

So the Confederate forces marched gaily along the dusty Pennsylvania roads through the hot June sun, and by the 28th of the month they were strung out over a wide territory. Ewell, who had crossed the Potomac first, had advanced as far as Carlisle, and Lee had ordered him to move on to Harrisburg, the capital of Pennsylvania, and capture it. Early's division had already captured York. Lee was at Chambersburg with the corps of Longstreet and Hill, and the latter was ordered on the 28th to move eastward, cross the Susquehanna and seize the railroad between Harrisburg and Philadelphia. Two or three more days and Lee would have central Pennsylvania firmly within his grasp—but all these movements were based on the theory that the Federal army was still on the Potomac, miles away.

While at Chambersburg, General Lee issued a general order to the troops specifically and emphatically forbidding pillaging and unauthorized foraging and insisting upon the proper respect for private property. Officers were ordered to "arrest and bring to summary punishment all who shall in any way offend against this order." The inhabitants of Pennsylvania were not only pleasantly surprised at the forbearance of the invading troops, they were generally dismayed at having the war thus brought so suddenly and unexpectedly to their doorsteps. They did not know exactly how to act in the presence of a hostile army. A Lutheran minister in Chambersburg timidly asked General Ewell if it would be all right to continue to use that part of his church's regular service which included a prayer for the President of the United States. "Certainly! Certainly!" agreed the gruff old general. "I don't know anybody who needs praying for any more than old Abe Lincoln."

On the night of the 29th Lee received the report of Hood's scout, Harrison, telling him that the Federal army had crossed the Potomac several days previously, had reached Frederick, was rapidly moving northward and showed signs of crossing the mountains into the Cumberland Valley in Lee's rear. Harrison also brought the news that Meade had succeeded Hooker.

Lee was disturbed by this information about the movements of his opponents. He felt that it would be fatal to permit them to get in his rear and cut his communications; and he decided to try to prevent this by concentrating his army east of the Blue Ridge, threatening Washington and Baltimore, and thus forcing Meade to stay on that side of the mountains. Accordingly he countermanded all his previous orders and arranged for a concentration of his forces at Cashtown and Gettysburg, two small towns about six miles apart.

Ewell's advance had reached the banks of the Susquehanna opposite Harrisburg, but he turned back in obedience to his orders and moved in the direction of Gettysburg. Early also turned in that direction; and Longstreet and Hill, accompanied by Lee, moved on leisurely to Cashtown. Lee was still without his cavalry and had no idea that Meade was anywhere near him. If he had known that Meade's army was so close at hand he would have stayed at Chambersburg, as it was not a part of his plan to provoke a battle.

On the morning of July 1st a detachment of Hill's corps marched from Cashtown to Gettysburg for the purpose of getting a store of shoes said to be available there—the Army of Northern Virginia always needed shoes—and thus, unconsciously, the first move was made in one of the bloodiest battles ever fought on this hemisphere. A force of Federals, the advance guard of Meade's army, had already gone to Gettysburg to get those shoes; and three miles west of that quiet little Pennsylvania village the hostile troops collided and the fighting began.

After exchanging a few volleys reinforcements were brought up until each side had in the neighborhood of about 25,000 men engaged, and a terrific battle ensued, with heavy losses on both sides. The Confederates had four divisions in action, the Federals five; but early in the fighting the Federals lost General Reynolds, who was in immediate command, and that was just enough to turn the tide against them. Slowly but steadily the Confederates pressed them back fighting through the streets of Gettysburg to the ridge on the other side of town; and when the day was over the Confederates could very justly claim a victory.

As soon as General Lee heard the firing he hastened to the front, arriving on the scene about two o'clock in the afternoon. He had no idea of the

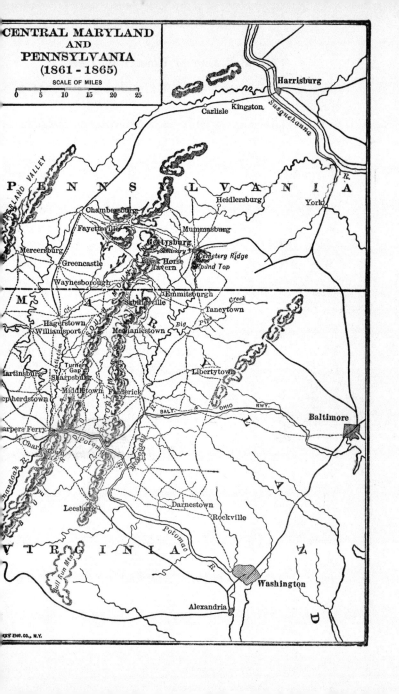

CENTRAL MARYLAND
AND
PENNSYLVANIA
(1861 – 1865)

SCALE OF MILES

0   5   10   15   20   25

Harrisburg

Carlisle   Kingston

Susquehanna

R.

PENNSYLVANIA

CUMBERLAND VALLEY

Chambersburg

Heidlersburg

York

Fayetteville

Mummasburg

Mercersburg

Gettysburg

Seminary

Cemetery Ridge

Greencastle

Black Horse Tavern

Round Top

Waynesborough

Emmitsburgh

Creek

Taneytown

Sabillasville

Big

Pipe

M

A

R

Hagerstown

Mechanicstown

Williamsport

Y

Turner's Gap

Libertytown

Martinsburg

Sharpsburg

Middletown   Frederick

BALT.

OHIO   RWY.

Baltimore

epherdstown

Harpers Ferry

Charlestown

Potomac   R.

Monocacy   R.

andoah   R.

BLUE

Leesburg

Darnestown

Rockville

Potomac

V   I   R   G   I   N   I   A

Bull Run Mts.

R.

Washington

D

Alexandria

KAY ENG. CO., N.Y.

strength of the enemy in his front; but he suspected that he was in contact with the whole Army of the Potomac; and he promptly ordered Ewell to advance and force the disorganized enemy out of their position on the ridge about a mile south of town. But Ewell's men were exhausted by the day's fighting; Ewell himself was upset by the fact that a fragment of shell had smashed his wooden leg and temporarily disabled him. Furthermore, he received a report that the enemy was moving on his rear (which was a false report); so he decided to stay where he was and try to take the hill the next morning. The next morning it was too late. Ewell's men rested that night where the end of the day's fighting found them. A part of his line extended right through the town of Gettysburg, and the men camped there in the streets, the Dutch burghers staring open-eyed at the novel spectacle of Rebel soldiers, laughing and joking, cooking their suppers at fires in the street, and at last lying down to sleep on the village's clean-swept sidewalks.

The ridge to which the Federals had retreated was occupied by the town's graveyard and was known as Cemetery Ridge. Prominently displayed at the entrance to the cemetery was a sign reading: "All persons shooting off firearms on this property will be prosecuted to the full extent of the law." That regulation was violated several thousand times during the next two days—but there were no prosecutions.

During the night of the 1st, Meade strongly occupied Cemetery Ridge with all of his men who had come up—and they were coming up rapidly; and as his forces arrived during the night and through the morning of the 2nd they were placed in position along the crest of this strong natural defense, the ridge stretching six miles southward from Gettysburg.

General Lee, before leaving Virginia, had closely studied a map of Pennsylvania which the far-seeing Stonewall Jackson had had prepared by his chief of engineers, Jed Hotchkiss, during the preceding winter. After his study of the lay of the land, Lee had told his aides that he expected to encounter the enemy either at Chambersburg, York or Gettysburg, and that he might have to fight a battle at one of those places. He was therefore not entirely unfamiliar with the nature of the country around Gettysburg. He had anticipated the possibility of fighting there. But it had been his idea that he would not fight at all in Pennsylvania unless he could choose the battlefield; and now he found it necessary to fight on a field where the enemy had already occupied the strongest natural position.

The absence of Stuart's cavalry was exceedingly embarrassing to Lee now, not only because it had kept him in ignorance of the enemy's whereabouts and had caused him to stumble up on Meade unexpectedly, but also because an army can hardly exist in a hostile country without cavalry to collect provisions and supplies. This fact made it impracticable for Lee to retreat west of the mountains and force Meade to follow and attack him; it also made it impossible for him to maneuver Meade out of his position. His best plan in the absence of his cavalry, it seemed, was to attack the enemy before the whole army could get up, and try to drive them out of their strong position before they could get firmly established there.

Lee therefore decided to attack the next morning "as early as practicable," and he so instructed Longstreet, who was getting into position on the Confederate right. Ewell on the left was to attack when he heard Longstreet's guns. "The enemy is here," Lee said, "and if we don't whip him he will whip us."

Longstreet suggested to Lee that a flank movement around Meade's left would be the best strategy, but Lee did not agree with him. Lee had already considered this plan but had dismissed it because of many reasons. He was still uncertain of the position of Meade's forces; in the absence of his cavalry such a flanking movement could not be undertaken unobserved; and the armies were so close together that such a movement would have been dangerously exposed to attack. Longstreet was a poor subordinate. He could not bear to see his suggestions over-ruled. The consequence was that he sulked throughout the rest of the battle and failed to give the proper co-operation. He took full advantage of Lee's generous practice of giving his corps commanders his general ideas of desired movements, leaving the details to them. Stonewall Jackson had worked perfectly under this arrangement, but Longstreet imposed on the liberty of action thus granted him by his commander and carried his stubbornness almost to the point of insubordination. He took his time about bringing his men into position; and instead of attacking at daybreak on the 2nd as Lee desired, it was 4 P.M. before he got his lines organized and his offensive started. By this time the whole Army of the Potomac was on Cemetery Ridge, and the opportunity to defeat Meade in detail had passed.

The best explanation that Longstreet could offer of his delay was that he was waiting for the arrival of Pickett's division which had been guarding the wagon trains and was the last to leave Chambersburg. Longstreet knew very well that his tardiness was wrecking Lee's plans, but he seemed to take an impish delight in it. Watching Lee walking impatiently up and down on the morning of the 2nd, Longstreet said to Hood: "The General is a little nervous this morning. He wants me to attack. I do not want to do so without Pickett. I never like to go into battle with one boot off."

Cemetery Ridge terminates at its southern end in two high knobs called Round Top and Little Round Top, which commanded that part of the battlefield. To the east of the northern end of the ridge was an elevation called Culp's Hill, also occupied by the Federals; so Meade's line was roughly in the shape of a big J or fish-hook. The road from Gettysburg to Emmittsburg, Maryland, runs to the west of Cemetery Ridge, and west of the road is another ridge called Seminary Ridge on account of the Lutheran theological seminary located on its end nearest town. Seminary Ridge formed the center of Lee's line, occupied by General Hill's corps. Ewell's corps was bent around through the town and to the east so as to oppose Culp's Hill. Longstreet was at the southern end of Seminary Ridge on the Confederate left.

The attack on the afternoon of the 2nd was strongly delivered when it was at last launched. Longstreet's men were valiant fighters once he got them into action. There was fierce and bloody fighting all along the line. Hood's division came within a hair's breadth of capturing Little Round Top, and did occupy with their sharpshooters a rocky position called The Devil's Den. The Federals' advanced line in the peach orchard along the Emmittsburg Road was driven back to the ridge, thus enabling Longstreet to occupy a part of the field which he might have had unopposed during the morning. But Longstreet's men were exhausted by their hard driving; they were unable to gain a foothold beyond the foot of the ridge, and there they bivouacked when the day ended. Ewell got into action even later than Longstreet; and although one of his divisions was able to capture and hold a part of the Federal position on Culp's Hill, Ewell's general attack was made in a disjointed and ineffective manner. Hill's corps in the center kept up a demonstration during the day, while the principal assaults were delivered by Longstreet and Ewell on the flanks.

Late in the evening of the 2nd, General Stuart's cavalry clattered into Gettysburg, both horses and men worn out and bedraggled by their constant movement during the past week. Stuart had the satisfaction of knowing that he had again executed the brilliant maneuver of riding around the Army of the Potomac, and he brought back with him a train of 125 wagons he had captured; but, incidentally, he had contributed to placing Lee's army in a most precarious and unwelcome position. When Stuart rode up to headquarters and saluted, Lee was scarcely able to conceal the irritation he felt at his cavalry leader's long absence. "General Stuart, at last!" he said acidly; and Stuart knew his commander well enough to know that even that much sharpness from him was a stinging rebuke.

The Confederate successes on the second day, slight as they were, coming after the heavy losses suffered by the Federals on the first day of fighting, caused General Meade to become uneasy. He called a council of war that night and the retirement of the army was suggested; but his corps commanders voted unanimously against any such plan, so he decided to stay and fight it out. The two armies therefore slept on the field, both resolved to see the fight to a finish the next day.

During the night General Lee, after examining the lines, decided to attack again on his right and left, hoping to follow up the advantages gained. But early on the morning of the 3rd the Federals delivered a concentrated surprise attack on the Confederates lodged on Culp's Hill and succeeded in driving them off, which forced Lee to change his plans again.

Mounting to the cupola of the theological seminary, with field-glasses in hand, he surveyed the Federal lines and came to the conclusion that the weakest spot was the center; and so he decided to attack there. In preparing for the attack, Longstreet's corps was brought over in front of Hill's line so that the latter could support him. Pickett's division of Longstreet's corps was selected to lead the assault. They had come up during the night, had not been in the fight so far, were fresh and eager to get into action. Pickett was to be supported by Longstreet's other two divisions under McLaws and Hood, with such other support as Hill could give.

In preparation for the attack, the Confederate guns ranged along Seminary Ridge opened fire at noon, and the Federal batteries promptly answered. Then ensued what was perhaps the greatest field artillery duel ever staged before the days of the World War. There were 228 guns firing at the same time, and the ground shook and quivered beneath the thunderous roar. After two hours of continuous uproar the Federal artillery ceased firing, for the purpose of bringing up fresh guns and ammunition; and thirty minutes later the Confederate batteries were also silenced on account of the increased scarcity of ammunition.

Now was the critical moment of the whole campaign. Even now the Confederates had an excellent chance of winning a conclusive victory if the infantry attack, well supported, had been immediately launched. But Longstreet, to whom was left the duty of ordering Pickett's advance at the proper moment, was still sulky. While the cannonading continued he sat on a rail fence, in the shade of a tree, placidly whittling a stick. When the roar of the guns ceased, Pickett waited impatiently for the order to advance; but Longstreet remained silent. Finally Pickett went in person to where Longstreet sat and asked him pointedly if he should launch his charge, but Longstreet seemed reluctant to order the attack and whittled on in silence. At length Pickett said: "Sir, I shall lead my division forward!" Longstreet nodded his head, and the historic charge began.

It was nearly a mile to the top of Cemetery Ridge from where Pickett started, across open fields fully exposed to the Federals' fire; but Pickett's men moved forward in well-closed ranks and with elastic step, as though on dress parade. The first part of their advance was made in silence, save for the music of the Confederate bands on the top of the ridge which, strangely enough, were playing not martial music but a selection of waltzes and polkas. As soon as the advancing soldiers reached the Emmittsburg road the Federal guns opened up on them with a murderous fire of grape and canister which mowed them down in masses; but bravely they closed up their ranks and kept straight on through the pelting rain of fire until they encountered the advanced line of Federal skirmishers. The force of their charge drove the skirmishers back before them onto the artillery and the supporting infantry. There was desperate hand-to-hand fighting there on the crest of the hill. For a few minutes a foothold was gained there; some of the Federal guns were captured; the Stars and Bars floated briefly in triumph above the stone wall that had sheltered the Federal guns. But it was only for a moment. The success was short-lived. Pickett's supports were feebly handled. The divisions of Hood and McLaws never were advanced at all. Of nine Confederate divisions on the field only two were actively engaged that day. The remaining seven were spectators.

The valor of Pickett's men was not sufficient to overcome the unequal odds. The recoil of the Federals stopped their furious charge in spite of their mad bravery. Gallantly they fought to hold the position they had gained, but by overpowering force they were driven in broken ranks from the top of the ridge, down the slope and back across the fields, leaving the ground spotted with dead. Their loss was frightful —six out of seven did not return to the Confederate lines. All three of the brigadier generals fell mortally wounded, one within the Federal works. Only one officer above the rank of captain survived.

As Pickett's shattered division came streaming back to Seminary Ridge, General Lee, mounted on his horse, rode out to meet them with words of sympathy and condolence. "All this will come out right in the end," he was telling them. "We'll talk it over afterwards; but, in the meantime, all good men must rally," for a counter-attack was feared. Pickett, almost in tears, rode up to Lee bewailing the fate of his men; but Lee comforted him with: "Never mind, General; all this has been *my* fault. It is *I* that have lost this fight, and you must help me out of it the best way you can."

The repulse of Pickett's charge, with the tremendous loss of brave men, was the kind of thing that tore at the strings of Lee's heart. The failure of the supports was distressing to him. But as he rode along the line, rallying and encouraging the broken troops, his face showed no signs of disappointment, care or annoyance. He took time to stop and speak courteously to a visiting British army officer, saying: "This has been a sad day for us, Colonel; but we can't always expect to gain victories." And then he urged the Colonel to get into a safer and more sheltered position where he would not be in danger from the Federal shells.

All the next day the two armies remained in their positions inactive. Lee by this time had despaired of taking the Federals' strong position by direct attack, especially as his supply of ammunition was gradually growing less. His communications with Virginia had been interrupted, cutting off his supply from his base, nor had he been able to rely on his usual method of capturing needed ammunition from the enemy. So he determined to stand in position on Seminary Ridge, thinking that perhaps Meade might attack him, and feeling that he had just about enough ammunition left to repulse an attack.

So that Fourth of July passed without a shot being fired. Meade, it developed, had no idea of attacking. Colonel Biddle of Meade's staff said: "General Meade realized fully the exact condition of affairs. Lee had been repulsed, not routed; and if Meade had yielded to his own inclination to attack he would have been repulsed himself and would thus have thrown away the fruits of his victory." Meade's men were about fought out, for the time being; also the commands had become hopelessly snarled in fighting off Pickett's desperate charge, and time was required to reorganize his forces. Lee's soldiers were glad to celebrate the day by resting and catching up on their sleep, for neither officers nor men had been able to do much sleeping during the past 48 hours. During the day the dead were buried, the severely wounded were provided for, and the wounded who could be moved were placed in ambulances and wagons and started to the rear.

That night Lee withdrew his men from their positions and began his retreat. It was about all there was left for him to do. He could not resume the offensive until he renewed his ammunition supply. Meade had made it abundantly plain that he had no idea of attacking him. Furthermore, he was now burdened with about 5,000 prisoners, thousands of his own wounded, and the wagons captured by Stuart and Ewell which formed a train fifteen miles long. The withdrawal of the troops from Seminary Ridge started soon after dark, and it was nearly daybreak before the whole army was in motion. Meade's cavalry and a small force of infantry put up some show of harassing the retreat, but it was not very forcefully carried out.

Nevertheless the retreat was a wretched affair. There was the sting of failure; the rain was falling steadily; the roads were muddy; the moaning and praying and cursing of the wounded in the wagons added to the gloom. As the column passed through one Pennsylvania town citizens armed with axes swarmed out suddenly and cut the spokes of the wheels of the artillery and wagons, throwing things into temporary confusion. But the men plodded on, and by the 7th the bulk of the Confederate forces had closed up at Hagerstown, where Lee established his headquarters.

A vivid picture of Lee, the unsuccessful commander, after the third day's hard fighting, is provided by General Imboden who was called to Lee's headquarters that night for orders. Lee was not there when Imboden arrived, so he sat down on the grass to wait for him. At length, about 1 A.M., Lee rode up, reined in his horse and attempted to dismount.

"The effort to do so," says Imboden, "betrayed so much physical exhaustion that I hurriedly rose and stepped forward to assist him, but before I reached his side he had succeeded in alighting and threw his arm across his saddle to rest, and fixing his eyes upon the ground leaned in silence and almost motionless upon his equally weary horse, the two forming a striking and never-to-be-forgotten group. The moon shone full upon his massive features and revealed an expression of sadness that I had never before seen upon his face. Awed by his appearance, I waited for him to speak until the silence became embarrassing, when, to break it and change the silent current of his thoughts, I ventured to remark in a sympathetic tone and in allusion to his great fatigue: 'General, this has been a hard day on you.' He looked up and replied: 'Yes, it has been a sad, sad day to us,' and immediately lapsed into thoughtful mood and attitude. After a minute he straightened up to his full height and said, in a voice tremulous with emotion: 'I never saw troops behave more magnificently than Pickett's division of Virginians did to-day in that grand charge upon the enemy. And if they had been supported as they were to have been—but, for some reason not yet explained to me, were not—we would have held the position and the day would have been ours.' Then, after a moment's pause, he added in a loud voice, in a tone almost of agony: 'Too bad! *Too bad!* TOO BAD!' "

The retreat from Gettysburg was a masterly exhibition of Lee's genius and of his power to impart confidence to all under his command. It had been begun with the idea of crossing the Potomac at Williamsport; but when the river was reached it was found that it was unfordable on account of the heavy rains, so Lee was forced to throw up entrenchments between Hagerstown and Williamsport and place his army in position to defend itself if attacked before he could get it across the river.

It was a ticklish position. The swollen river formed an impassable barrier before him; Meade was scarcely a day's march in his rear, with greatly superior numbers. But Lee did not lose his poise. He selected a strong position, dug in, and invited attack. Stuart's cavalry, while the fortifications were being prepared, went back and held the pursuing troops at bay. Meanwhile the engineers were working like beavers, throwing a pontoon bridge across the Potomac.

Meade showed no great enthusiasm about attacking Lee in his entrenchments, although he had about twice as many men. He had a wholesome respect for the Confederate commander, and advanced with caution. By the 12th he had attained a position on the road between Hagerstown and Sharpsburg, not far from where the battle was fought a year before. Still he did not move to attack; and on the night of the 13th Lee's whole army crossed to the Virginia side, the artillery and trains using the new bridge and the men crossing at the fords, now passable. On the 14th Meade moved forward—but he found Lee's trenches unoccupied.

Those were trying days and nights while the Army of Northern Virginia was effecting its crossing of the river and many of the officers' nerves were on edge, worn down as they were by anxiety and fatigue. Colonel Venable of Lee's staff tells of how on the night of the 13th he rode up to General Lee and reported an unsatisfactory state of affairs at the Williamsport ford, speaking of another officer's failure in what Lee thought was too loud a tone of voice. This caused him to speak sharply in reproof to Venable, who promptly retired to his tent in a sulky mood. Lee had his hands full that night, with many vexatious troubles and responsibilities, but he could not get the fact out of his mind that he had hurt his staff officer's feelings; and so a little later he sent to him an invitation to come to his tent and join him in a glass of buttermilk. Venable came, but he was obviously still pouting at what he considered an unmerited rebuke. The next night Venable completed his duties about 3 o'clock in the morning; and after making his report to the General threw himself wearily on the ground, in spite of the falling rain, and soon fell asleep. When he awoke he found that he was protected from the rain by General Lee's oil-cloth poncho which he had taken from his own shoulders and thrown across the exposed form of his sleeping aide. No wonder one of his men said in later years: "He was always more like a father to us than a commanding officer."

The Gettysburg campaign was over. Viewed as a whole, the campaign was a failure; and Lee assumed all the blame. In his report he said nothing about Stuart's wandering off; he did not mention Ewell's failure to follow up the first day's success; he did not censure Longstreet. "It is all my fault," he said— but some of Lee's admirers have thought that his greatest fault was in dealing so leniently with the shortcomings of his subordinates.

Meade did not cross the Potomac until July 17th, and even then his pursuit of Lee was so hesitating as to raise a question as to whether he really wanted to over-take him. The Washington authorities were harassing Meade with urgent telegrams insisting that he engage Lee in battle; and when Halleck telegraphed him that "The escape of Lee's army without another battle has created great dissatisfaction in the mind of the President," Meade promptly replied that he had performed his duty conscientiously and to the best of his ability, that he considered the censure of Lincoln undeserved, and that he felt compelled to ask to be immediately relieved from the command of the army. Halleck quickly sent Meade an apologetic telegram and he consented to retain his command; but he was exasperated at the long-distance criticism of his conduct in the face of the enemy and he bluntly notified Stanton and Lincoln that he was ready to be relieved at any time they thought they could supplant him with somebody they thought could do better.

Curiously enough, Lee was at the same time offering his resignation to President Davis. He realized that his return to Virginia was a disappointment to the Southern people and he wrote to Davis pointing out that "The general remedy for want of success in a military commander is his removal" and stating that "everything points to the advantage to be derived from a new commander—a younger and abler man than myself." He paid a glowing tribute to the army of which he was the commander and closed by saying that "I have no complaints to make of anyone but myself." President Davis immediately wrote Lee a gentle, kindly letter, emphatically rejecting his proffered resignation and assuring him of his abiding confidence in him.

Following his return from the Pennsylvania invasion, Lee camped on the Rapidan near Orange, and Meade stopped in the vicinity of Culpeper Court-house; and there the two armies remained comparatively inactive for several weeks. Longstreet's corps was detached from the Army of Northern Virginia temporarily and sent to help Bragg in Tennessee; and Meade's army was also reduced by the transfer of two corps to New York City where there had been rioting in opposition to the conscription laws.

When Meade's army was reduced, Lee considered that he was justified in again assuming the offensive; and the next three months were occupied in an interesting campaign of maneuvers, interspersed with occasional engagements of cavalry and infantry, but without any real battles of serious importance. The last clash of the campaign came during the very last days of November along the banks of Mine Run, in the tangled Wilderness not far from Chancellorsville. Here Meade tried to outwit Lee by a surprise movement; but the watchful eye of Stuart detected the first movement of the enemy, and Lee moved swiftly across Meade's path and had his men there in entrenchments when Meade arrived. The Federal commander, despite his preparations, recognized the fact that his expected attack must certainly be repulsed, so he withdrew without firing a shot.

The year ended with Meade back at Culpeper and Lee on the Rapidan near Orange—about the same relative position of the two opposing armies as in the summer of 1862 before the battle of Second Manassas.

The Christmas of 1863 was one of the saddest of General Lee's life. Rooney was still in prison; and his young wife, already an invalid, began to fade so rapidly that early in December her life was despaired of. Efforts were made to have Rooney granted a leave of absence so he could see his wife before she died, and Custis Lee offered to go to the prison at Fort Lafayette and take his place while he went to her bedside. But these efforts were unsuccessful. Young Mrs. Lee died on Christmas Day; and Rooney, pining in a cell at Fort Lafayette, was crushed. During his imprisonment death had taken both his children and then his wife. General Lee was overwhelmed; but he wrote to Rooney a fatherly, comforting letter—as comforting a letter as could be written under such tragic circumstances.

The winter of 1863-1864 spent in the bleak country near Orange Court-house might well be called the Valley Forge of the Army of Northern Virginia. Again, as at Fredericksburg, the soldiers had to resort to the building of huts and rude shelters to protect themselves from the rain and snow, tents being scarce and unobtainable in the Confederacy. Lee shared the privations of his army. Four old army tents on a steep hillside sheltered him and his staff. He and his aide had cots in one tent together; and sometimes when they had visitors the two of them had to sleep together, so that blankets might be provided for the guests.

Supplies for the army were very scarce, and there was actual suffering from hunger. One day a desperate private soldier wrote a letter to the General, enclosing between two oak chips the small fragment of meat which was the soldier's daily ration, saying that he wanted to know if the General knew to what extreme the soldiers in the ranks were reduced. Lee knew only too well, and suffered deeply because of it. He had been bombarding Richmond with protests against the inefficiency of the commissary department; and, recognizing the feeling of the soldiers, he issued a general order on the subject in which he said:

"The commanding general considers it due to the army to state that the temporary reduction of rations has been caused by circumstances beyond the control of those charged with its support. Its welfare and comfort are the objects of his constant and earnest solicitude, and no effort has been spared to provide for its wants. It is hoped that the exertions now being made will render the necessity of but short duration, but the history of the army has shown that the country can require no sacrifice too great for its patriotic devotion.

"Soldiers! You tread, with no unequal steps, the road by which your fathers marched through suffering, privation and blood to independence.

"Continue to emulate in the future, as you have in the past, their valor in arms, their patient endurance of hardships, their high resolve to be free, which no trial could shake, no bribe seduce, no danger appall; and be assured that the just God who crowned their efforts with success will, in His own good time, send down his blessings upon yours."

The general himself was living on very scant rations, although the people who lived nearby would occasionally send him some tid-bit or delicacy. One of the few things that was fairly plentiful in the neighborhood was cabbage, and this was generally the leading (and sometimes the only) item on the headquarters menu. One day there was company for dinner and Bryan Lynch, Lee's old steward, surprised the staff by serving a steaming dish of cabbage surmounted by a fragrant slice of middlin'-meat. There being only the one piece of meat, everybody courteously refused it; but that night at supper Lee remembered that tempting morsel of meat and asked for it. But, alas, the cook reported sadly: "Marse Robert, that wasn't our middlin'; that was borrowed middlin', and I've done sent it back to the man I borrowed it from!"

CHAPTER XV

—And It Took All Summer

B Y THE spring of 1864 the military situation was decidedly favorable to the North. Vicksburg had fallen and the whole Mississippi River was open to the Federal gunboats, cutting the Confederacy in two. Bragg had been whipped at Missionary Ridge, and the Confederates had been driven out of nearly all of Tennessee.

But Lee and the Army of Northern Virginia still maintained their position between Richmond and Washington; and three years of fighting in this territory had not produced the slightest crack in the defense of the Confederate capital. The Commander of the Army of the Potomac had been changed six times, but all the Northern generals had bounced off Lee's lines. The authorities in Washington were worried.

Down in Tennessee there was a commander in charge of the Federal forces who had been having a remarkable run of good luck. There was nothing flashy or showy about him; but, somehow or other, he got good results. He was producing victories, and victories were what the Federals sorely needed in Virginia. So, more or less in desperation, Stanton in March ordered General U. S. Grant to leave Nashville and proceed to Washington for orders.

Arrived in Washington, Grant was promoted to the rank of lieutenant-general (the only officer of that rank in the United States army) and put in supreme command of all the Federal forces, charged with the duty of keeping them in cooperation; but especially entrusted with the task of doing something to the Army of the Potomac that would get it out of its distressing habit of being outwitted and outfought by the Army of Northern Virginia.

Grant immediately went to Culpeper Court-house and personally assumed charge of the operations in Virginia. Meade was still nominally the head of the Army of the Potomac, and Grant issued all his orders to that army through Meade; but everybody recognized that there was a new hand at the helm.

Grant's genius consisted largely in an ability to make the best use of the powers at his command. He knew that the United States had more men and more money and more resources than the Confederate States; and he determined to make use of that superiority. He took the position that his true objective was Lee's army, not Richmond. In fact, he said that "Richmond was fortified and entrenched so perfectly that one man inside to defend was more than equal to five outside besieging or assaulting"—a well-deserved tribute from a high source to the system of fortifications which Lee had planned for Richmond in the spring of 1862.

Grant in the ensuing campaign had one great advantage over Lee. He had not only the enormous resources of the United States government behind him, he had the far greater advantage of being in undisputed command of all the troops in the field. He could order up reinforcements when he needed them, and he could direct the movements of other armies so as to contribute to the support of his plans. Lincoln and Stanton had at last decided that a soldier should be given the responsibility and the power of directing the armies; and, once they came to that conclusion and selected a military leader, they backed him up to the fullest possible extent. Lee, on the other hand, was still merely the commander of the Army of Northern Virginia. He had no authority whatever over any other Confederate troops. President Davis not only continued to direct the grand strategy of the armies in the field; he had rewarded the unsuccessful Braxton Bragg by promoting him to the rank of General and had him at his side in Richmond as his military adviser and nominal commander of all the Confederate armies.

Lee and his generals spent the spring days of 1864 on Clark's Mountain, near Orange, watching through their field-glasses the Federal preparations for the coming campaign. Lee had done everything possible to recruit and strengthen his army, but the man-power of the Confederacy was waning and there was not much he could do except watch his adversary and wait for him to make the first move. Longstreet and his corps had returned from Tennessee, but Pickett's division was still in the Petersburg field. Rooney Lee had been exchanged in March and was back with his cavalry brigade, and that was one load lifted off Lee's heart. But, with everything he could do, his total force was but little over 60,000 men. Grant had more than 125,000 men under arms, aside from nearly 15,000 cavalry.

Finally, in May, Grant was ready to make his grand advance—a carefully prepared plan of campaign along the whole front, involving the forward movement of all the armies in the field, east and west, at the same time. Sherman was to advance against Joseph E. Johnston in Georgia; Crook marched southeastward from the mountains of western Virginia and Siegel was sent up the Shenandoah Valley. In letters to President Davis, Lee had shrewdly predicted all these movements and urged that defensive steps be taken.

The advance of the Army of the Potomac was preceded by feints at the various fords along the Rapidan; but Lee, after studying the position of the Federals and the maps, with uncanny accuracy predicted to his division commanders that Grant's strategy would be an effort to turn his right flank and threaten Richmond and that the actual crossing of the river would be at the Germanna and Ely fords. On the 4th of May the Army of the Potomac crossed at these fords, Lee's forces making no opposition to the crossing. The Federals then struck boldly out southward on the direct road to Richmond, probably feeling that they had outwitted their opponents; but they were moving exactly in the way he wanted them to go, down through the western edge of the Wilderness where Hooker had been so badly used up.

Waiting until the whole body of Federals had moved out of their camp and started on the march, Lee moved his force quickly eastward from his encampment near Orange. The Confederates marched along the two roads leading from Orange to Fredericksburg, known as the Prank Road and the Old Turnpike—the roads that had figured in the fighting a year before at Chancellorsville—the route of the Federals lying directly across these two roads.

Lee's men marched in parallel bodies along the two roads, and on the morning of the 5th they blasted into the flank of Grant's columns within a mile of where Jackson had surprised Hooker's exposed wing almost exactly a year before. Lee knew this ground well. He had hoped that Grant would move this way and had left the fords unguarded so as to entice him in this direction. He had deliberately chosen this point in the tangled Wilderness as the best place where he could make his inferior numbers count to the utmost, and where he could reap the advantage of a surprise attack.

Grant's men, although surprised, fought savagely. Artillery could not be used in the close underbrush, so it was a grim and desperate fight between the infantry at close quarters continuing through two days, a bitterly contested struggle on both sides. The Battle of the Wilderness was fought with the added disadvantage to both Confederates and Federals that the woods caught fire and the fighting was carried on to a great extent through the flame and smoke of a forest fire.

Only two of Lee's corps were up in time for action the first day, but Longstreet arrived on the morning of the 6th (late again), Hood's division in the lead. The fire of battle burned strongly in Lee that morning in his impatient desire to follow up the advantages gained the preceding day, and he rode to the head of Hood's division for the purpose of personally leading them into the battle. At first sight of him there was a rousing cheer from Hood's Texans for "Marse Robert," but when the men realized that he was intending to lead them into action there was an uproar of protest. "Lee to the rear!" rolled down the line, and "We won't go on unless you go back!" One of the men seized the General's bridle-rein and turned Traveler's head away from the front, one of his generals added his remonstrance; and at length

Lee reluctantly consented not to expose himself, and rode off to join General Longstreet.

After a few hours of fighting in the heavy woods and amid the rolling clouds of dense smoke, the commands became hopelessly tangled and involved and soon were so mixed up that the Confederates were firing on each other in the confusion. Longstreet was shot down and seriously wounded by his own men and as a result of this there was a delay of several hours and his men were not able to follow up their early successes. The battle ended that night, with the advantages on the side of the Confederates, since Grant's attempted turning of Lee's flank had been foiled; but Lee was disappointed in that he had not been able to cripple Grant's forces as seriously as he had hoped. The losses were terrific on both sides: 17,000 Federals and 12,000 Confederates.

During the heat of the battle in the Wilderness Lee did not lose his sense of the importance of details. Some steers had been captured from Meade's train and promptly slaughtered for the benefit of the hungry Confederate soldiers. The officer in charge was interested entirely in getting meat for the men to eat; but Lee, riding by where the steers had been butchered, reprimanded him because he had thoughtlessly thrown the hides aside. Lee's mind was ever on the wants of his army, and he ordered that the hides be salvaged and sent to Richmond for shoe-making purposes. Nor did the fury of the battle dim his love and feeling for dumb animals. In full gallop to the front, he reined up to give a stinging tongue-lashing to a driver who was brutally beating an artillery horse; and when a courier dashed up with a message from one of his division commanders he insisted, before reading the despatch, that the courier dismount so as to rest his tired horse. Not satisfied with this, he dug down into his saddlebags and produced a buttered biscuit placed there for his own lunch and gave half of it to the courier's panting mount.

The next day after the battle was spent in skirmishing, Lee carefully watching Grant for signs of his next movement. During the afternoon the ever-watchful Stuart detected the movement of the Federal trains to their left. Lee quickly decided that Grant's next objective was Spotsylvania Court-house, southwest of Fredericksburg, which would put him between Lee and Richmond, so Lee hastily set his own men in motion for that point. The two armies moved that night in almost parallel columns; and when Grant arrived at his selected destination the next morning, there was the Army of Northern Virginia waiting for him. Grant's left was two miles closer to Spotsylvania than Lee's right, but Lee won the race from Grant.

The next few days were spent in maneuvering and fighting, without decisive result. Both armies prepared entrenchments, the Confederates being forced to dig theirs with bayonets, sharpened sticks and tin cups for want of more suitable implements. There were five pitched battles in six days; and early on the 12th a general attack was made by Grant on Lee's position in one grand effort to break through by main strength.

Again during the course of the desperate struggle on that day did Lee attempt to take an active part in the combat by riding at the head of Gordon's division in a counter-attack. Again the cry of "Lee to the rear!" rang out from the ranks, and for a second time within a week the beloved commander was led away from the front line as Gordon's men, inspired by his spirit, rushed to the front and hurled the Federals back.

General Gordon in his reminiscences paints a graphic picture of this terrible battle: "To Spotsylvania," he says, "history will accord the palm, I am sure, for having furnished an unexampled muzzle-to-muzzle fire; the longest roll of incessant, unbroken musketry; the most splendid exhibition of individual heroism and personal daring by large numbers who, standing in the freshly spilt bloods of their fellows, faced for so long a period and at so short range the flaming rifles as they heralded the decrees of death. This heroism was confined to neither side. It was exhibited by both armies, and in that hand-to-hand struggle for the possession of the breastworks, it seemed almost universal."

After the fighting on the 11th, and just before the grand assault on the 12th, Grant sent his famous message to Washington in which he said: "I propose to fight it out on this line if it takes all summer." But that was before the next day's fighting showed him how stern a resistance the ragged Rebels could put up. Before Grant reached Richmond he was forced to change his chosen line of attack. He was not able to fight it out on that line—and it took not only all summer, but almost another twelve months before his hammer was able to break down the keen defense of Lee's rapier.

Again at Spotsylvania the loss was appalling. The Federals lost 18,000, the Confederates not less than 9,000. Included in the Confederate loss was General Ewell whose horse was shot and fell on him, disabling him.

Grant had entered into this campaign with the avowed purpose of waging a campaign of "attrition" —breaking down the strength of the Confederate forces by steady fighting that would wear them out from sheer exhaustion and loss of men. He closed his eyes to his own losses, knowing that the populous North could fill his depleted ranks and that he could stand heavy losses far better than Lee. He even stopped the exchange of prisoners, so as to cut off that source of renewing strength to the Confederate ranks. It was a cruel but effective way of making the most of the North's superior man-power. But after the Wilderness and Spotsylvania Grant shuddered at the tremendous loss of life resulting from those two unsuccessful battles and so expressed himself to General Meade. But Meade replied drily: "General, we can't do these little tricks without heavy losses."

The Confederates had suffered one crushing loss during the campaign. On the 9th Grant had sent Sheridan's cavalry on a raid towards Richmond. At Yellow Tavern, just six miles outside the capital city, they were intercepted by Stuart's forces. The Confederate cavalry fought desperately to save Richmond and succeeded in driving Sheridan off; but when the fighting was over, Stuart lay on the ground mortally wounded. Stuart's death was a blow to Lee second only to the loss of Stonewall Jackson. "He never brought me a false piece of information," Lee said—and the courtly Stuart would not have wanted a more glorious epitaph.

There was continued skirmishing for a week after the big battle on the 12th, with Grant continually trying to find a weak place in Lee's lines. At length he decided that it was hopeless to try to force the Confederates out of their entrenchments, and so the Federals pulled out and moved to a position on the North Anna to Lee's right. Again Lee's men, marching promptly and swiftly, threw themselves in front of Grant and between him and Richmond. Again Grant was completely checkmated. Indeed, Lee had gained such an advantage in position on the field that he might have been able to do some serious damage to the Federals had he been able to take action promptly. But at this critical moment General Lee, already weakened by the strain and loss of sleep during the preceding twenty days, was stricken with an attack of ptomaine poisoning, and for several days the army was without the services of its great leader. In fact, with Longstreet and Ewell both disabled at the same time, the Army of Northern Virginia was in a bad way for leadership for a few days; and during that time Grant hastily re-crossed the river and withdrew from Lee's front.

This time Grant made a big swing around to the southeast until he reached Cold Harbor on the Chickahominy—scene of a hard day's fighting during the Seven Days early in 1862. And again he found the thinning but unterrified ranks of Lee's army across his front.

At Cold Harbor Grant's army was within eight miles of Richmond. The Northern newspapers were clamoring for him to capture the Confederate capital and end the war, and Grant gathered all his strength to make this the decisive battle of the campaign. At Spotsylvania he had telegraphed Halleck to send him "all the infantry you can rake and scrape," which resulted in 40,000 fresh replacements being furnished him.

After a few days of maneuvering and skirmishing, on June 3rd at daybreak Grant threw his men forward in a furious general assault on the Confederate line of breastworks, resulting in one of the bloodiest repulses of the whole war. The Federals moved forward in masses rather than in the customary lines of battle, and the Confederate works were so arranged that the attackers were subjected to both frontal and enfilading fires of musketry and artillery. The execution was frightful. One observer said: "It was not war; it was murder!" It was more than flesh and blood could stand, no matter how brave, and the shattered Federals fell back to their own works. Once more a general assault was ordered, and there then ensued one of the strangest episodes of the war—the men, as by common consent, refused to move forward at the command, recognizing the futility of carrying the Confederate works in the face of that tempest of fire! Thus the day's fighting ended within less than an hour after it started; but within that short time the attacking Federals had suffered a loss of 13,000 men. It was estimated that 10,000 were killed within the first twenty minutes of the fight, when the attacking troops were mowed down in masses. The Confederates, fighting behind their breastworks, lost only a few hundred.

The Northern press and public were shocked at the wholesale slaughter suffered at Cold Harbor. Grant had enjoyed the greatest popularity in the North, but now some of the newspapers were beginning to refer to him as "The Butcher" and to murmur against what they said was his reckless disregard of his soldiers' lives. One of Grant's own generals wrote: "In the opinion of a majority of the survivors, the battle of Cold Harbor never should have been fought. There was no military reason to justify it. It was the dreary, dismal, bloody, ineffective close of the Lieutenant-General's first campaign with the Army of the Potomac." Grant himself, writing after the war, said: "Cold Harbor is, I believe, the only battle I ever fought that I would not fight over again under the circumstances."

Military critics could not help pointing out that Grant had arrived at the position he then occupied only after fighting a series of unprecedentedly bloody battles, his total loss in which had exceeded the entire strength of his opponent; and that, after paying this great price, he was in a position which might have been attained without the loss of a single life by the simple expedient of moving his army there by transports as McClellan had done in 1862.

Grant had started out from Culpeper with about 140,000 men and had received about 50,000 reinforcements. His losses were about 60,000. Lee started out with nearly 64,000 and had had 14,000 reinforcements sent him. His losses were more than 20,000.

Less than a month had elapsed since the start of the campaign. The summer was not over—was, in fact, hardly started. But Grant saw that it would not be possible for him to fight it out on that line. Accordingly he decided on the move which had been proposed by McClellan two years before and rejected. He moved his entire army to the south side of the James River, and planned to approach Richmond by way of Petersburg.

Petersburg, all this while, had been menaced by a Federal force of about 30,000 under General Butler, whose lumbering attacks were skilfully fought off by Beauregard who was in command at Petersburg with a makeshift army composed of a few veteran troops, some militia and a Petersburg home guard composed of boys and old men. Grant, after crossing the river, consolidated Butler's army with his; and Lee moved into Petersburg to defend it against the movement on Richmond from that direction.

CHAPTER XVI

The Stretched Line Breaks

G RANT's move to the south of the James marked an entire change in his plan of operations. Up to that time he had been actively on the aggressive, hammering away at Lee's army, trying to wear it away by killing and capturing as many as possible. A month of this was enough to convince him that it was not getting the desired results; so he abandoned the aggressive offensive and settled down to the patient siege of Petersburg, the key to the back-door of Richmond. If Petersburg could be captured it would cut off Richmond's two lines of communication necessary for its support. The fall of Petersburg meant the fall of Richmond.

Richmond, to be sure, was of no particular military value to either side. From the strictly military standpoint it would have been wise for the Confederates to abandon that city and draw the army far enough into the interior to be able to fight Grant to the latter's disadvantage. Lee knew this all too well, and suggested it to Davis: but the politicians of the Confederacy insisted upon the defense of the capital city to the last ditch, and Lee had been trained in the belief that the civil government's authority over the military forces was supreme. He was still getting a crick in his neck looking over his shoulder at Richmond; but, obedient to the wishes of his superiors, he settled down to the almost hopeless task of defending Petersburg and Richmond from the superior army that assailed them.

For ten long months the siege continued, Lee with never more than 45,000 or 50,000 men holding the works against Grant's host of more than twice that many. During the first few days of the siege Grant made repeated efforts to storm the Confederate lines before they could get their system of breastworks established; but, after losing 10,000 men in four days, he abandoned this idea and settled down to the investment of the city. From then on Grant's activities consisted principally in a continual reaching out with his left wing in an effort to cut Lee's lines of communication with the South. There were repeated cavalry raids and infantry sorties in these attempts; but, for the most part, the siege dragged wearily on, month after month, through the summer, autumn and winter and into the following spring. The men lived in the great system of trenches and dug-outs, with sharpshooters on both sides constantly at work picking off unwary enemies. Trench mortars hurled their heavy missiles into the opposing trenches. Shells from the Federal guns went screaming into the houses in Petersburg. It was a nerve-wracking ordeal for soldiers and citizens.

During the early part of the siege Grant attempted literally to blast his way into Petersburg by exploding a charge of 8,000 pounds of powder directly under the Confederate lines—one of the most dramatic and sanguinary episodes of the war, resulting in what has come to be known as the Battle of the Crater. The plan was suggested by an officer of a regiment composed largely of Pennsylvania coal-miners, the officer himself being a skilled mining engineer. After weeks of hard work in the underground darkness, these miner-soldiers constructed a tunnel 500 feet long ending in a chamber directly under the Confederate breastworks where the charge of four tons of powder was carefully placed in position. At 4:30 A.M. on July 30th all was in readiness, and the fuse was lighted.

The Confederate camp was wrapped in sleep when the tremendous explosion rocked the ground with the force of an earthquake. More than two hundred Confederate soldiers were instantly killed, literally blown to pieces by the blast which tore a great gap in the Confederate works leaving a "crater" 135 feet long, 90 feet wide and 30 feet deep. The brigade of Federals assigned to charge through the breach made by the explosion rushed with headlong bravery into the crater; but they found it easier to get into that big hole than to get out of it, and while they scrambled around in confusion in the death-trap they had made for themselves, the Confederate shell and canister tore them to pieces.

Hastily the Confederates formed an emergency line of defense back of the shattered earthworks, and although the Federals came on repeatedly with great determination and bravery, the crater proved to be more of an obstacle to them than a help, and after six hours of fighting the attempt to break the Confederate lines by storm was abandoned. Grant suffered a loss of more than 5,000 men in the effort to charge through the breach; the Confederate loss was only a few hundred.

The tragic failure of this surprise movement was enough almost to insure that it would not be repeated; but General Lee, always careful, designed an arrangement of extensive underground works for the purpose of checking any future attempts along this line.

The Confederate defenses covered not only Petersburg, but extended on north of the James River on the east so as also to protect Richmond on that front. Lee was constantly in the saddle, superintending the strengthening and maintenance of the thirty-five miles of earthworks and fortifications which sprang up under his guiding hand. His aide tells an interesting story of these times, illustrative of the general's thoroughness and also of his diplomacy and his ability to administer a reproof delicately but at the same time effectively:

"On one of his daily visits to the lines, General Lee asked one of his officers who was riding with him if a work he had ordered to be performed was finished. The officer replied, hesitatingly, that it was. Lee then proposed to ride to the spot and inspect it. On arriving there he found that the work had made very little progress since his last visit to it, a week before. The officer, in much confusion, sought to excuse himself for his negligence, saying that he had ordered it to be completed at once and had been told that it was finished, but had not himself been there. General Lee simply remarked: 'We must give our personal attention to the lines,' and rode quietly on. While doing so he began to compliment his companion on the fine charger he rode. 'Yes, sir,' replied the officer, 'he is a splendid animal, and I prize him the more highly because he belongs to my wife and is her favorite riding-horse.' 'A magnificent horse, indeed,' was General Lee's reply, 'but I should not think him safe for your wife to ride. He is entirely too spirited for a lady, and I would advise you by all means to take some of the mettle out of him before you suffer your wife to ride him again. And, by the way, general, I would suggest to you that the rough paths along these trenches would be admirable ground over which to tame him.' It need scarcely be said that the rebuked officer did not trust to the reports of subordinates from that time forward, and that he found a new field for the exercise of his horse."

Grant had a pontoon bridge across the James and he was able to shift his forces rapidly from in front of Petersburg to Richmond and back again, keeping up a constant threat against both cities. The gray line of defense, stretched out to cover thirty-five miles, was mighty thin in some places, and it required constant vigilance to meet all of Grant's raids. One of the South's noted generals, John H. Morgan, was killed in Tennessee in August, and he was given a military funeral in Richmond. A detachment of soldiers from the Richmond outer works under General Ewell marched in the funeral procession; and as the cortege approached the cemetery a courier dashed up to Ewell and delivered a message telling of an attack on the lines which disclosed such an urgent need for defenders that Ewell marched his men right out of the funeral procession and double-quicked them to the scene of the attack.

As the months dragged by, the privation of the citizens of Petersburg and of the soldiers increased. Provisions were still scarce, and the soldiers were always hungry. Again and again Lee wrote to Richmond telling of the suffering of the men from hunger and exposure, and urging an improvement in the system of supplies. But nothing was done about it. As late as February, Lee was writing to the War

Department: "Yesterday, the most inclement day of the winter, the troops had to be maintained in line of battle, having been in the same condition two previous days and nights. I regret to be compelled to state that under these circumstances, heightened by the assaults and fire of the enemy, some of the men have been without meat for three days and all are suffering from reduced rations and scant clothing, exposed to battle, cold, hail and sleet. Their physical strength, even if their courage survives, must fail under this treatment." The food profiteers were in the saddle in Richmond at this time. Bacon was selling for $20 a pound, meal was $140 a peck and flour $1,500 a barrel.

Although close to Richmond, Lee's attention to his duties made it impossible for him to see his family except at very long intervals. Mrs. Lee and the girls were busy knitting socks for the soldiers, which they sent directly to the general and which he distributed where they were most needed. During the summer Mrs. Lee was ill and, in her feverish condition, expressed a desire for fruit and for cold lemonade. His daughter wrote him about it, and he momentarily dropped everything else to scour the country for some apples and a pear which he sent her along with a little dried-up lemon he had been carrying in his trunk.

The General's mess was frugal in the extreme most of the time; but he and his staff took it all good-naturedly. One day General Hampton took a meal with them, and when a tureen of soup was placed on the table it was obvious that there was not enough to go around. The general calmly divided it between himself and his guest saying, with a twinkle in his eye, "I am credibly informed that the young men of my staff never eat soup."

Among Lee's visitors during those hard days was the Honorable Thomas Connally, an Irish Member of Parliament from Donegal, who was on a tour of observation in this country. During his visit at the army headquarters he had a room in a nearby farmhouse, but had his meals with General Lee; and he was astonished, though not critical, at the sparse rations available. "You should have seen 'Uncle Robet's' dinner to-day," he said one day. "He had two biscuits and he gave me one." On another occasion he reported: "We had a glorious dinner to-day. Somebody sent 'Uncle Robert' a box of sardines." A witty Irish officer in the British Army who visited the Confederate camp during these lean days said, after returning home: "It's a wonderful army—but they don't eat often enough." About this time an item was printed in one of the Northern newspapers quoting General Grant as saying that his system of espionage was so perfect that he knew what General Lee had for breakfast every morning. When Lee saw this he laughed and remarked with a rueful

smile: "I'm sure he does not, for if he did he would surely send me over something better!"

All of General Lee's sons were actively engaged in the ten months of continuous fighting around Petersburg and Richmond. Custis, at last successful in his efforts to get out of President Davis's office and into active service, was put in charge of the division stationed at Chaffin's Bluff on the James, one of the defenses of Richmond. Rooney and Rob were still riding with the cavalry, and the cavalry was kept mighty busy through summer and winter fighting off the never-ending efforts of Grant's horsemen to break the railroads and cut the Confederate lines of communication with the South. Rooney had a horse shot from under him in one of their many brushes with the blue troopers, and Rob suffered a gunshot wound in the arm during the early part of 1865 which kept him out of action for several weeks. But both of them found time to ride by the General's headquarters occasionally; and their father mentioned these visits with great pleasure in his letters home to his wife.

During the latter days of the siege, an interested participant on the other side was Robert Lincoln, the President's 23-year old son, who had just finished his four years' course at Harvard and had been given an honorary position on Grant's staff.

One of the things that worried Lee the most during these trying days was the steady reduction in the numbers under his command and the difficulty in getting replacements. The Confederacy some time before had followed the example of the North and had abandoned the volunteer system for conscription. During the time he was at Petersburg, however, General Lee complained that the conscript service was falling down in its appointed task and that it was not sending enough men to him.

Grant's army was full of conscripts also; and a strange feature of the siege of Petersburg was the steady stream of desertion suffered by both sides. Grant's ranks were, however, steadily filled with new recruits; but Lee had no such good fortune. Desertion from the Confederate army was aggravated by the fact that the men were getting insufficient food and clothing, and many of them were harassed by thoughts of the sufferings and privation of their families at home. The Federals shrewdly promoted Confederate desertions by practicing a form of propaganda that was used successfully by the Allies during the World War. Taking advantage of the close proximity of the two lines to each other and the fraternizing that went on between the opposing troops, the Federals distributed hand-bills among the Confederates offering all deserters food, clothing, a parole and safe passage through the lines so they could get home. As prisoners were not being exchanged, a parole was equivalent to a discharge from the service, and many worn-out and discouraged

Confederates succumbed to the temptation to get home the easiest way. Every morning at roll-call a few would be found to be missing; and the trickle of recruits was not sufficient to replace them, although the Confederates were now enlisting old men and young boys—"robbing the cradle and the grave." The man-power of the South was pretty nearly exhausted. Lee's army was slowly dwindling away.

Lee forcefully warned Davis again and again of the desperate necessity for reinforcing him. "Unless we can obtain a reasonable approximation to his (Grant's) force," he wrote in November, "I fear a great calamity will befall us." At frequent intervals he repeated this warning. Early in February he wrote Davis that Richmond would have to be abandoned unless he could be reinforced—but he was not reinforced.

While Grant was slowly strangling Petersburg and and Richmond and the fate of the Confederate capital was trembling in the balance, President Davis made one of the most serious errors of the war. Expressing dissatisfaction with General Joe Johnston's management of his defensive campaign against Sherman's army invading Georgia, Davis dismissed Johnston and over Lee's advice replaced him with Hood, a brave but reckless man. Hood threw his army away in a bold but ineffectual campaign to recapture Nashville; and while he was doing this, Sherman unmolested conducted his famous march through

Georgia to the sea. After Sherman reached Savannah he turned northward through the Carolinas, with the obvious intention of joining Grant and crushing Lee. Beauregard took the remnants of Hood's army, added to it such fragments of other commands as he could muster, and planned to try to stop Sherman's northward march somewhere in North Carolina if possible.

In February, 1865, recognizing that some desperate step must be taken to save the Confederate cause, Congress conferred on Robert E. Lee the title of general-in-chief of all the Confederate armies. Davis did not disagree with Congress this time. Gracefully and heartily he wrote to Lee: "The honor designed to be bestowed has been so fully won that the fact of bestowing it can add nothing to your fame." But it was too late now for such a step as this to prove of much material benefit. Lee's hands were too full, trying to save the Army of Northern Virginia from destruction, for him to be able to make good use of the supreme authority thus tardily conferred on him; but one of the first things he did do was to restore Joseph E. Johnston to active service and put him at the head of the troops charged with the duty of stopping Sherman.

Lee, despite his courageous determination to fight to the bitter end if necessary, was not blind to the great difficulties in the way of his ultimate success. As early as 1863 he had suggested to President

Davis the advisability of making an honorable peace if possible; and now, in the trenches of Petersburg, he was still willing to accept peace without victory, and gladly grasped an opening that seemed to point in that direction. General Longstreet had a discussion under a flag of truce with General Ord of Grant's staff regarding steps to stop the fraternizing of the troops. Ord and Longstreet had been friends in the old army, and Ord told him that the Federal officers thought that the war had gone on long enough and that the officers of the two armies should "come together as former comrades and friends and talk a little." Ord said that he believed that Grant would be glad to discuss with Lee the matter of bringing the war to an end on a basis that would be satisfactory to both sides, and suggested to Longstreet that Lee get into communication with Grant. Lee promptly wrote to Grant telling him of his willingness to hold a conference with him on the subject, and Grant forwarded Lee's letter to Lincoln; but Lincoln slammed the door in Lee's face by sharply commanding Grant to hold no communication with Lee for any other purpose than to accept his surrender. So Lee settled down to his task of sustaining the waning Confederacy as long as possible.

At this time Lee had about 45,000 men. Grant had 110,000. Sherman had 80,000. If Sherman ever united with Grant, nothing could save Lee.

Johnston pulled his little army together and

fought one battle with Sherman at Bentonville, but on March 23rd he telegraphed Lee that with his small command he could not seriously hinder Sherman's advance. "It is no longer a question whether you leave your present position," Johnston bluntly warned Lee. "You have only to decide where to meet Sherman."

Spurred to action by this discouraging message, Lee on March 25th made a desperate effort to capture Fort Steadman, a stronghold of the Federal position east of Petersburg. He hoped that if this were successful it would force Grant to shorten his line and then he would be able to hold Grant off with a portion of his troops and with the remainder unite with Johnston to battle Sherman in North Carolina. He figured that if the outcome of such an encounter with Sherman should be successful he could at once return to the Petersburg line; and that if it were not successful he would be in no worse position than if he waited for Sherman to join Grant and force his withdrawal.

But the attack on Fort Steadman was not successful. The Confederates, to be true, captured the fort by a sudden onslaught; but they could not hold it, and were forced back to their lines with losses amounting to nearly 3,000. That night Lee wrote to Davis: "I fear now it will be impossible to prevent a junction between Grant and Sherman, nor do I deem it prudent that this army should maintain its position until the latter shall approach too near."

After the repulse of Lee's attack on Fort Stead-man, Grant continued steadily to extend his left flank, massing here 50,000 men under Sheridan for the purpose of turning the Confederate right. Lee rushed General Pickett's division and all the available cavalry to the threatened point, and at first they fought off Sheridan's advance; but on April 1st Sheridan brought all his force into play at Five Forks and crushed General Pickett's brave but insufficient command.

Lee instantly recognized that this was probably the beginning of the end, and immediately notified Davis of the grave state of affairs. Affairs were too critical for him to leave the front and go to Richmond, so he suggested that the President or the Secretary of War should come to the front to confer with him; but nobody came.

The Confederate line of defense had been woe-fully weakened to reinforce Pickett, and at daybreak of the next day Grant smashed an irresistibly strong blow at the line southwest of Petersburg, sending the Confederate defenders reeling back in confusion. As Lee saw his men falling back through the early morning mist, he shook his head sadly and said to his aide: "It is as I feared it would be. The line has been stretched until it had to break." Promptly he notified the Secretary of War that it would be necessary to abandon Petersburg and Richmond. Then with painstaking carefulness he caused orders to be issued to all his subordinates to withdraw from the positions before Petersburg and Richmond and re-assemble at Amelia Court-house, west of Petersburg, where he had asked that supplies for the troops be deposited.

In spite of all Lee's warnings, the actual announcement of his retreat seemed to come as a shocking surprise to everybody in Richmond, including the authorities. President Davis was in his pew at church on the morning of that fateful Sunday, when the sexton tiptoed down the isle with the message just received from General Lee. Davis hastily left the church and spread the word, and all that day was spent in feverish preparations to abandon the capital city.

By the morning of the 3rd all the officials, with their archives and baggage, had arrived at Danville, on their way to North Carolina to join Johnston's army. Lee's army, now reduced to less than 30,000, was tramping along in the direction of Amelia Court-house.

Mrs. Lee and the Lee girls were among those who stayed in Richmond to take the consequences of the occupation of the city by the enemy. During the forenoon a detachment of Federal cavalrymen galloped into Richmond and planted the Stars and Stripes on Capitol Square. Soon the city was full of blue-coated soldiers. The mayor formally surrendered the city to General Weitzel. In the confusion of the retreat the tobacco warehouses had been set on fire, and the fire was roaring through the lower part of the city. The fire-bells were ringing as the blue cavalry came clattering through the streets. It was just the fire-bells; but they were tolling the death-knell of the Confederacy.

CHAPTER XVII

Surrender

FOR the Army of Northern Virginia the next seven days was a tortured nightmare. Days and nights were a dizzying muddle of marching and fighting, without enough food and without enough sleep. How they stood it as long as they did is hard to understand.

By the morning of April 5th the whole army had reached Amelia Court-house, where Lee had ordered supplies to be deposited. To his dismay he learned that through some misunderstanding the train loaded with provisions that had been sent there from the South had gone on through to Richmond without unloading. There was no food there for the hungry soldiers, who had been living for three days on parched corn.

This was a crushing blow to Lee's plans. He had hoped by rapid marching to get his little army into the hilly country of southwestern Virginia where he could occupy a strong defensive position and fight off attack while drawing to him the forces of Joe Johnston and other scattered Confederate commands.

Swift movement was his only hope of success. Grant's superior force was swarming in pursuit, led by Sheridan's vigorous and well-mounted cavalry. Delay was almost certain to be fatal.

But Lee, despite the shocking disappointment, did not lose his poise and composure. Hastily sending out foragers to scour the country for something to eat, he halted his men for a day at Amelia and waited anxiously for the foragers to come in with the scanty supply of food they had been able to collect. Then that night they moved on—with Grant's pursuing forces a day's march closer.

During the 6th the vanguard of Grant's army caught up with Lee's rear at Sailor's Creek. The troops bringing up the rear were mostly those who had occupied the defenses of Richmond and were under the command of General Ewell. Ewell, after being disabled at Spotsylvania, had had to retire from the command of his corps; but, although one-legged and in bad health, he refused to leave the service entirely, and so was assigned to the defense of Richmond. In his crippled condition he could not stay on a horse unaided, and in his work around Richmond he rode from point to point in a sulky; but when the evacuation was ordered he strapped himself on his war-horse and led his motley force of soldiers, sailors, marines and government clerks down the muddy road that led to defeat and disaster.

The Federal assault at Sailor's Creek was overwhelming and irresistible, aided by the slashing drive of the cavalry. Ewell's men, who had been marching all night and were weary, weak, hungry and sleepy, were cut off and surrounded. They fought desperately as long as their strength lasted, but resistance was useless. Overpowered and hemmed in on all sides, Ewell succumbed to the inevitable and surrendered. Custis Lee was serving under Ewell and he was included in the capture, along with several other general officers.

This wholesale capture of Confederate officers and men brought together many old class-mates at West Point who had been fighting against each other for several years; and, in spite of the circumstances, there were some pleasant reunions of old friends. The captors acted with the greatest kindness and consideration, sharing their rations with the famished prisoners; and the courtly Custer showed his good-natured sportsmanship by having one of his regimental bands that night play "The Bonnie Blue Flag," which evoked a rousing rebel yell from the miserable prisoners. Another gracious act of thoughtfulness was when General Williams of Grant's staff arranged to send word through the lines to General Lee that his son had been captured and was safe.

This disaster at Sailor's Creek was just about the last straw added to the heavy burden of trouble that Lee was carrying, but he still pressed on with the remnant of his command, now reduced to no more than 10,000 men. Late into the early morning hours he worked that night, issuing orders to his commanders in one last desperate effort to consolidate his forces and get them out of danger. A messenger found him, after midnight, standing wearily with his hand on the wheel of a wagon in which his adjutant-general was seated, with lap-desk and lantern, writing orders. "Every effort," Lee was dictating, "must be made to get up all stragglers and all such men as have fallen asleep by the campfires or by the wayside." But the tired soldiers, many of them now beginning to lose heart for the first time, were dropping by the wayside in large numbers—and not a few of them, with a premonition that the end was at hand, were slipping quietly away during the night hours.

On the 7th the marching men reached Farmville, where a train of rations awaited them—precious bread and meat—the first issue of supplies since leaving Petersburg. But a Federal battery galloped up on a commanding hill, quickly got the range and drove off the train before the rations could be distributed. So, most of the men, as they plodded on, still had nothing to eat but corn on the cob, and not much of that. They parched the corn at their camp-fires, stuffed it into their pockets along with their cartridges, and munched it grain by grain as they stumbled wearily along the muddy road, dazed and discouraged at the plight in which they found themselves, but still hoping and believing that Marse

Robert would find some way out of their difficulty
for them.

Grant's men were pursuing closely, fired with the
spirit of victory. Says the historian of one of their
regiments: "The men were singing, laughing, joking
and apparently happy. Along the road were evidences of the rapid retreat of the enemy, all sorts of
ammunition lying around loose, dead horses lying
where they had dropped, others abandoned because
they could no longer carry their riders, and here and
there a dead soldier, lying in the road where he had
halted for the last time, with every appearance of
having died from hunger and exhaustion."

It was on this morning of the 7th that General
Lee was visited by General Henry A. Wise, whose
brigade, now reduced to a few hundred, had safely
escaped from the encounter at Sailor's Creek. Wise
was an old man with a white beard, wearing spectacles
and chewing tobacco, a stooping, sickly figure,
wrapped in a ragged blanket as a protection against
the chilly April morning air; but he was still full of
fire and strong language. He found General Lee
washing his face in a tin basin on the back porch of a
farmhouse by the roadside. Wise had washed that
morning in a puddle of rain-water, and his face was
streaked with the red Virginia mud. Wrapped in his
blanket, and with his clay-streaked face, he bore a
grotesque resemblance to a painted Indian chief; and
Lee, despite the load of care resting on his spirit,

greeted him with a laugh. "Come in, general," he said, smiling, "I am glad to see that you have not given up hope; you have your war paint on this morning," and then proceeded to compliment him on the behavior of his brigade. But Wise was in no mood for pleasantries. Bitterly he complained that his men had been fighting for a week without food and declared that they should not move another step until somebody gave them something to eat. The rations train was there then, so Lee was able to promise him that his men would be relieved; and then he asked Wise to share his breakfast with him, meanwhile asking him what he thought about the situation.

"Situation!" roared Wise excitedly. "There is no situation! Nothing remains, General Lee, but to put your poor men on your poor mules and send them home in time for spring ploughing. This army is hopelessly whipped and is fast becoming demoralized; and I say to you, sir, emphatically that to prolong the struggle is murder, and the blood of every man who is killed from this time forth is on your head!"

As he paused for breath, Lee protested: "Oh, general, do not talk so wildly. My burdens are heavy enough. And what would the country think of me if I did what you suggest?"

"Country be damned!" exclaimed the fiery old man. "There is no country. There has been no country, general, for a year or more. You are the country to these men. They have fought for you. They have shivered through a long winter for you. Without pay or clothes, or care of any sort, their devotion to you and faith in you have been the only things which have held this army together."

That very day a group comprising most of the division and brigade commanders of the Army of Northern Virginia held a conference, there on the hills overlooking Farmville, and concluded that their cause was a lost cause and that further resistance was hopeless. They recognized, however, the odium attaching to the surrender of any army in the field; and, so that Lee might not have to bear alone the responsibility of asking for terms of peace, they selected General Pendleton, Lee's chief of artillery, as the messenger to take to their commander the news of their conclusion that the army should be surrendered.

Lee, however, was still reluctant to believe that the end was truly at hand. "Oh, no!" he exclaimed to Pendleton, "I trust it has not come to that. We have yet too many bold men to think of laying down our arms." But Wise's blunt words and this message of despair from his generals' council—all this must have combined to shake his confidence.

While he was turning over in his mind these counsels of despair, there was received that same day from General Grant a message saying that the events of the past week must have convinced Lee of "the hope-

lessness of further resistance" and asking for the surrender of Lee's army so as "to shift from myself the
responsibility of any further effusion of blood." Lee
promptly replied that he did not agree as to the hope-
lessness of his position, but asked Grant to outline
the terms he would offer on condition of surrender.
Grant answered the next day that peace was his only
desire and that all he would ask was that the men and
officers surrendered should be disqualified from taking up arms again against the government of the
United States. He offered to arrange for a meeting
to agree on definite terms; and Lee replied with the
suggestion that he should meet Grant "at ten A.M.
tomorrow on the old stage road to Richmond, between the picket lines of the two armies"—although
he closed his message with a reiteration of the statement that he did not intend to surrender his army.

Lee had still not given up all hope. He was pressing onward in the direction of Lynchburg; and he
planned, if he found a supply of provisions at Appomattox, to move on to the Staunton River and
establish himself behind that stream until he could
effect a junction with Joe Johnston.

Appomattox Court-house was reached on the afternoon of the 8th; and upon arrival there he found that
the Federal cavalry had got to Appomattox Station
ahead of him and captured the stores placed there for
his army. This was a staggering piece of news; but
even now Lee's great heart did not give up. He called

a council of war that night, the last council of the leaders of that great army of fighting men, and it was determined to make one more desperate effort the following morning to force a way out of the ring of Federals who now surrounded him. He now had fewer than 10,000 men with arms in their hands, and was immediately confronted—practically surrounded—by a force out-numbering him by about five to one; but he was so accustomed to fighting against superior numbers that he found it hard to believe that he was at last over-powered.

The attack was arranged for the early morning, and at 3 A.M. Lee, who had been in the saddle all night, rode forward with Colonel Venable to see whether Gordon, entrusted with the advance, could cut his way through. Gordon launched his attack as planned, and had some temporary success; but he soon found that he was up against a greatly superior force and could advance no further. He promptly sent word to General Lee: "I have fought my corps to a frazzle, and I fear that I can do nothing unless I am heavily supported by Longstreet's corps." Longstreet was holding Meade back in the rear (and having his hands full doing it) and he could not be moved from that position. So, when he received Gordon's despairing message, Lee said simply: "Then there is nothing left for me but to go and see General Grant—and I would rather die a thousand deaths."

Even then, hopeless as was the outlook, some of

Lee's staff found it impossible to believe that their great leader had reached the end of his resources and must at last give up. "Oh, general," one of them said in despair, "what will history say of the surrender of the army in the field?" General Lee replied: "Yes, I know they will say hard things of us. They will not understand how we were overwhelmed by numbers. But that is not the question. The question is: Is it right to surrender this army? If it is right, then I will take all the responsibility."

Major Wilmer McLean was a quiet, peace-loving country gentleman who had lived in 1861 on his farm on Bull Run in the northern part of the state. When the two great armies collided there in July of that year, and he saw his fields stained with blood and his home menaced by flying shells, he promptly decided that he would move so far into the interior that the war's alarms could not reach him. Accordingly he moved to Appomattox Court-house and lived there quietly for four years, until the rolling tide of the war overtook him that April morning in 1865; and it was in the parlor of his house that Lee and his aide waited for Grant and his staff to come and arrange the terms of surrender.

Two days previously the Confederates, to speed their march, had destroyed all their surplus baggage, and Lee had saved nothing but the brand-new uniform, cavalry boots, gauntlets and sash which had been sent him through the blockade from Liverpool by some English admirers during the preceding summer. When he prepared to go to meet General Grant he carefully dressed himself in this new uniform, the first time he had ever had it on, and also dug up his handsome dress-sword out of his trunk and buckled it at his side. When he stepped out of his tent that morning his staff saw him more splendidly dressed than had ever before been their experience, and one of them said: "He looked, as he was, a full-blooded cavalier, a type of high chivalrous manhood, to be remembered by those who beheld him through all time."

Lee and Grant greeted each other affably when the latter arrived, and the two engaged in general conversation regarding old army matters and incidents during the Mexican War. General Grant in later years said that the conversation grew so pleasant that he almost forgot the object of the meeting; and it was General Lee who finally had to bring up the subject of the surrender, suggesting to Grant that he put his terms in writing.

Lee and his officers had feared that perhaps Grant might live up to his nickname of "Unconditional Surrender"; but the Federal commander soon set them at ease on this score. The terms were simple and generous. The men were to lay down their arms, and all public property was to be surrendered. Officers were to retain their side arms and personal baggage. Lee suggested to Grant that the Confederate cavalrymen furnished their own horses, and that the men would need them when they went home to plough and plant their crops. Grant answered generously that every man who claimed to own a horse or mule should be permitted to take the animal home. "That will have a very happy effect," said Lee; and the terms were written out on that basis. Lee mentioned the fact that he had about 1,500 Federal prisoners for whom he had no food, having none for his own men; and Grant promptly ordered Sheridan to have sent to the Confederate commissary 25,000 rations—"for our men and his men".

That was all there was to it. Lee did not offer his sword to Grant, and Grant therefore had no opportunity to refuse or return it. Grant himself disposed of this widely-believed myth when he said: "The much talked of surrendering of Lee's sword and my handing it back, this and much more that has been said about it is the purest romance."

There was a conspicuous lack of gloating on the part of the victorious Federals, and they seemed just about as much embarrassed as the Confederates during the surrender proceedings. Lee's demeanour, said one of Grant's staff, "was that of a thoroughly possessed gentleman, who had a very disagreeable duty to perform, but was determined to get through with it as well and as soon as possible." Lee had carefully dressed himself for the important occasion; but Grant came in from the field in his fatigue uniform, dusty and rather soiled, and he seemed to be rather concerned about it, apologizing to Lee especially for not having his side arms with him. Nearly twenty years had elapsed since that day in General Scott's headquarters in Mexico when Captain Lee had to reprove Lieutenant Grant for the informality of his costume, but remembrance of that episode flashed through Grant's mind as they sat there that day in Major McLean's parlor.

The papers signed, and the casual conversation ended. Lee prepared to return to his army and announce to them the sad news. Waiting on the front steps of the McLean house for his horse to be brought to him, there was a far-away look of sadness in his face and he struck his gauntleted hands together two or three times as he waited. But he gave no other sign of the sorrow that engulfed his heart.

When he rode back through the Confederate lines he was greeted with cheers, despite the rapidly spreading news that he had surrendered. Tears streaming down their faces, his men crowded around him, halting Traveler's progress. "Men," he said to them, "we have fought through the war together. I have done the best I could for you. My heart is too full to say more." And there were tears starting in Marse Robert's eyes as he rode on to his tent, through the heart-broken ranks of his faithful and devoted remnant of an army.

The next day he issued to them his farewell address:

"After four years of arduous service, marked by unsurpassed courage and fortitude, the Army of Northern Virginia has been compelled to yield to overwhelming numbers and resources.

"I need not tell the survivors of so many hard-fought battles, who have remained steadfast to the last, that I have consented to this result through no distrust of them; but, feeling that valour and devotion could accomplish nothing that could compensate for the loss that would have attended the continuation of the contest, I have determined to avoid the useless sacrifice of those whose past services have endeared them to their countrymen.

"By the terms of agreement, officers and men can return to their homes and remain there until exchanged.

"You will take with you the satisfaction that proceeds from the consciousness of duty faithfully performed; and I earnestly pray that a merciful God will extend to you His blessing and protection.

"With an unceasing admiration of your constancy and devotion to your country, and a grateful remembrance of your kind and generous consideration of myself, I bid you an affectionate farewell."

The war was over. True, there were other Confederate troops in the field for several more weeks. President Davis and his Cabinet were trying to escape through the South across the Mississippi to make a last stand in Texas. But when Robert E. Lee ordered the Army of Northern Virginia to furl their flags and stack their muskets, then the Southern Confederacy really ceased to exist.

CHAPTER XVIII

A Paroled Prisoner of War

For days following the surrender at Appomattox the Virginia roads were crowded with Confederate soldiers, singly and in groups, on foot and horseback, returning to their homes. One such group, composed of General Lee and several members of his staff, including Rooney, set out for Richmond three days after the surrender. They had a wagon containing their personal baggage, and they camped by the roadside at night, Lee still pursuing his policy of refusing to intrude on private homes for lodging.

On the morning of the 15th the party crossed the pontoon bridge into Richmond, and although their return was unheralded, the General mounted on Traveler was soon recognized and before he had gone far he was surrounded by a crowd of men, women and children, cheering him as they waved their hats and handkerchiefs. Though deeply affected by their greeting, he made no other response than to doff his hat; and as rapidly as possible he rode to the house on Franklin Street where his wife and daughters awaited him. His military career was now behind him. Robert E. Lee was a private citizen.

The spring and summer were devoted to obtaining the rest he so much needed after four years of the exposure and fatigue of campaigning; but it was mighty little rest he got those first few weeks. His house was besieged with visitors—friends and former enemies, old soldiers, Northern tourists prompted by curiosity, all these crowded to his door.

One day the door-bell rang and there stood a burly Irish sergeant in the blue uniform of the Regular Army. An old trooper of the Second Cavalry he turned out to be; he had heard that his old Colonel was in need, suffering for want of food, and he had brought along a big basket packed with everything the market afforded. There was a mist of appreciation in Lee's eyes as he assured the old soldier that he was not in such dire distress as to need a contribution of food; but Pat was so insistent that he be permitted to do something for his old Colonel that Lee finally agreed to accept the proffered basket, with the reservation that he would send it to a hospital.

Another day two ragged ex-Confederates came shyly to the door, explaining that they had heard that the General was about to be indicted for treason and they wanted to offer their help. They had it all figured out; they said they spoke for sixty other ex-members of the Army of Northern Virginia who lived in the mountains of the southwestern part of the state and they had a farm there which they wanted to offer the General as a refuge, where they would defend him with their lives. Although his heart was touched at the offer, he assured them that he needed no place to hide.

As a matter of fact, Lee and some of the other Confederate leaders were indicted by a carpet-bagger grand jury in Norfolk. Lee wrote to General Grant pointing out that in his understanding his parole as a surrendered soldier protected him against civil prosecution; but he stated plainly that he had no objection to facing a court trial if the United States government cared to subject him to it. Grant was indignant when he learned of the indictment and immediately notified the Secretary of War that such action was an act of bad faith on the part of the government; and the indictment was promptly quashed.

President Andrew Johnson in May had issued an "amnesty proclamation"; and Lee, wishing to set an example to the people of the South to bring themselves into affiliation with the government and secure their old rights as citizens, made formal application for "amnesty and pardon" and sent it to General Grant with the request that he forward it to President Johnson. Grant did so, with the strong recommendation that it be granted—but that was the last that was ever heard of it. Johnson was a vindictive man, determined, as he expressed it, to "make treason odious"; and he never acted on Lee's application, so the commander of the Confederate armies remained a paroled prisoner of war, denied the privileges of citizenship.

Despite his own shabby treatment, however, he repeatedly advised those who sought his counsel—and they were many—to submit to all authority and become law-abiding citizens of the United States. The questions which had been in dispute, he told them, having been referred to the decision of war and "having been decided against us, it is the part of candor to recognize the fact and the part of wisdom to acquiesce in the result." And he sternly rebuked a Virginia woman who was speaking bitterly of the North, telling her that she should bury her old animosities and raise up her sons "to be loyal Americans."

At the same time, although he did with a fine sense of sportsmanship acquiesce in the result of the war, General Lee never receded from the position that he was right in 1861 when he cast his lot with Virginia and the South, and before he died he repeated that "I could have taken no other course save with dishonor; and if it were to be all gone over again, I would act in precisely the same way."

Further regarding his course, he said after the war: "I fought against the people of the North because I believed that they were seeking to wrest from the South dearest rights; but I have never cherished towards them bitter or vindictive feelings, and have never seen the day that I did not pray for them." Lee deeply resented the often repeated statement that he had fought to maintain the slaves in bondage. "So far from engaging in a war to perpetuate slavery," he said, "I am rejoiced that slavery is abolished. I believe it will be greatly to the interest of the South. So fully am I satisfied of this, as regards Virginia especially, that I would cheerfully have lost all I have lost by the war and have suffered all I have suffered to have this object attained."

Lee spent only a few weeks in Richmond. Repeatedly he expressed a desire to retire to the peace and quiet of a little farm somewhere, and during the latter part of June he leased a modest place in the country called "Derwent" where he spent the summer. Riding on Traveler, he passed the time quietly and pleasantly, visiting his relatives and old friends in the surrounding country. As his son said: "The pains of the past, the worries of the present and the cares of the future were, for the time being, banished."

All this time he was being besieged by offers to ally himself with various business enterprises, and many financially attractive proposals were made to him. He was offered $50,000 a year to go to New York to head a company being organized to promote business with Southern firms. An insurance company offered him $25,000 a year to act as president. Another company proposed to pay him $10,000 a year merely for the use of his name. But his sense of honor did not permit of his accepting any of these efforts to capitalize his fame. "My name is not for sale at any price," he said simply. Nor did he give a moment's consideration to the offer made by a British nobleman to give him an estate in England to live on if he would come there, together with a yearly income of $15,-000. He wrote a grateful letter of appreciation to his generous admirer, but concluded: "I must abide the fortunes and share the fate of my people."

As offer after offer of this kind came in, one of his daughters one day remarked to a friend: "They are offering my father everything except the only thing he will accept: a place to earn honest bread while engaged in some useful work." This remark was repeated to a gentleman of Staunton, Virginia, who was one of the trustees of Washington College at Lexington, and he mentioned it a few weeks later when the trustees were holding a meeting to decide on the future of the college and were discussing the selection of a president.

Washington College was an old and honored educational institution, more than a hundred years old, which had changed its name in honor of George Washington when he bestowed on it an endowment. The war had dealt harshly with the school. The investments in which its endowment was placed were unproductive of revenue and of doubtful value. The small sum remaining in its treasury was in Confederate money. It had only four professors and forty students; and, worst of all, the college buildings had been damaged and its equipment and library destroyed when General Hunter raided Lexington late in the war.

The trustees hesitated about offering the presidency of such a run-down and impoverished institution to such a distinguished man, but finally they mustered up their courage and passed a resolution offering Robert E. Lee the position at a salary of $1,500 a year. So destitute was the college that it was a serious problem to meet the expenses of sending a member of the board of trustees to notify the general of his nomination. The member selected to make the trip to "Derwent" had to borrow a suit of clothes to wear, and also was forced to borrow the money to cover the expenses of the trip.

Lee was in some doubt about accepting the position offered him. Not, we may be sure, because of the pitifully small salary, but because he questioned whether his failing health would enable him to fulfill the duties of the office and also because, he said, he was "an object of censure to a portion of the country" and he feared that his occupation of the office of president "might draw upon the college a feeling of hostility." He had already rejected an offer to act as vice-chancellor of the University of the South at Sewanee, Tennessee. But the trustees of Washington College over-rode all his objections, Lee's election as president was announced, and the college almost instantly took on new life.

Late in September General Lee arrived in Lexington after a leisurely four days' ride on Traveler and dismounted in front of the hotel all unannounced, but he was instantly recognized by one of his old soldiers on the street who yelled "There's Marse Robert!" and ran to have the honor of holding his horse for him. Soon the street was filled with a cheering crowd, and then he was escorted to the home of one who had served with him in the Army of Northern Virginia, where he was hailed as an honored guest.

It was a discouraging prospect that greeted Lee when he took hold of the job of trying to re-establish this poverty-stricken school from the ruins that had been left by the ravages of war; but he was no mere figure-head president, and he attacked his task with enthusiasm and energy. He had had educational experience as superintendent of the Military Academy at West Point, and he knew how a successful school should be run. He went over and enlarged the course of study and engaged additional professors; replaced the scientific equipment that had been destroyed; and obtained new books for the library. Before the end of his first year it was plain to see that the college was on its way to becoming what it is to-day—one of the influential institutions of the country, Washington and Lee University.

Many of his former soldiers in the Army of Northern Virginia were still young enough to go to school and were eager to take advantage of the opportunity to resume their studies under him. Southern families with young sons were delighted to enroll them under Robert E. Lee, the idol of the South. The boys who had served in the army were very proud of that distinction and were commonly called the "Confeds," as distinguished from the non-combatant students who were known as "yearlings."

On account of his long life in the army and his experience at West Point, it was thought that perhaps General Lee would want to change Washington College to a military school with strict martial discipline, but nothing was further from his thoughts. "Young gentlemen," he told two young students who had come from Tennessee, "we have no printed rules. We have but one rule here: that every student be a gentleman." He instituted the honor system in place of the rigid discipline then common in schools and colleges; and he also replaced the old hard-and-fast compulsory course of study with the then new and modern elective system, which gave the students a voice in the studies they should undertake.

The general took his new work very seriously. "I have led the young men of the South in battle," he said; "I have seen many of them die on the field; I shall devote my remaining energies to training young men to do their duty in life." How well he succeeded in his efforts is indicated in the tribute paid him by Mr. Gamaliel Bradford when he says of this period of Lee's life: "In point of fact he was creating, or re-creating, a great nation still. His patience, his courage, his attitude toward the future, his perfect forgiveness, his large magnanimity, above all his hope, were reflected in the eager hearts about him and from them spread wide over the bruised and beaten South which stood so sorely in need of all these things. It is almost impossible to over-estimate the immense importance of his general influence in bringing about reconciliation and peace."

Those years at Lexington were happy years for General Lee, the Indian Summer of his life. After four years of hard campaigning, it was a pleasure to him to find congenial, useful work, and to take his part in the life of the little town of Lexington. Out of school hours he was a familiar figure, riding on Traveler in the streets of the town and on the roads of the countryside. He made it his business to know all of his students by name, and he never passed one of them without speaking cordially and pleasantly. One of his greatest delights was to stop and talk with the little boys and girls he passed on the road; and he nearly always returned from his rides with some happy child riding behind him on Traveler's broad back.

During the summer seasons he went with his wife and daughters to some of the health resorts in the nearby mountains, his favorite being White Sulphur Springs where the family had a simple cottage. At the

Springs he was always a center of interest, and his kindly courtesies and thoughtfulness added to the pleasure of the others at the resort. A horseback ride on Traveler was a daily feature of his life there, and generally he was joined in these rides by a group of the young people in whose company he took so much pleasure. In the evenings he was always surrounded by a gay group of young girls during the merry-making in the big ball-room after dinner; and he made it a part of his duty to see that everybody knew everybody else and that the newcomers and the wall-flowers were absorbed into the general gayety.

It was at "The White" that General Lee met and became friendly with the great Northern philanthropist, George Peabody; and the Peabody College for Teachers at Nashville, liberally endowed by him, is said to have been established as the result of General Lee's suggestion in answer to his inquiry as to how he might best do something to benefit the South.

Lee's home life at Lexington was simple but pleasant. Upon his arrival there he found that the house assigned to the school's president was in a very bad state of repair, and he immediately set to work to get it ready for the occupancy of his wife and family, meanwhile living himself in a single room on the third floor of the Lexington Hotel. The new home was carpeted with the rugs saved from Arlington, but most of the other family furnishings had been left behind when Arlington was deserted in 1861 and providing the new home with furniture was a problem, as the Virginia manufacturers had not yet got back into business. To meet this emergency a Lexington lady drew designs for a complete outfit of household furniture. It was made by a one-armed ex-Confederate soldier who was a cabinet maker by trade, and so President Lee's house was furnished. The old family silver was dug up, tarnished and mouldy, from the hiding-place where it had been buried; and while it was being restored and polished the family used the pewter-ware out of General Lee's camp chest. The general himself laid out a vegetable garden, planted roses and flowering shrubs and fruit and shade trees; and soon the dilapidated old house blossomed out into a real home. Mrs. Lee was almost totally disabled with rheumatism, being able to get about only by means of a wheel-chair; but in spite of her suffering she was cheerful and uncomplaining and kept busy with her knitting and her water-colors.

Custis Lee had been made a professor of civil engineering at the Virginia Military Institute in Lexington and, still unmarried, made his home with his father. Rooney and Rob were farming on their plantations, the White House and Romancoke; and General Lee kept up an active correspondence with them, giving them advice and assistance wherever possible, and extending his sympathies to Rob when he was stricken down with chills and fever and poison-oak all at the same time.

During the latter part of November, 1867, Rooney was married at Petersburg to Miss Mary Tabb Bolling, and General Lee and Custis went down from Lexington to attend the ceremony. Both the bride and her father were old friends of the Lees and they had been kind and attentive to the general during the siege of Petersburg. He was glad to see them again; but he seemed to dread returning to Petersburg and meeting its people. Any such feeling, however, was immediately removed by the tremendous ovation given him when his train reached the city. He was met by General Mahone, in whose home he was to be a guest, with a carriage and four white horses; and, but for Lee's emphatic protest, the cheering citizens would have removed the horses and drawn the carriage themselves.

During his stay in Petersburg his old friends and old soldiers crowded around him wherever he went, anxious to show their admiration and devotion; and his visit was one continuous ovation. But he found time, somehow, to go out into the country near where his old headquarters had been located in 1864-65 to visit with an old woman who had kindly sent him butter and eggs when he was there during the siege.

After his return to Lexington, General Lee wrote of his visit: "When our armies were in front of Petersburg, I suffered so much in body and mind on account of the good townspeople, especially on that gloomy night when I was forced to abandon them, that I have always reverted to them in sadness and sorrow. My old feelings returned to me as I passed well-remembered spots and recalled the ravages of the hostile shells. But when I saw the cheerfulness with which the people were working to restore their condition, and witnessed the comforts with which they were surrounded, a load of sorrow which had been pressing upon me for years was lifted from my heart."

In 1869 Lee visited Baltimore, one of a delegation from the Shenandoah Valley in connection with efforts being made to have the Baltimore & Ohio railroad extended in the Valley. It was his first visit outside the state of Virginia since the war, but everywhere he went on the streets of Baltimore he was enthusiastically welcomed by cheering people. At this time Cyrus H. McCormick, through a Baltimore friend, invited him to come to New York to visit him. Lee expressed an unwillingness to go, whereupon the friend, thinking that perhaps he would appreciate privacy, offered to procure for him a compartment in the sleeping-car and have a closed carriage meet him at the station in New York so that nobody need see him. "Oh, no," exclaimed Lee, "I couldn't go sneaking into New York. If I do go there I'll go in the daylight and go like a man." On his way back from Baltimore he stopped off at Alexandria for several days, visiting friends and members of his family in that vicinity; and he also paid a brief formal visit of courtesy to President Grant at the White House in Washington.

Under General Lee's guidance, the affairs of Washington College prospered. Additional endowments and appropriations were obtained; and in 1867, at Lee's suggestion, a new chapel was built, in the basement of which he established his office. As the prosperity of the school increased, the trustees decided to build a new house for the president, and this was completed and occupied in 1869.

During his leisure time Lee had been engaged in a labor of love, preparing to bring out a new edition of his father's book "Memoirs of the War of '76 in the Southern States," and the book appeared in 1869. As an introduction to this new edition of Light-horse Harry's celebrated book, General Lee wrote a biographical sketch of his father—the only literary work he ever did. He had in mind writing a history of the operations of the Army of Northern Virginia, but experienced some difficulty in getting to work on this as all his own records were destroyed or captured in the retreat from Petersburg. He had written to all of his generals asking them to furnish him with their recollections of the battles in which they had been engaged, but responses from the generals were slow and this work was never accomplished.

CHAPTER XIX

The End

As THE days and weeks went by at Lexington, General Lee's health grew increasingly feeble. That attack of pneumonia he had suffered while in his bleak camp at Fredericksburg in the early spring of 1863 had left its mark on him in a chronic rheumatism of the heart sac; and as the years rolled around he found it harder and harder to recover from its attacks.

During the winter of 1869-70 he contracted a severe cold, which held on persistently despite all efforts to shake it off. At last, in March of 1870, his doctors prevailed on him to take a trip to Florida to try the effect of a warmer climate on his trouble; and, with his daughter Agnes as his companion, he set out on what proved to be a fruitless search after health.

The first stop on the southward journey was at Warrenton Springs, in North Carolina, where his daughter Annie had died during the war and where she was buried. From there they proceeded on to Savannah, traveling in one of the new sleeping-cars, "very handsome and comfortable." At every station where the train stopped the news of his passage had preceded him and there were bands of music playing martial airs and crowds of cheering people crying "Lee! Lee!" Little boys named for him by admiring parents were brought to the stations to see him and have their heads patted. Old ladies craned their necks to look in the windows and murmur: "He is mightily like his pictures." One-armed and one-legged soldiers were very much in evidence. Little girls with bouquets; veterans of the Confederate army, from privates to generals; admirers with baskets of fruit—all these met the train wherever it stopped. It was the first opportunity that the people of the South had had to see him since the war; and the passage of five years and the fact that he was a defeated general had not dimmed their enthusiasm for him. They cheered him whenever he appeared where they could see him; and they serenaded him when he tried to go to sleep at night.

"I do not think that traveling in this way procures me much quiet and repose," he wrote his wife. "I wish I were back home." But he went on with his trip—to Cumberland Island to visit the grave of his father, then on to Palatka in Florida. They returned to Savannah, thence to Charleston, Wilmington, Norfolk and Richmond; and before he returned to Lexington he visited Rooney at the White House and Rob at Romancoke, and also paid a visit to Shirley on the James, the girlhood home of his mother, and to the homes of other relatives.

The trip to the South was a diversion, but it did the general's health no permanent good. In June he went to Baltimore to consult the doctors there, but without much benefit. The pains in his chest still continued, and grew worse. Back to Lexington he went; and then on to the Hot Springs where he took the baths and drank the water, read with close interest the newspaper accounts of the Franco-Prussian War in Europe, and wrote letters home telling the gossip of the Springs and giving emphatic orders about the proper care of Traveler. But his health did not improve; in fact, he felt that he was growing weaker.

Early in September he returned to Lexington to look after the details of the opening of the college term, and the stimulation afforded by his interest in the school's affairs seemed to be of greater benefit to his health than all his visits to doctors and health resorts. On the morning of September 28th he wrote a cheerful letter to a friend in Baltimore in which he remarked that his health was improving. "My pains are less and my strength greater," he wrote.

That afternoon he attended a meeting of the vestry of Grace Church, in whose affairs he took great interest. The day was rainy, with the chill of the early mountain autumn in the air. The church was damp and cold, and the general shivered a little as he sat there with his military cape wrapped around him.

The meeting was long drawn out, with discussion of church finances. There was not enough money for the salary of the minister—Reverend W. N. Pendleton who, during the four years of the war had been General W. N. Pendleton in charge of Lee's artillery. When the amount of the deficit was stated General Lee quietly said: "I will give that sum," and the vestry meeting adjourned.

It was seven o'clock when he returned home and found his family seated at the table waiting to have tea with him. He took his place, standing at the head of the table, bowing his head to say grace; but no words came from his lips. His dismayed family saw him sink without a murmur into his chair; and, thoroughly alarmed, they hastily called the family physicians.

For two weeks he lingered, never able to leave the couch on which he was placed when first stricken, and never showing any interest in what was happening about him. Vainly the doctors tried to rouse him by talking of Traveler: "You must make haste and get well; Traveler has been standing so long in the stable that he needs exercise." But even the mention of his old war-horse did not stir his interest in living, and slowly he sank.

One who sat by his bedside during those last sad days has written: "As the old hero lay in the darkened room, or with the lamp and hearth-fire casting shadows upon his calm, noble front, all the massive grandeur of his form and face and brow remained; and death seemed to lose its terrors and to borrow a grace and dignity in sublime keeping with the life that was ebbing away."

It was on the morning of October 12th that the end came. Not until then did his great brain lose contact with reality and begin to wander. "Tell Hill he *must* come up!" he cried out, seeing in his last fancy that same gallant general whose name had been on Stonewall Jackson's dying lips. Then, after a few moments of silence, he said: "Strike the tent!"; and, with a deep-drawn sigh, closed his eyes forever.

Bibliography

ALEXANDER, E. P., *Military Memories of a Confederate*. Charles Scribner's Sons, New York, N. Y., 1907.

BOWEN, J. J., *The Strategy of Robert E. Lee*. Thomas Y. Crowell Company, New York, N. Y., 1914.

BOYD, T. A., *Light Horse Harry Lee*. Charles Scribner's Sons, New York, N. Y., 1931.

BRADFORD, GAMALIEL, *Lee, The American*. Houghton Mifflin Company, Boston, Mass., 1912.

BROCK, R. A. (edited by), *General Robert Edward Lee: Soldier, Citizen and Christian Patriot*. B. F. Johnson Publishing Co., Richmond, Va., 1897.

CHILDE, EDWARD LEE, *Life and Campaigns of General Lee*. Chatto & Windus, London, England, 1875.

COOKE, JOHN ESTEN, *A Life of General Robert E. Lee*. D. Appleton-Century Company, Inc., New York, N. Y., 1875.

DAVIS, JEFFERSON, *The Rise and Fall of the Confederate Government*. D. Appleton-Century Company, Inc., New York, N. Y., 1881.

DEARING, JOHN R., *Lee and His Cause*. The Neale Publishing Company, New York, N. Y., 1907.

ELLIS, EDWARD D., *The Camp-fires of General Lee*. Henry Harrison & Co., Philadelphia, Penna., 1886.

FREEMAN, DOUGLAS SOUTHALL (edited by), *Lee's Con-*

fidential Dispatches to Davis. G. P. Putnam's Sons, New York, N. Y., 1897.

FREEMANTLE, COL. A. J. L., *Three Months in the Southern States.* Goetzel & Son, Mobile, Ala., 1863.

GORDON, GEN. JOHN B., *Reminiscences of the Civil War.* Charles Scribner's Sons, New York, N. Y., 1904.

JOHNSTON, J. E., *Narrative of Military Operation.* D. Appleton-Century Company, Inc., New York, N. Y., 1874.

JONES, J. B., *A Rebel War Clerk's Diary.* J. B. Lippincott Company, Philadelphia, Penna., 1866.

JONES, REV. J. WILLIAM, *Life and Letters of Robert Edward Lee, Soldier and Man.* The Meade Publishing Co., New York, N. Y., 1906.

——*Personal Reminiscences, Anecdotes and Letters of General Robert E. Lee.* D. Appleton-Century Company, Inc., New York, N. Y., 1875.

LEE, FITZHUGH, *General Lee.* D. Appleton-Century Company, Inc., New York, N. Y., 1894.

LEE, CAPT. ROBERT E., *Recollections and Letters of General Robert E. Lee.* Doubleday, Doran & Company, Inc., New York, N. Y., 1924.

LONG, A. L., *Memoirs of Robert E. Lee.* J. M. Stoddart & Co., Philadelphia, Penna., 1886.

LONGSTREET, JAMES, *From Manassas to Appomattox.* J. B. Lippincott Company, Philadelphia, Penna., 1896.

MCCABE, JAMES D., *Life and Campaigns of General*

Robert E. Lee. National Publishing Company, Philadelphia, Penna., 1870.

McCLELLAN, G. B., *McClellan's Own Story.* Charles L. Webster & Co., New York, N. Y., 1887.

McKIM, RANDOLPH H., *The Soul of Lee.* Longmans, Green and Co., New York, N. Y., 1918.

MASON, EMILY V., *Popular Life of General Robert Edward Lee.* John Murphy & Co., Baltimore, Md., 1872.

MAURICE, MAJ.-GEN. SIR FREDERICK (edited by), *An Aide-de-Camp of Lee.* Little, Brown & Company, Boston, Mass., 1927.

——*Robert E. Lee, the Soldier.* Houghton Mifflin Company, Boston, Mass., 1925.

MEAD, EDWARD C., *Genealogical History of the Lee Family.* University Publishing Co., New York, N. Y., 1871.

PAGE, THOMAS NELSON, *Robert E. Lee, Man and Soldier.* Charles Scribner's Sons, New York, N. Y., 1911.

——*Robert E. Lee, the Southerner.* Charles Scribner's Sons, New York, N. Y., 1909.

PRYOR, MRS. ROGER A., *Reminiscences of Peace and War.* The Macmillan Company, New York, N. Y., 1905.

RILEY, FRANKLIN L., *General Robert E. Lee, After Appomattox.* The Macmillan Company, New York, N. Y., 1922.

STILES, ROBERT, *Four Years Under Marse Robert.* The Meade Publishing Co., New York, N. Y., 1903.

TAYLOR, WALTER H., *Four Years with General Lee.* D. Appleton-Century Company, Inc., New York, N. Y., 1878.

——*General Lee, His Campaigns in Virginia.* Nusbaum Book & News Co., Norfolk, Va., 1906.

WHITE, HENRY ALEXANDER, *Robert E. Lee and the Southern Confederacy.* G. P. Putnam's Sons, New York, N. Y., 1897.

WISE, JOHN S., *The End of An Era.* Houghton Mifflin Company, Boston, Mass., 1900.

Battles and Leaders of the Civil War. D. Appleton-Century Company, Inc., New York, N. Y., 1897.

Confederate Veteran, Nashville, Tenn.